OPENING MINDS
The Evolution of Videodiscs
& Interactive Learning

George R. Haynes, Ph.D.

With a Foreword by Rockley L. Miller

Future Systems Inc.

KENDALL/HUNT PUBLISHING COMPANY
2460 Kerper Boulevard   P.O. Box 539   Dubuque, Iowa 52004-0539

Cover Art Designed by Deborah A. Prelaz.

Copyright © 1989 by Future Systems Inc.

Library of Congress Catalog Card Number: 88–83895

ISBN 0–8403–5191–7

Printed in the United States of America
10 9 8 7 6 5 4 3 2 1

For
Regina Shipman Haynes
and
Robert Anderson Haynes
in recognition of
and gratitude for
their wisdom and ongoing inspiration.

Contents

Foreword

The American education system is in deep trouble and the only thing on the horizon that might deal with its major problems is technology.

Alfred Bork, Director
Educational Technology Center
University of California
February 1984

Not a lot has changed since Dr. Alfred Bork made the above observation at the Second Annual SALT conference on Interactive Instruction Delivery. Four years later, Bork is still waving the technology flag as his pessimistic assessment of our educational system continues to be born out by the statistics.

- Of the nation's 16,000 high schools, roughly half have no physics curriculum and a quarter have no chemistry courses.
- In academic skills, students from Japan and Europe consistently outperform American students nearly across the board.
- With up to half of all teachers retiring within the next ten years, we will need 1.6 million new teachers to replace them—two ninths of all college graduates expected over that period.
- With an average teacher salary of $25,000, we are very unlikely to attract that number of graduates to turn to teaching.
- And the SAT scores of those that are attracted to the field rank lowest of any category.

The educational problems are not limited to the academic world. Industry is paying a bigger and bigger price not only to remediate employees who have failed to master basic skills but also to retrain employees who are being surpassed by technology.

According to an estimate by the American Society for Training and Development, US business already spend about $30 Billion on education and training each year—a number that is expected to rise by five percent per year over the next five years. It is further estimated that by the year 2000, about 75% of today's workers will need retraining.

Add to that a population that includes 23 million adults who are considered functionally illiterate and you might agree with Dr. Bork that today's education and training methods are not winning the war.

But hope is on the horizon. According to Bork, "the key to rebuilding education is the computer, the videodisc, and CD-ROM." And just as the statistics demonstrate the magnitude of the problem, they also highlight the potential for these technologies to offer a solution.

- The IBM Principals of the Alphabet Literacy System, an interactive video based course, is achieving remarkable increases of over two years in reading and writing skills with only 100 hours of instruction.
- The Texas Learning Technology Group reports numerous benefits from an interactive physical science curriculum: reduced behavior problems; better lesson management; high motivation levels; high enjoyment levels for both students and teachers; and better performance by students.

On the business side:

- Xerox reports saving $6 million each year by training 15,000 field-service technicians with interactive videodiscs.
- IBM reports in a 1984 study that interactive video was about three times more effective at teaching than an instructor.
- Massachusetts Mutual Insurance reports cutting training time in half with the use of interactive video.
- And, a published summary of thirty research studies called "The Use and Effectiveness of Videodisc Training," by Michael DeBloois, supports the assertion that time savings can indeed range from one third to one half.

These are mere examples of the kinds of results being achieved in both the education and business sectors through the use of interactive technologies.

I have been tracking the evolution of interactive technologies for over ten years and remain convinced that they will be broadly adopted for education and training in the future. Not because they are effective, which they are. Not because they are inexpensive, which they are in proportion to other types of costs. And not because they are a panacea for all that ails the system, which they are not.

They will be adopted because the problems are growing faster than any alternative solution on the horizon can deal with. Interactive technologies will be adopted because we have no other choice.

John Henry Martin, creator of IBM's PALS program, describes his instructional methodology as being based on the thinking and cognitive structures of Piaget. These emphasize the need to discover how a given body of material can be "lined up" or organized in a meaningful structure. Thus, Martin observes, the job of an interactive system is "to make learners aware that there is a structure and invite them to think their way into learning."

I trust this book will help its readers discover how the interactive technologies line up and the dynamic role that they can play, indeed must play in the future of education. And I hope that it will succeed in opening the minds of readers to the roles that they might play in the continuing evolution of interactive learning.

ROCKLEY L. MILLER

Preface

Modern civilization can survive only if it begins again to educate the heart, which is the source of wisdom, for modern man is now far too clever to survive without wisdom.

E. F. Schumacher

The Creativity of Change: A Historical Perspective

The diffusion of any innovation is quite frequently a complex and arduous process requiring substantial amounts of insight, empathy, credibility, and patience on the part of a "change agent." While occurring within particular social systems, the nascent state of innovation involves uncertainty, but also a creating and sharing of information as a means of reducing that uncertainty. The communication process involved is one that is interactive, or, according to Everett Rogers, a "two-way process of convergence," in order to achieve, ideally, greater understanding that is mutually beneficial.[1]

Change, of course, is inevitable—as is substantial resistance to such evolution. The rapid technological advancements of recent years, however, focus attention on the electronic revolution— frequently to the exclusion of what history records. A myopic view may limit our perspective. Change agents have always been with us, and they have often been treated poorly at first.

The historian Arnold Toynbee provides insight to innovation by outlining what he calls a pattern of withdrawal and return. In *A Study of History*,[2] Toynbee describes Plato's simile of the cave dwellers who never ventured out of their darkness. They lived facing the cave walls and were terrorized by the multiple shadows that were reflected daily. Their energies were directed toward mere existence, to finding some semblance of security in their immediate surroundings. Anything that threatened the firm walls of familiarity became the enemy. As time progressed, one member of this community was compelled to step from the cave into the bewildering blaze of light that existed outside. Alone, he ventured out into the unknown. Some time later, having experienced a new world, he returned to share his experiences with family and friends in the cave, and to encourage them to venture forth as well. But his enthusiasm and new insights attracted no one. Instead, he was greeted with ridicule and hostility.

Toynbee then moves through the ages of recorded history, giving numerous examples of how change and progress have come from creative and courageous individuals willing to step from the familiar and the secure into the unknown. Seminal advances have come about as such individuals then return to share their wisdom with others—Peter the Great of Russia, Jesus, Mohammed, Buddha, Confucius, Kant, and Ibn Khaldun, to name a few. (Some religious sects might argue the degree of awareness or nature of some of those mentioned here. Nonetheless, their significant roles as change agents is undeniable.) The process or movement is one of withdrawal and return, and each creative person motivated in such a way becomes, in his or her own way, a change agent.

Toynbee also records the reason for the collapse of the mighty Egyptian civilization.[3] Those in power at the height of the Egyptian dynasty became selfish with their possessions and came to ignore those who enabled them to acquire and maintain what they had—the people they ruled. The governing minority, having lost the art of ruling by leadership, turned instead to dictatorial repression. Alienation grew until the entire system collapsed within.

Such an elitist orientation has stymied many civilizations and organizations. Its lesson emphasizes the importance of sharing the new developments and the varied potential of the electronic age with everyone. Of course, change agents need to understand the resistance to change, and, respectfully and creatively, need to help the resisters overcome the initial fear of something mysterious and new.

Videodisc: A Contemporary and Creative Medium for Educational Change

Technology, in Everett Rogers' model,[4] "is a design for instrumental action that reduces the uncertainty in the cause-effect relationships involved in achieving a desired outcome." This definition "implies some need or problem" and, when technology is employed, hardware and software components are usually involved.

As an information storage medium, the laser optical reflective videodisc is revolutionary. For a variety of reasons, however, it has not yet been very influential in educational environments, wherein may lie its most trenchant potential.

The videodisc is a high-density carrier of both audio and video information. Shaped like a long-playing phonograph record, it is commonly 12 inches in diameter and has a silvery, prismatic, grooveless surface that is encoded and read (played back) by a laser beam. Each side of a Constant Angular Velocity (CAV) disc can store 30 minutes of motion, video or film, or 54,000 individual frames, and each frame can contain a single picture, such as a 35-mm slide. Perhaps even more impressive is that the laser is able to locate and display any one of the 54,000 frames in 1.5 seconds or less, while the videodisc is spinning at the rate of 1,800 revolutions per minute. With the single video track are two independent audio tracks: these can be used to mix narration with music, record two different languages associated with the same video, or record instructive information on one channel and remediation or answers on the other. Such sophisticated use is commonly associated with interactive video, which couples the visual capabilities of the videodisc (or videotape) with the memory capacity of the computer.

The creative educational use of interactive video, as well as other interactive technologies, has the potential to overcome the elitism that continues to prevail in our school systems today. The National Task Force on Educational Technology, established by Terrel H. Bell when he was United States Secretary of Education, concurred with an earlier report, "A Nation at Risk," stating that the educational system in this country does not serve all students effectively. Information technology, they concluded:

> "when creatively applied and appropriately integrated will help meet three fundamental goals: improving the quality of learning; increasing equity of opportunity, access and quality; and ensuring greater cost effectiveness."[5]

Consistent quality and mastery learning can be achieved through interactive video, and extended to all students. Instructional designers who use interactive video can incorporate a foundational academic discipline and, at the same time, move beyond a pedagogy that attempts to

Pioneer LaserDisc. (Courtesy Pioneer Electronics)

The 54,000 frame capacity of a single videodisc side equals the capacity of 675 standard carousel slide trays. (Courtesy Sony Corporation of America)

instruct and control too rigidly. The latter is accomplished by including data bases (visual or textual, for example) that the student can access as needed or as desired.

A philosophy that would serve this developing model well is one offered by Rilke in his advice to a young military student struggling with the polarity of stringent control versus encouragement of the creative spirit within. Rilke's response was

> to be patient toward all that is unsolved in your heart and . . . try to love the questions themselves like locked rooms and like books that are written in a very foreign tongue . . . And the point is, to live everything. Live the questions now.[6]

Such a model of encouraging questions is fundamentally different from seeking or providing answers in order to limit, or terminate, the inquiry. Rilke's paradigm emphasizes that education is life, and as such is an ongoing process.

Interactive video, when creatively and appropriately integrated, augments traditional instruction and encourages the best of the Socratic method. In the process it has the potential to demonstrate that education is life, and that the process can be dynamic and challenging. Art and science unite in this medium.

This historical perspective traces the use of technology in public education and presents a comprehensive chronology of videodisc technology, from the 1890's to the present. It includes personal interviews conducted with experts who were primary decision makers during the early development of the videodisc.

Research findings and applications of visual and computer based components and various levels of interactive video demonstrate a representative diversity of educational and training investigations. Included are a model used by a progressive public school district and one developed for medical information management at a university health center. In addition, an evolving paradigm for a regional interactive learning center for representatives from education, industry, and government is described. Such a cooperative and synergistic initiative may enable academic researchers and educators to direct, rather than be led by, technology.

Hopefully this book will expedite the implementation of high quality interactive technology, especially interactive video, in learning environments. Educational institutions involved in this process have an opportunity to assume a vital new role in society and to demonstrate what Benjamin Bloom has concluded after 40 years of intensive research on school learning:

> What any person in the world can learn, almost all persons can learn if provided with appropriate prior and current conditions of learning.[7]

Endnotes

1. Everett M. Rogers, *Diffusion of Innovations*. Third Edition (New York: The Free Press, 1983), pp. 1, 5, 6, 20, 21, 24, 28, 312–330.
2. Arnold J. Toynbee, *A Study of History, vol. 3: The Growths of Civilizations* 8th ed. (London: Oxford University Press, 1963), pp. 248–377.
3. Ibid., pp. 212–217.
4. Rogers, *Diffusion of Innovations,* pp. 12, 138.
5. The National Task Force on Educational Technology, "Transforming American Education: Reducing the Risk to the Nation," T.H.E. Journal 14,1 (August 1986): 58.
6. Rainer Maria Rilke, *Letters to a Young Poet* (New York: W.W. Norton & Company, Inc., 1954), p. 35. The German-born Rilke was a prodigious letter-writer as well as a distinguished poet and philosopher whose works offer enduring insight. He died in 1926.
7. Benjamin S. Bloom, quoted in Robert J. Trotter, "The Mystery of Mastery," *Psychology Today* 20,7 (July 1986): 38.

Acknowledgments

The list of contributors to this book is substantial and significant gaps would have been evident without their valuable aid. For the creative guidance, constructive criticism, and enduring support and encouragement of Robert A. Cox, Omar K. Moore, Clark D. Rogers, and Blanche E. Woolls, I am deeply grateful.

In addition, the following videodisc experts (in research, manufacturing, hardware, software, evaluation and applications) provided invaluable and, for the most part, unavailable information:

James J. Bosco, Thomas L. Elmquist, Kenneth E. Farr, Anthony Ferralli, Kathryn Ferralli, James N. Fiedler, Larrie E. Gale, Rus Gant, Douglas Howorth, George R. Jones, Donald J. Kerfeld, Mark H. Kryder, John C. Messerschmitt, Sam P. Petruso, Frank M. Price, Lou L. Prudhon, Verel R. Salmon, Lloyd A. Troeltzsch, Lynn A. Yeazel. The visual and technical additions provided by Rockley L. Miller of The Videodisc Monitor are also indispensable components.

For insightful contributions, bountiful support, and technical assistance I am indebted to two of my brothers—Richard and Ronald. The masterful work of Erika Van Sickel in translating my cryptic writing to manuscript form has been an inspiration, as has been the skillful editing by Joan C. Cash and Tracey Linton Craig. Essential as well, to the intellectual, physical, and spiritual challenges and endurance requisite to this process, has been the perspicacity, patience, and gentle strength of Bay Hallowell.

1

Educational Technology: A Historical Perspective

Effective teaching and learning with the use of technology has yet to have its potential realized in most academic environments. Optical laser reflective disc technology, with its mass storage capacity, durability, immediate random access, and interactive proficiency (especially when coupled with a microcomputer) is the latest and most promising medium to be introduced to educators. Whether it is accepted and widely used will be determined in large part by instructional designers, administrators, and teachers themselves.

A new era in education with technology leading the way is not a recent proclamation. Shortly after inventing the motion picture projector in the 1890s, Thomas Alva Edison announced his belief that it would revolutionize education to the extent that textbooks would no longer be necessary. In 1922 Edison said, "I believe that the motion picture is destined to revolutionize our educational system, and that in a few years it will supplant largely, if not entirely, the use of textbooks in our schools. Books are clumsy methods of instruction at best."[1]

In 1925 he further emphasized this belief: "Maybe I'm wrong, but I should say that in 10 years textbooks as the principal medium of teaching will be as obsolete as the horse and carriage are now. I believe that in the next 10 years visual education—the imparting of exact information through the motion picture camera—will be a matter of course in all of our schools. The printed lesson will be largely supplemental—not paramount." Since then radio, television, language laboratories, and teaching machines have all been introduced and promises for the educational environment have run high. Each has made a contribution, some more significant than others. Unfortunately, though, as useful educational tools, they have tended to be "misunderstood, overbought, under-used and eventually largely discarded."[2]

In similar fashion the microcomputer has been over-merchandized in ways that make efforts by hucksters of earlier educational technology seem like neophytes in comparison. If it is to escape the fate of its predecessors, substantial application alterations will be necessary on the part of teachers and school administrators.

Programmed Instruction

Educational television, programmed instruction with "teaching machines," and its extension under computer-assisted instruction have all been hampered by excessive emphasis on hardware and system issues to the detriment of effective and creative programming, according to Cambre[3] and Gayeski.[4] With respect to the failure of language laboratories, Joseph Hutchinson, a specialist in foreign languages for the U.S. Office of Education, reported that one significant hindrance was that of the more than 12,000 high selected secondary school teachers trained in the foreign language summer institutes during this period, early 1960s with funding from title III of the National Defense Education Act, the majority were not functionally competent enough in the languages they taught to be models for their students. Teachers needed "new skills and new insights" to use the new materials effectively.[5] With programmed instruction, which is a sequential or linear instructional design,[6] such concerns were seemingly addressed by making programs, particularly the early ones, self-contained and teacher-proof. This left the role of the teacher unspecified and many, understandably, felt threatened.[7,8] In the public school system of Denver, Colorado and Manhasset Junior High School of Long Island, New York,[9] it was demonstrated that teacher attitude toward programmed instruction was a critical factor in its success. The more enthusiasm a teacher had for programmed instruction reflected in better work by the students on the program. At Manhasset it became apparent that a classroom environment with more teacher-individual student interaction and less formality enhanced the learning process as well.

A notable exception to Cambre's and Gayeski's observations—and an exemplary use of programmed instruction—was designed and implemented by the Denver schools working with a research team from the Stanford University Institute for Communication Research in the early 1960s. The intent of the research project was to test the teaching of Spanish through the use of programmed materials coupled with instructional television. The researchers used television to facilitate the transition from a wholly audiolingual method of language teaching to a combination of speaking-listening and reading-writing. Based on what the Denver-Stanford team learned in its first experiment with programmed instruction teaching English, particularly in relation to effective implementation or program introduction, this time the team structured paid workshops for the Spanish teachers so they would become familiar with the new program prior to classroom use.

More than 6,000 students participated in this Spanish program experiment, which was designed from the start to be used in conjunction with regular classroom teaching. The results demonstrated a substantial increase in learning with students progressing at the same rate in their respective groups. In a substantive way, the innovative instruction used with technology enhanced the teaching and learning environment without threatening or supplanting the teacher, which is both the ideal and the potential of educational technology.

The success in this instance encouraged teachers as well as administrators to welcome and further promote such instructional innovation. Unfortunately, such models that use technology to encourage the revolutionizing of educational practice do not abound.

Educational Television

The Ford Foundation supported research in educational television as early as 1951, and, by 1953 the first station, KUHT in Houston, Texas, was broadcasting. In April of 1954 station WQED opened in Pittsburgh as the first community-sponsored educational television station in America. In 1955 it was the first to telecast classes to elementary schools. Experimentation and implementation grew rapidly in school systems for primary grades through college in such areas as Montgomery County, Maryland; Pittsburgh, Pennsylvania; Chicago, Illinois; and central Indiana. As the shortage of teachers became more critical during the 1960s, many lauded educational television as a panacea.

In 1966 the Ford Foundation ended its funding of educational television experimentation with the recommendation that the FCC establish a satellite system for television broadcasting in place of telephone transmission of signals and, with the accumulated savings from commercial television, implement a national non-commercial network that would include educational programming.

Nearly 20 years later the satellite system remains on drawing boards and public television totters on the brink of financial insolvency. . . .

The impact of television on instruction cannot be said to have been dramatic, influential, or even significant. Educational television in the school, once oversold, is now under-utilized. . . . An unmitigated disaster by overuse in the home, television is a disaster by default in the classroom.[10]

The American Elementary-Secondary Classroom Model

The American elementary-secondary classroom model of today is akin to the traditional "teaching" model that has endured for organized mass education in this country for some 135 years. In more than 100 years of this system there has been little change in the student-teacher ratio, which averages around 20–25 to 1. After summarizing the history of mass education in the United States, Arthur Melmed[11,12] goes on to detail its declining reputation over the past 25 years, as well as the receding average annual teacher salary over the past 15 years. In the Rand Corporation report titled "The Evolution of Teacher Policy" that was released in April of 1988, it was found that average teacher salaries rose 31-percent from 1981–86 to the mid-$20s.[13] More recent figures from the National Education Association and other sources estimate average salaries in 1988 to be around $28,000.[14] Even so, the professional status of teachers is still in question. Albert Shanker,[15] the president of the American Federation of Teachers, sees salaries beginning to rise, significantly in some states such as New York, with its model for educational reform in Rochester, but he fears that as many as half of the nation's teachers will leave the profession by 1992. The reason, says Shanker, is primarily low salaries—low in comparison to other professions—combined with poor working conditions.[16,17]

To further complicate matters, Melmed[18] reports that while "the social, intellectual and cultural diversity of the student population has increased substantially," the "academic competence of teachers" has already "on average, declined." Drawing estimates from the National Science Teachers Association, Shanker relates that 30 percent of those currently teaching science do not have the proper academic background to do so. Clearly, a complementary or new model is needed.

Accordingly, Shanker is exerting much effort to raise the standards, the salaries, and the working environments of teachers to the quality of comparable professionals. As with the medical profession, professional teachers in his restructured model need paraprofessionals, interns, technologists and others to assist them and to manage a large portion of the tasks that currently overextend them. New technology will play a vital role—particularly computer and video technology. With such collaborative efforts, professional teachers "will be freed up to practice their profession" and finally able "to begin to move in the direction of more individualized learning, fitting the structure to the child rather than the other way around."[19]

Educational researchers and practitioners from Dewey to the present time have much discussed and pursued, through various inventions, the rather elusive ideal of providing for differences among learners amidst mass education. Dewey contended that the learning process involved a two-way action, or interaction between learner and environment, and that reflection was at the center of this process aimed always at advancing intelligence. As an educational paradigm, Dewey's experimental curriculum, which he implemented at the Laboratory School that he founded in 1896 at the University of Chicago, was much more individualized than was the standard model of the day; and his instructional approaches were clearly more effective. Even so, a quarter of a century later Dewey himself would declare progressive education a failure because "it had too hastily destroyed the traditional instructional pattern without replacing it with something better."[20]

The traditional and demanding academic program of the 1930s and 1940s was, in practice, quite good. The quality of teacher and curricula were high, and the schools had their pick of the best students. Unfortunately, such an environment was achieved at the expense of the majority of students. In 1940 the dropout rate for high school students was nearly 80 percent.[21]

Requisite Changes

What has not been tried with much careful and sustained effort is the use of technology, coupled of course with scientific advances, in mass educational environments.[22,23,24,25,26] Carter and Wedman, surveying classroom media use, conclude that simple technologies are more attractive to teachers, as are materials that are least expensive to produce. They recommend teachers receive more instruction both in frequently used classroom equipment—such as overhead projectors, audio cassette recorders, and 16mm projectors—as well as less frequently used equipment, such as video. Such training would help teachers better understand and use appropriate media technology in order to enhance the learning environment. Cost, of course, remains a significant impediment.

Omar Moore sketches the cultural impact of technology and emphasizes its importance to learning environments, as well as the necessity of change. He writes,

> "The last 300 years, in the technologically sophisticated parts of the world, have been convulsively dynamic, with the past 20 years bringing us to morphogenic changes almost on a yearly basis. A learning environment that is to constitute a distillation, i.e., a model, of our present situation must be dynamic. The learner must get used to sudden changes; . . . he must . . . somehow cope with series of new worlds instead of mere variations on a theme."[27]

This emphasis on change is vital.

New educational technologies frequently necessitate new theories of learning and new instructional design strategies rather than developments that are extensions of existing models. Interactive learning technology requires such change.[28,29,30] [An interactive program is one in which the selection and sequencing of information is determined by the user's response, which is generally processed through a computer.] Even so, Reigeluth and Garfield[31] recommend a progressive approach that includes:

(1) making better use of present instructional design knowledge;
(2) development of new models as well as meta-models to expand and better integrate the interactive designs available to educators; and
(3) the designing of both software and hardware that truly enhance effective learning.

Such a method complements and expands current and traditional instructional models. Alterations in work patterns and attitudes have also proven essential in corporate environments integrating the computer into the work place.[32,33]

For educators, this conceptual change in teaching and, consequently, in learning, offers increased potential for active, individualized, and dynamic learning by those using the medium. It need not, though, pose a threat to more traditional ways of teaching and learning. Reigeluth[34] writes that "different instructional theories and different theoretical perspectives should not be thought of as competing with one another. . . . Each theory or 'knowledge base' provides a partial understanding of the real world of instruction in much the same way that each window in an unknown house provides a partial understanding of what the inside of the house is like and therefore how to move around in that room."

The focus on instructional change also underscores the evident fact that the technology itself does not insure substantive learning. James Bosco[35] accentuates that "because an instructional system is called interactive does not mean that it provides a higher level of interactivity than does a well-organized book on the same topic with a good table of contents and index." Further, having a highly efficient means of storing and manipulating information is no guarantee that high quality information "gets stored and retrieved in a way to improve instruction." The instructional effectiveness of this medium as well as the extent of its use is, and will be determined by, the availability of high-quality programs (software).[36, 37,38,39] Rockley Miller[40] concurs in his discussion regarding the development of videodisc and CD-ROM by pointing out that the markets for both are "inexorably software-bound and software driven. Users will purchase hardware only if there is either available software of sufficient value or if need warrants the expense of developing their own."

This emphasis on the marketplace driving the development of the technology is rather foreign to most academics. Gabriel Ofiesh points out that

> educational technology is a science which too often has been based on the adaptation of present technological developments to educational purposes rather than on developing technological innovations from learning needs. When the microcomputer and interactive videodisc were invented, the educational technologist began to explore its learning applications. The result was computer-assisted instruction (CAI) and interactive training packages used in vocational and technical education.[41]

Such application has resulted in most computer-assisted learning being "highly controlling and directive." Should interactive technology be applied in similar fashion, it would "be a gross misuse of the medium."[42] By giving students greater flexibility they are encouraged to accept greater responsibility for their learning and are able to access broader variations of stored data, according to their course of study and/or particular interests. Effective instruction, however, requires a great deal of knowledgeable and creative planning. Such a process is the foundation of a dynamic learning environment—particularly one that truly is adaptive to specific learner needs. Flexibility follows a disciplined core that serves as the hub of this interactive learning process.

Moore, in exploring the nature of human potential—particularly in relation to learning, which has been the impetus of most of his research—developed four heuristic principles for "clarifying environments" [perspectives, autotelic, productive, and personalization] that are effective in creating a dynamic learning environment. Much of his work in the early 1960s centered on a computer-based electric typewriter that used programmed instruction coupled with auditory responses from this "talking typewriter." The system was adaptive to individual learning responses and needs. Experimental research demonstrated improvements in levels of reading, as well as motor dexterity and control by three grade levels or more. Moore is presently working with interactive video which is an advanced model of the responsive devices he wrote about in 1965.[43]

5

Excellent instructional designers thoroughly familiar with interactive technology and its capabilities are essential to its effective educational use. Such work by knowledgeable and creative designers needs to be coupled with a strong working commitment by teachers and administrators who want to implement this medium in their environment. Working together, they clarify learning goals and objectives that are particular to the students for whom the program is designed.[44] Ideally, this disciplined core then opens out to excellent and multifarious knowledge bases that the student/user can access easily.

Educational Technology Potential

The interactive technologies today—specifically, optical laser reflective discs controlled by a microcomputer—are highly efficient and very durable storage media of text, pictures and motion sequences, graphics, computer programs and data, as well as sound with immediate and random display when desired. The discs referred to are encoded and read by laser, and include: videodisc and CD-ROM (compact disc read-only memory)—which can store up to 600 megabytes of digital information, or the equivalent of more than 200,000 pages of typed text.

Emerging variations on this optical disc medium include CD-I (Compact disc-interactive), DVI (Digital Video Interactive), and CVD (compact videodisc). CD-I is a multimedia disc format with application and operating software implementations encoded along with a variety of other digital information, such as speech, music, photographs, graphics, and computer programs. DVI is a format that uses digital data compression and decompression techniques to store up to 72 minutes of full motion video on a CD-ROM. Finally, CVD is a hybrid CD format that combines analog video with digital audio and data. Each of these formats is expected to come to market during 1989. (For more detailed descriptions of these media, see glossary.)

A variety of interactive videotape and compact disk technologies are also being developed for introduction to the market in 1989 or soon thereafter. These are primarily aimed at the home market and are coming from game companies such as the ViewMaster-Ideal Group and Mattel Incorporated. A historical perspective on earlier interactive videotape systems for educational use will be addressed in the research review in Chapter 3.

One obvious and exciting application for optical technologies is in libraries where information is not generally consulted, but, rather, "nibbled at by a few." Having so stated, Vanevar Bush, the first director of the federal Office of Scientific Research and Development, chairman of the National Advisory Committee for Aeronautics, and president of the Carnegie Institute in Washington, D.C., perspicaciously outlined a vision he had in 1945 that is just now coming to fruition with the interactive technologies described above.

> Our ineptitude in getting at the record is largely caused by the artificiality of systems of indexing. When data of any sort are placed in storage, they are filed alphabetically or numerically, and information is found [when it is] by tracing it down from subclass to subclass. It can be in only one place, unless duplicates are used; one has to have rules as to which path will locate it, and the rules are cumbersome. Having found one item, moreover, one has to emerge from the system and re-enter on a new path. The human mind does not work that way. It operates by association. With one item in its grasp, it snaps instantly to the next that is suggested by the association of thoughts, in accordance with some intricate web of trails carried by the cells of the brain. It has other characteristics, of course; trails that are not frequently followed are prone to

fade, items are not fully permanent, memory is transitory. Yet the speed of action, the intricacy of trails, the detail of mental pictures, is awe-inspiring beyond all else in nature.

Man cannot hope fully to duplicate this mental process artificially, but he certainly ought to be able to learn from it. In minor ways he may even improve, for his records have relative permanency. The first idea, however, to be drawn from the analogy concerns selection. Selection by association, rather than by indexing, may yet be mechanized. One cannot hope thus to equal the speed and flexibility with which the mind follows an associative trail, but it should be possible to beat the mind decisively in regard to the permanence and clarity of the items resurrected from storage.[45]

Ofiesh[46] solidifies this foresight by describing emerging applications today that use interactive technology. Unlike most written text on paper, such as a book, which is by design sequentially and logically ordered, information that is accessed through advanced communication and storage systems need not be so restricted. Rather, by using non-sequential text [or hypertext], such as material stored on CD-ROM, the creative and critical thinking process can be given extended rein while reading, researching, or otherwise seeking knowledge.

With massive storage now possible,[47] and various documents as well as different drives (videodisc players and CD-ROM players, for example) networked together and manipulated by a microcomputer, cross references of articles and books, pictures and graphics are available almost instantly. John Vries, neurosurgeon and assistant vice president for health sciences at the University of Pittsburgh, has created such a workstation. [see Appendix]. Further, such information retrieval is possible with split-screen (or monitor) option for comparison, if desired, without losing the primary focus or reference point.

"Now we are talking about interactivity in learning in a way we never talked about it before," Ofiesh writes. "Exploratory and discovery learning!"[48] Such a system indeed positions reflection at the center of a learning process firmly affixed to the advancement or improvement of intelligence. Dewey would find this most heartening. The limitations of interactive technology are those imposed by the imagination and time constraints of the instructional designer/producer.[49,50]

At its best, interactive learning technology can be a "master teacher" that brings expert knowledge and instruction to "ordinary people," with the further potential of opening to them seemingly boundless educational treasures at the beckon of their fingertips—literally. Such strategic use of this medium has the long overdue potential of bringing substantive educational programs of high quality to greater numbers of students—to the benefit of more equal educational opportunity.[51]

In the process of adjusting to interactive media, teachers may find their prestige and authority threatened by such technology—at least initially, as they themselves adjust to it. Also, in a very labor-intensive marketplace, monies re-allocated to educational technologies may impinge upon job security for some teachers. The economic dilemma is that mechanization in education has tended to increase costs since "nothing is ever deleted."[52] With the issues of teacher quality as well as declining numbers that have been raised by Shanker, interactive media may be looked to more and more as an aid by some, as a panacea by others. Still others may view its potential as a threat. "Putting resources behind educational technology turns out to be a political decision," as Jim Mecklenberg of the National School Boards Association has said.[53] These important concerns will require much deliberation and collective resolution for real progress to be realized.

Despite the rather discouraging history of educational technology, most new technologies, according to Miller,[54] go through three basic marketing stages. First is the "unbridled optimism" or panacean stage. Next, when the hype wanes, a "pessimistic depression" sets in. If the technology is a genuinely useful tool, the slump is followed by a substantive acceptance resulting in "real benefit and real value."

This last step seems slow in coming to academic environments in general, but there are exceptions, as in the Denver project, where administrators and teachers with vision and the means to experiment are able to work together to advance the learning environment. Such development, though, or the extent to which current and emerging technologies will be used advantageously in academic settings will be determined by seven factors:

Determining Factors for Use of Educational Technology

1. the quality of the educational environment and its ability to adapt to ongoing dynamic changes;
2. the quality of the educational technology;
3. the appropriateness of the technology to particular educational applications;
4. the acceptance of such technology as instructional aids to augment the learning environment, rather than as nemesises to educators;
5. how effectively such technology is implemented or introduced to teachers and by teachers,[55] and the extent to which it is actively used;
6. the educational quality of the instructional designs (software) that accompany such information technology; and, related to this,
7. the motivational capacity of such technology.

Interactive technologies, and particularly optical laser reflective discs governed by microcomputers,[56] now present the opportunity for educators to supersede much of the technological maelstrom that has bedeviled them in the past. With the ability to access huge databases of information in the form of audio, video, and computer data—and in any desired combination almost immediately—the germane issue will be how best to use such information technology. Ongoing research focused on creative and successful implementation and the instructional effectiveness of this medium, which only recently has begun to expand, will also be necessary, as will research on ways to use it effectively.

Endnotes

1. See Dagobert D. Runes, ed., *The Diary and Sundry Observations of Thomas Alva Edison* (New York: Philosophical Library, Inc., 1984), pp. 78–79, 65.
2. John F. Ohles, "The Microcomputer: Don't Love It to Death," *T.H.E. Journal* 13,1 (August 1985): 49–53.
3. Marjorie A. Cambre, "Interactive Video," *Instructional Innovator* 29,6 (September/October 1984): 24–25.
4. Diane M. Gayeski, "Interactive Video: Integrating Design 'Levels' and Hardware 'Levels'," *Journal of Educational Technology Systems* 13,3 (1984–85): 146.
5. Joseph C. Hutchinson, "The Language Laboratory—How Effective Is It?" *School Life* 46,4 January/February 1964, pp. 14–17, 39–41.
6. B. F. Skinner, with his delivery of a paper titled "The Science of Learning and the Art of Teaching" in 1954, is generally considered to be the first to strongly emphasize the scientific study of instruction. His

programmed instruction movement clearly demonstrated the educational possibilities of this medium to the academic community. For the first time, "how information is presented to the student" (instructional variables) was focused on rather than "how learning occurs" (learning variables). See Charles M. Reigeluth, C. Victor Bunderson, and M. David Merrill, "What Is the Design Science of Instruction?" *Journal of Instructional Development* 1,2 (Spring 1978): 11. Also see Ohles, "The Microcomputer: Don't Love It To Death," pp. 51 -52; and Paul Saettler, *A History of Instructional Technology* (New York: McGraw-Hill, 1968), pp. 253–254.

7. Ohles, "The Microcomputer: Don't Love It To Death," pp. 51–53.
8. Saettler, *A History of Instructional Technology,* pp. 250–267.
9. Ibid., pp. 256–261.
10. Ohles, "The Microcomputer," pp. 50–51. For an insightful discussion of the dispute over what public television should be—pitting traditionalists such as Bill Moyers against audience-responsive station managers—see Peter J. Boyer, "Public TV: That Delicate Balance." *The New York Times,* 25 October 1987, sec. 2, pp. 1, 40.
11. Arthur S. Melmed, "The Technology of American Education: Problem and Opportunity," *T.H.E. Journal* 14,2 (September 1986): 77–81.
12. This traditional and passive learning mode that endures today in most schools as well as universities is also addressed by Alfred Bork, "Education and Computers: The Situation Today and Some Possible Futures," *T.H.E. Journal* 12,3 (October 1984): 95.
13. "Teachers Still Not Full-Fledged Professionals, Study Says." *The Pittsburgh Press,* 12 April 1988, p. A6.
14. Melinda Beck, et. al. "A Nation Still At Risk," *Newsweek.* May 2, 1988, pp. 54–55.
15. Albert Shanker, "Our Profession, Our Schools: The Case for Fundamental Reform," *American Educator* 10,3 (Fall 1986): 12–13. See also Shanker's address to 3,000 delegates (representing 630,000 members of the federation) at the union's convention in July 1986 that was reported by Jane Perlez, "Improvement in Teachers Is Viewed as Threatened," *The New York Times,* 6 July 1986, sec. Y, p. 14.
16. Albert Shanker. "Impatience Short-Circuits Reform: Tough Problems Need Time and Effort," Where We Stand column, *The New York Times,* 13 March 1988, sec. 4, p. 9.
17. Jerry Buckley, "A Blueprint for Better Schools," *U.S. News and World Report,* January 18, 1988, pp. 60–65.
18. Melmed, "The Technology of American Education: Problem and Opportunity," p. 77.
19. Shanker, "Our Profession, Our Schools: The Case for Fundamental Reform," pp. 17, 44–45.
20. Saettler, *A History of Instructional Technology,* p. 55.
21. Albert Shanker, "An Open Letter to Education Secretary Bennett," Where We Stand column, *The New York Times,* 1 May 1988, sec. 4.
22. Isaac I. Bejar, "Videodiscs in Education: Integrating the Computer and Communication Technologies," *BYTE* 7,6 (June 1982): 78–104.
23. Bork, "Education and Computers: The Situation Today and Some Possible Futures," *T.H.E. Journal* 12,3 (October 1984): 95.
24. James J. Bosco, "Interactive Video: Educational Tool or Toy?" *Educational Technology,* April 1984, pp. 17–19.
25. Alex Carter and John Wedman, "A Survey of Classroom Media Use," *Instructional Innovator* 29,6 (September/October 1984): 36–37, 41.
26. Gabriel D. Ofiesh, "The Seamless Carpet of Knowledge and Learning," in *CD-ROM: The New Papyrus,* eds. Steve Lambert and Suzanne Ropiequet (Redmond, WA: Microsoft Press, 1986), p. 300.
27. Omar K. Moore, "The Clarifying Environments Program: 1960–1980" in *Organizing for Social Research,* eds. Burkart Holzner and Jiri Nehnevajsa (Cambridge: Schenkman Publishing Company, 1982), p. 137.
28. Vicki Blum Cohen, "Interactive Features in the Design of Videodisc Materials," *Educational Technology,* January 1984, p. 16.
29. Gayeski, "Interactive Video: Integrating Design 'Levels' and Hardware 'Levels'," p. 150.
30. Phyllis M. Levenson, James R. Morrow, and Barbara Signer, "A Comparison of Noninteractive and Interactive Video Instruction About Smokeless Tobacco," *Journal of Educational Technology Systems* 14,3 (1985–86): 201.

31. Charles M. Reigeluth and Joanne M. Garfield, "Using Videodiscs in Instruction: Realizing Their Potential Through Instructional Design," *Videodisc and Optical Disk* 4,3 (May/June 1984): 206–213.
32. Bosco, "Interactive Video: Educational Tool or Toy?" p. 17.
33. William Bowen, "The Puny Payoff From Office Computers," *Fortune,* May 26, 1986, pp. 20–24.
34. Charles M. Reigeluth, ed., *Instructional-Design Theories and Models: An Overview of Their Current Status* (New Jersey: Lawrence Erlbaum Associates, 1983), p. 474.
35. Bosco, "Interactive Video: Educational Tool or Toy?" pp. 15, 18.
36. Bejar, "Videodiscs in Education," p. 100.
37. Diane Gayeski and David Williams, *Interactive Media* (New Jersey: Prentice-Hall, Inc., 1985), pp. 119–147.
38. Reigeluth and Garfield, "Using Videodiscs in Instruction: Realizing Their Potential Through Instructional Design," pp. 206–207.
39. Judith Paris Roth, "The Coming of the Interactive Compact Disc," *High Technology* 6,10 (October 1986): 46.
40. Rockley L. Miller, "CD-ROM and Videodisc: Lessons to be Learned," in *CD-ROM: The New Papyrus,* p. 38.
41. Ofiesh, "The Seamless Carpet of Knowledge and Learning," p. 306.
42. Diana M. Laurillard, "Interactive Video and the Control of Learning," *Educational Technology,* June 1984, pp. 7–15.
43. Omar Khayyam Moore and Alan Ross Anderson, "Some Principles for the Design of Clarifying Educational Environments," in *Handbook of Socialization Theory and Research,* ed. David A. Goslin (New York: Rand McNally & Company, 1969), pp. 571–613; Omar K. Moore, "The Clarifying Environments Program: 1960–1980," in *Organizing for Social Research,* eds. Burkart Holzner and Jiri Nehnevajsa (Cambridge: Schenkman Publishing Company, 1982), pp. 105–167; and Omar Khayyam Moore, "From Tools to Interactional Machines," in New Approaches to Individualizing Instruction, report of a conference to mark the dedication of Ben D. Wood Hall, Educational Testing Service, Princeton, N.J., 11 May 1965. See also Saettler, *A History of Instructional Technology,* pp. 262–263. Moore is a professor of Sociology at the University of Pittsburgh and director of the Clarifying Environments Program. He is co-inventor of the Talking Typewriter and author, with Francine E. Jefferson, of a videodisc for IBM and World Book. He has also authored more than 140 publications and in the area of applied research is primarily interested in the education of America's "underprivileged."

     For an extensive study of Moore's work and its application to interactive video, see Andrew J. Peterson, "The Clarifying Environments Program: An Application to Interactive Videodisc Courseware." Ph.D. dissertation, University of Pittsburgh, 1987–88.
44. Reigeluth and Garfield, in discussing current problems, cite "the shortage of professionals qualified to produce such (interactive) courseware, coupled with the expectations by institutional policy makers that faculty can do such courseware development on their own time!" Reigeluth and Garfield, "Using Videodiscs in Instruction: Realizing Their Potential Through Instructional Design," p. 206.
45. Vannevar Bush, "As We May Think," in *CD-ROM: The New Papyrus,* eds. Steve Lambert and Suzanne Ropiequet (Redmond, WA: Microsoft Press, 1986) pp. 3–20. This article was originally printed in The Atlantic Monthly, July 1945.
46. Ofiesh, "The Seamless Carpet of Knowledge and Learning," pp. 299–317.
47. For example, the Grolier Encyclopedia is currently available on one CD-ROM. Also, it is possible to place all forty volumes of the Encyclopaedia Britannica on one CD-ROM, with remaining room for additional information. See Peter R. Cook, "Electronic Encyclopedias," *BYTE* 9,7 (July 1984): 151–170.
48. Ofiesh, "The Seamless Carpet of Knowledge and Learning," p. 310.
49. Alex van Someren, *Interactive Video Systems* (London: Century Communications, 1985), p. 63.
50. John Eggert, "Lessons Learned in the Development and Implementation of Computer-Based/Interactive-Video Instruction" (Center for Instruction Development and Evaluation, University of Maryland, no date given), pp. 5–7.
51. Isaac I. Bejar, "Videodiscs in Education," p. 104.
52. Bosco, "Interactive Video: Educational Tool or Toy?" p. 18.
53. Jim Mecklenburger of the National School Boards Association, quoted in Sally Banks Zakariya, "Here's Why Most Schools Don't Use Videodiscs—Yet," *The American School Board Journal* (June 1984): 27.

54. Rockley L. Miller, "CD-ROM and Videodisc: Lessons to be Learned," in *CD-ROM: The New Papyrus,* eds. Steve Lambert and Suzanne Ropiequet (Redmond, WA: Microsoft Press, 1986), pp. 37–41.
55. Gayeski and Williams, Interactive Media, p. 143.
56. There are predictions that "every personal computer will have a CD-ROM drive built in by 1990," and, further, "that the larger and less expensive storage capacity of optical discs will eventually bring about the replacement of magnetic disks." See Jeffrey Bairstow, "CD-ROM: Mass Storage for the Mass Market," *High Technology* 6,10 (October 1986): 44–51.

2

Videodisc to Optical Media: An Industry Emerges

Early History

The late 1800s were a fertile time for inventions and discoveries. The skyscraper, the electrical spark plug, a rabies vaccine, the electric elevator, as well as the fountain pen, zipper, incandescent light bulb, and the portable typewriter all emerged. With the discovery of how to convert sound into electrical impulses and then back to sound came the inventions of the telephone, radio, and phonograph.

In 1884, Paul Nipkow of Germany patented a disc for visual images that was created by way of a mechanical scanning process.[1,2,3] At about the same time, Alexander Graham Bell produced 12-inch audio discs that were optically recorded. His audio recording patents were leased to Thomas Edison.[4] Also introduced, in 1889, was transparent film on a flexible support, which opened the door for modern photography. Two years later, using this development by George Eastman, Thomas Edison invented the Kinetoscope, or motion picture projector,[5] and in 1894 demonstrated the first moving picture show—which actually gave the illusion of motion by showing still or individual pictures in rapid succession.

Edison expected this new medium to revolutionize the educational process by giving greater vitality to curricular content while at the same time increasing motivation significantly. After predicting that it would replace textbooks,[6,7] he returned to his work on the phonograph. Thirty-five millimeter rapidly became the standard film format and it required expensive and bulky projection equipment. It also was highly flammable due to its cellulose nitrate base. While it was quickly and profitably welcomed as an entertainment medium, its very success in that mode automatically made it suspect as an educational tool.

Motion pictures were first used extensively for educational purposes during World War I by the U.S. Army, which produced a number of films on venereal disease. Though hampered due to the lack of sound (it was still the "silent" era of film), they proved to be effective as an instructional medium.

When motion pictures with sound arrived in 1926, it was a boon to the entertainment industry. Warner Brothers developed this electronic sound recording and reproduction process which was a byproduct of telephone and radio technology. Interestingly, Thomas Edison had the first "talking pictures" in his laboratory almost 30 years earlier. "Do you know that one of my first thoughts for the motion picture camera was to combine it with the phonograph? In fact, that was what primarily interested me in motion pictures—the hope of developing something that would do for the eye what the phonograph did for the ear.

"My plan was to synchronize the camera and the phonograph so as to record sounds when the pictures were made, and reproduce the two in harmony. As a matter of fact, we did a lot of work along this line, and my talking pictures were shown in many theatres in the United States and foreign countries. . . ."[8] Many educators were further put off by what they perceived to be explanations and interpretations "imposed" by the producers. They wanted to be able to add their own narration. Too, for administrators who had begun to accept motion pictures into their academic environments, the addition of sound to silent film meant new projectors and new films. Expense was a renewed obstacle. During and following World War II, educational film received much greater impetus. As interest and use evolved, so did the technology, as well as available programs. Sixteen millimeter and 8 mm. film came to be accepted as more suitable for classroom use.

Vladimir Zworykin

Some years earlier but parallel with the development and improvement of instant picture equipment and film, a new field of electronic research and development was underway. A scientist at Westinghouse Electric, Vladimir Zworykin, who had studied under Boris Rosing in Russia, filed a patent application in 1923 (issued in 1938) on a tube that would permit electronic television. His work on this and on the cathode-ray tube (CRT) attracted the attention of RCA and they lured him away to be the director of their electronic research laboratory in 1930. There he further developed the Kinescope (cathode-ray tube) and perfected his work on the iconoscope electronic television camera and tube. (Note: The word television means "the ability to see at a distance," and is half Greek and half Latin).[9,10,11] Substantial television experimentation was taking place during this time. Ernst F.W. Alexanderson, a Swedish engineer working for General Electric (GE), advanced video transmission on a mechanical scanning disc. In 1928, the year GE began experimental telecasting with station WGY, his system was used to broadcast television's first drama—a 40-minute play titled "The Queen's Messenger."[12] By 1930, NBC was operating station W2XBS in New York.[13]

John Logie Baird

Another early television pioneer was John Logie Baird, the Scotsman generally considered the first person to achieve recognizable television pictures via a mechanical system.[14,15,16,17] An inveterate experimenter with an inventive mind, Baird drew substantially from the insights of others (though he did not always acknowledge them).[18,19,20] His early endeavors were financed by selling waterproof socks, marmalade (which he made), and honey. While opting to ignore the electronic television ideas of Rosing and Alan Campbell Swinton, a Scottish engineer, Baird instead chose to further develop the mechanical scanning disc work of Nipkow.[21] Baird's "system used a Nipkow disc both to scan the subject at the transmitter and to scan a modulated neon bulb at the receiver."[22]

One transmitting method he used was to send television signals as a series of tones by way of AM radio stations. However, the speed and synchronization of the scanning wheels in the transmitter and receiver of this mechanical system needed to be matched. This synchronization dilemma remained a major problem, as did low definition, and was particularly troublesome to viewers since broadcasts, at the time, commonly lasted only half an hour, and no more than a total of one to two hours per day. It was not uncommon for a would-be viewer to spend 20 minutes or more tuning up and intercepting a signal. The problem was obvious. In response, Baird explored the idea of recording (inscribing) the same signals, 30 scanning lines at 12.5 frames per second, on a waxed phonograph record (disc), which he called Phonovision.[23,24] The year was 1926 and Phonovision was the first operational videodisc[25] (although the term videodisc did not appear until David Paul Gregg coined the term, which he spelled "videodisk," in 1958).[26]

The Phonovision disc "played on an ordinary gramophone linked to the television receiver. [It] was made of the same brittle plastic as contemporary audio discs, and played at 78 rpm to produce a dozen grainy still images."[27] The intent was to use this disc as a "warm-up" prior to tuning-in reception of BBC broadcasts on their Baird Televisor receivers.

In 1935 Baird attempted to sell prerecorded discs in a London department store, of which some discs also employed his color television techniques. The venture, however, lasted only a few months and mechanical videodisc development seemed to abate while electronic broadcast television evolved. According to one of his biographers, Peter Waddell, Baird led the field in color television development until his death in 1946, and was, through a court injunction instigated by RCA, not given a chance to significantly influence American television. Further, he asserts, "the Baird Company believed that pre-recorded television on film to the home or a cinema was the way television would develop."[28]

U.S. Television Development

Commercial television broadcasting was authorized by the Federal Communications Commission (FCC) in 1941. Almost from the start it was apparent that television production needed the capability to store broadcasts for delayed playbacks. The time difference from east to west coast was a contributing factor in this need. Editing technical production errors after recording, in order to air the best possible performance, was of equal interest and concern. The technology, however, proved difficult. Minnesota Mining and Manufacturing Company (3M), a developer of magnetic tape, convinced Bing Crosby to try magnetic audio tape recording in 1948. One of the recording engineers at the initial test was John Mullin, who, while in England with the U.S. Army Signal Corps during World War II, had heard and later thoroughly investigated the Magnetophone, a superior magnetic tape recorder that the Germans developed.

Mullin used a modified version of this system to record Crosby for the first taped radio network program in the U.S. The Magnetophone served as the basis for the Ampex and Rangertone audio tape recorders. Mullin later worked for Crosby Enterprises, helping to develop the video tape recorder.[29] Bing Crosby Enterprises "demonstrated the first working magnetic videotape recorder" in 1951 that ". . . performed poorly, but was hailed as a magnificent engineering achievement nonetheless."[30] Researchers and engineers from 3M, Crosby Enterprises, and Ampex Corporation collaborated on this new frontier.[31] "But when Ampex developed a superior product, Crosby decided to stop independent developments and sold the Electronics Enterprises Division of the organization to 3M. It became 3M's Mincom Division in 1956."[32] In that same year, Ampex Corporation introduced a videotape recorder (VTR) that, within six months, would become a permanent part of operations at CBS, NBC and ABC.[33]

Mechanical editing, involving the cutting and splicing of tape, was popularized in 1958 and Ampex, again the leader, introduced electronic editing in the early 1960s. This innovation significantly enhanced and simplified the editing process and was itself enhanced when, in 1967, a time-code system was developed that enabled each video frame to be coded or labeled with a unique eight-digit number. This system permitted editing with reliable single-frame accuracy and became so widely used that it was standardized by the Society for Motion Picture and Television Engineers and became known as the SMPTE Time Code. In 1969 Sony Corporation introduced the 3/4-inch video cassette recorder, U-Matic, which added convenience to the technology as the first cassette format; and by the late 1970s, home videotape players/recorders, VHS or Beta 1/2 inch formats, were popular.

The electronic circuitry of television needs to process information individually, in contrast to film, which captures an entire frame. Accordingly, in converting light energy—light reflected off an image—to electrical signals, television dissects the image into countless and minuscule dots (picture elements) which it then processes and transmits in mosaic form to be reassembled by a receiver.

The signal sent is analog, which is representative of or analogous to an original image component. Since the information carried is steadily flowing and continually changing, there is commonly some degradation in signal fidelity. This is caused in large part by the electrical circuits that it is sent through. Electrical "noise" weakens and distorts the signal. An alternative, digital television, "is based primarily on the pulse coded modulation principle proposed by Alex Reeves while working with ITT's French subsidiary in 1938."[34] This method converts the analog signal to digital code or binary notation and is then capable of sending the information long distances without much distortion.[35,36] Bell Laboratories experimented with digitizing broadcast quality television pictures in the 1960s, but its use with television has generally been of lesser importance than its application for data processing and telecommunications. Consequently, its development is still in progress.

The standard television resolution (NTSC) in the United States uses 525 scanning lines per frame and the frames are processed at a rate of 30 per second. A group of American engineers from the Electronics Industries Association (EIA) developed the NTSC (National Television Systems Committee) commercial color television broadcasting standard that was approved by the FCC in 1953. Their hope was that it would be adopted worldwide. It was not, but it is used by the USA, Japan, Canada, Mexico, the Bahamas, and the Philippines. France developed SECAM (sequential couleur a memoire) which is also used in the USSR and some Middle Eastern and African countries. Another system, PAL (Phase Alternation Line), is a refinement of NTSC and was developed in West Germany and adopted by the United Kingdom and most of Europe, the Middle East, Africa, Australia, and South America.

Each NTSC frame contains approximately 11 million pieces of information. In transmitting this information, the electronic signals are measured by the number of times they vibrate in one second. These cycles per second (cyclical waves) are expressed in hertz (Hz) which determines the frequency of the signal. One hertz carries two pieces of television information, and the range of frequencies required to send the signal is referred to as the bandwidth. Thus, one television frame needs a signal bandwidth of approximately 4.0 MHz (4.0 million hertz). In contrast, the human ear has a bandwidth of only about 20,000 Hz.

Westinghouse Research Laboratories

At Westinghouse Research Laboratories between 1963 and 1966, Sziklai and Farr[37] frequently discussed videodisc recording and its merits in relation to magnetic tape recording. Their developmental work focused on the use of phonograph recordings for image as well as audio reproductions, on methods of increasing bandwidth capability of phonograph records (i.e., gearing down to 3 1/3 rpm), and on bandwidth compression of television signals, especially via digitizing. Although several former BBC research scientists worked with them, the American team leaders did not pick up on the work of Baird. A technically sound working system that emerged was Phonovid.[38] It employed a standard 33 1/3 phonograph record to store (inscribe) still images at a slow scan rate. Using two storage tubes (one for readout and one for writing) Phonovid could present still images at a quality comparable to broadcast television.

The timing of the read-out scanning [was] independent of the timing of the writing scanning, thus permitting the conversion of the scanning standards from slow-scan to standard EIA format (60-field per second rate) by switching the storage tube scanning rates between reading and writing.

A "freeze" frame was possible, because of the type of storage tubes used, and up to 400 still images with accompanying audio could be recorded on a 12-inch record. Phonovid's use as a visual/audio supplement in education and training environments held good potential; in addition, mass replication was inexpensive.

But no systems were sold. Even though Westinghouse had invested substantially in this system, their business at the time was not in software development, programming, and the marketing necessary to promote its use.

Sometime later the Westinghouse Learning Corporation was established, and between 1969 and 1972 Farr and those working with him applied their developing expertise to creating a magnetic videodisc system for the University of Wisconsin Medical Center Library. Still frame slides were recorded at standard television rate onto a videodisc. This analog signal was then slow-scan generated in order to be digitized and sent out from the Madison Medical Center over dedicated phone lines to other hospitals. At the receiving end, the signal was picked up and recorded onto another magnetic videodisc, at standard television rate; then played as needed. They came close to realizing standard television resolution. Because the project was federally funded, it had a time line and did not further evolve.

The next magnetic videodisc project for Farr and his group focused on helping Georgia develop its statewide educational television system in the early 1970s. With only one channel available and numerous locations to serve a variety of subjects, time was a factor. The system developed could send from the center in Atlanta, during a three-minute intermission, up to 48 half-hour lectures of compressed audio-only information. Each synchronized still frame that accompanied the compressed audio (up to 16 seconds per frame) would reduce the aggregate of information sent by 16 seconds. With the wide bandwidth of the television system (as opposed to the narrow bandwidth of the phone lines) single frames were sent in actual or real time (30 frames per second). Lesson plans, obviously, would determine the ratio or blending of visual and audio material sent.

Various educational lessons were sent around the state and recorded, when received, onto a magnetic videodisc with two tracks—one for images, the other for audio—that were synchronized according to lesson design. One frame per track was stored on the disc, and about 50 minutes of material could be recorded.

There were similarities between this system and the slow-motion ("slo-mo") magnetic videodisc unit used with telecasts of sporting events. The first slow motion color videodisc system was introduced by ABC in 1967. Information is recorded onto these flat, magnetic discs in a series of concentric tracks. Each video frame is contained on one concentric circle—which permits instant slow motion, "freeze" frame, as well as variable speed replays—and about 30 to 35 seconds of material can be recorded at normal speed. Once the disc is filled, it automatically begins to erase and replace recorded material with new information. The unit uses a large, metallic disc pack, which rotates rapidly as the recording head system sweeps across the disc.[39] The first black-and-white magnetic videodisc, which provided instant replay and stop action, was introduced by CBS for a football game on July 8, 1965. Such systems are very expensive and have been losing their popularity to higher quality videotape as was demonstrated by the NFL's decision to use videotape for its "replay official" during the 1986 season.

17

The Georgia videodisc system was essentially an electronic equivalent of a slide/tape program with automatic queuing. After this project, Farr and his group were involved with some classified magnetic videodisc work in conjunction with MIT. When several key researchers left Westinghouse in 1974–75, the Learning Corporation began to fold up, and new management was not as oriented toward video projects. Thus, videodisc undertakings began to wane.

3M and SRI

Rice and Dubbe[40] cite a patent for television recording on a disc that was filed in 1952 and issued in 1965 to P.M.G. Toulon. (Toulon worked at the Westinghouse Research Laboratories from the late 1950s to the mid 1960s.) The disc held "a spiral array of minute images recorded on a high-resolution photographic plate". It turned at 1.5 rpm, according to the patent, and the images "were read out by focusing the beam of a flying spot scanner so that it scanned each picture along the radius of the disc." Whether or not such a system was actually built is unknown.

Early in 1961, 3M Company engineers were searching for ways to develop an inexpensive home video system. From the start they opted for the videodisc in place of motion picture film or magnetic tape because programs could be replicated more economically on the disc and the storage capacity was much greater as well. To expand their efforts, 3M turned to the Stanford Research Institute (SRI) for assistance. Together they moved away from the possibility of an embossed record since neither was equipped for such record processing, and opted instead for recording on a high-resolution photographic plate (using high-resolution Lippmann emulsion). What they developed was the first videodisc capable of recording and playing back full bandwidth images on an optical videodisc.

Their work, however, did not make use of the laser which had just been invented in 1960. Instead, the work at SRI was "limited to using high-pressure short-arc mercury and xenon lamps."[41] Because the amount of light was not sufficient to record images in real time, analog video signals were recorded at 1/16 of real time, or 112.5 rpm. They could, however, be played back in real time. (Real time equals 1,800 revolutions per minute or rpm, which is derived from the U.S. television signals frame rate of 30 per second; 30 frames per second times 60 seconds per minute = 1,800 rpm). The first images recorded and played back in this fashion were black and white with no sound, and were made in October of 1962. Although it was recognized that other information could be recorded on this medium, such as computer data, this aspect was not pursued. The format developed for this disc would be used in all subsequent constant-angular-velocity (CAV) optical discs.

While SRI's work was in progress, 3M engineers focused on developing electron beam videodiscs using Lippmann emulsion that recorded analog signals at standard video rates. The first demonstration was in March of 1963, but with continued refinement, by 1964 they were able to make 15-minute television recordings that were a significant improvement over the mercury-arc optical recordings. Silver halide discs of high quality were also developed at 3M, as were several portable videodisc players. The evolving emphases, though, were on developing plastic coatings for videodiscs and on videodisc recording, including ongoing research, as well as videodisc replication.

3M was issued 19 patents during this period (1960–1966) related to videodisc technology. Even so, had gas lasers been available to 3M and SRI scientists in their early explorations, more extensive development of the videodisc would have been realized much sooner.

Introduction of the Laser

In a 1916 publication, Albert Einstein "speculated that under certain conditions atoms or molecules could absorb light or other radiation and then be stimulated to shed their borrowed energy."[42] His fundamental work was essential to the invention of MASERS in 1951 (MASER stands for Microwave Amplification by Stimulated Emission of Radiation) and their evolving application to optical wavelengths that resulted in the invention of the LASER (Light Amplification by Stimulated Emission of Radiation).

The first operational, experimental maser was built at Columbia University by a team of researchers headed by Charles Townes, who became interested in microwave spectroscopy earlier while working at Bell Laboratories. At the same time, though independently, research was being conducted at the Lebedev Institute in the Soviet Union, principally under the guidance of Alexander Prokhorov and Nikolai Basov. For their work with masers and lasers, Townes, Basov and Prokhorov were awarded the Nobel Prize for Physics in 1964.

Townes, also a consultant at Bell Laboratories, worked closely on laser development with his former post-doctoral student Arthur Schawlow,[43] a research physicist at Bell Laboratories. Their early work was written up and from it a patent was applied for in July of 1958 through Bell's patent office. The patent was issued in March of 1960.

A research assistant and doctoral student at the Radiation Laboratory where Townes taught was Gordon Gould. Townes contacted him at home in October of 1957 to discuss some of Gould's research. Prompted by his interest, and having been introduced by Townes to the practice of getting laboratory notes signed for the establishment of invention priority claims, Gould had his notebook notarized on November 16, 1957. It contained "some rough calculations on the feasibility of laser light amplification by stimulated emission of radiation."[44]

Unfortunately, Gould's dissertation pertaining to the laser was not approved. He left Columbia University in March of 1958 and went to work for TRG Inc. He did, though, file for a patent application in April of 1959. Some of the material was similar to the Schawlow-Townes patent.

In December of 1965, Gould's priority laser work was the subject of a trial held at the U.S. Court of Customs of Patent Appeal. It was brought by TRG which had taken on Gould's laser project against Bell Laboratories. Ironically, Gould could not work on "his" project at TRG. Substantial funding was received from the Pentagon and he did not get the requisite security clearance. A patent was finally issued in 1977, 18 years after filing, and additional patents followed that were related to the 1959 application. Others are pending. Seventeen years is the duration of U.S. patents. As Gould's patent commenced in 1977, those issued to Schawlow and Townes in 1960 expired. For this period, Townes received approximately $1 million in royalties.

The first laser, which used synthetic ruby as the active material, was developed by Theodore Maiman at the Hughes Research Laboratories in California in July of 1960. It prompted much activity and further experimentation, including the use of gas lasers. In early 1986, the government was directed to issue a patent to Gordon Gould for his invention of the gas discharge laser, as filed in 1959. His patent covers the majority of all lasers used today, including carbon dioxide lasers, used in scientific and industrial applications, and argon lasers used in medical applications. It also is the type used on the recording and playback equipment for laserdiscs. The royalties are expected to be in the tens of millions of dollars.[45]

Light from such sources as the sun, light bulbs, a fire, or the like, is made up of diffused wavelengths. In contrast, a laser is a device that excites electrons into emitting photons—the basic unit of light energy—of identical wavelengths and then pumping that coherent light into an intense, amplified beam.[46] When focused to a minuscule spot on light-sensitive material, a low-power laser beam can record and read information in the form of microscopic pits, or holes. This technology, when applied to a laser disc, provides a storage density that is approximately one hundred times greater than that of a rigid magnetic disc for computer applications.[47]

Laser videodiscs, however, did not emerge immediately. Further research and prolonged development were necessary. By the early 1970s, Philips, MCA (formerly Music Corporation of America) and Thomson-CSF were using laser sources to record and play-back videodiscs, and were replicating them by pressing or injection molding, as with conventional records. Their entrepreneurial ventures, however, were not concerted at first.

Other Videodiscs Requiring a Stylus

TeD System

While others were pursuing the use of lasers with videodiscs for home replay systems of prerecorded programs, the Teldec research organization rejected both optical and magnetic methods and opted instead for a mechanical system for reproducing video and sound that used conventional, albeit advanced, audio recording principles. Teldec was jointly owned by Germany's AEG-Telefunken (Radio and Television Corporation) and Britain's Decca Record Company, and the monochrome version of the TeD System was first demonstrated in 1970.[48] A full-color version with dual-channel audio followed, and in March of 1975 they launched the first videodisc system to be extensively marketed commercially. (Baird's efforts in 1935 were commercial but certainly not extensive, and of rather short duration.)

Worth noting is K.G. Thorne's letter to Douglas Howorth at the Westinghouse Research and Development Center, dated 27 May 1975. Thorne, manager of Decca's video disc division, referred to TeD (Television Disc) as a video disc system. In an undated press release, but seemingly from later in the same year, the director of the audio-visual department at Telefunken, Rolf W. Schiering, refers to the same product as a videodisk system. This divergence in spelling lingers today. "Videodisk" seems to be used primarily by those that are more computer oriented and who view the videodisk as a computer peripheral. "Videodisc" seems to be used more often by those with a primary television or video orientation. Schiering viewed TeD as the perfect augmentation to printed material.

A storage medium with one hundred-fold capacity was required to advance a program with only sound transmission, (such as a phonograph record,) to the same length program in video.[49] TeD accomplished this by storing signal information "in the form of vertical undulations in a shallow V-shaped spiral groove"[50] and by rotating the disc at 1800 rpm (NTSC). Each video frame occupied one full rotation, and playback was accomplished through the use of an electro-mechanical transducer (piezo-electric) with a diamond stylus.

The thin, sensitive, eight-inch disc was made of a plastic foil, weighed 5 gms, and was 0.1 mm thick. It required a protective sleeve, which the disc player removed when inserted. Disc playing time was limited to 10 minutes but cartridges to play 12 discs automatically in sequence were offered. Average life expectancy was comparable to a phonograph record.

More than 6,000 players and in excess of 300,000 videodiscs were manufactured, adaptation to the television standards of other countries was completed, and licensing agreements were signed with several companies in Japan.[51] Nonetheless, the system had a short life. Parsloe[52] cites poor picture quality and lack of programming (disc variety) as contributing factors. Sigel mentions several more, including disc mastering difficulties and economics.[53]

Visc System

In 1978, Japan's Matsushita introduced the Visc system which was quite similar to TeD but with a nine-inch disc made of the same material as an ordinary phonograph record. It rotated at 450 rpm (NTSC) and offered dual channel audio with two hours of color video. Its marketplace existence was of much shorter duration than was TeD's.

By 1978 numerous videodisc systems were being developed in various parts of the world with many, if not most, being incompatible—which only served to further divide and splinter an unsettled market.

RCA SelectaVision

In 1919 Westinghouse Electric, General Electric (GE), which was a successor to Edison General Electric, and American Telephone & Telegraph (AT&T) formed the Radio Corporation of American (RCA). In early 1927, RCA, Westinghouse, and GE formed the National Broadcasting Company as a subsidiary of RCA. AT&T withdrew from the broadcasting aspect to control all network relays. In 1930, under antitrust suit pressure, Westinghouse and GE transferred their radio and television activity to RCA.[54,55] (This encouraged Zworykin's move from Westinghouse to RCA.)

When color was introduced to television, it was assumed that the medium would become much more popular to the general public. RCA, accordingly, began to rerun existing programs in color as a cost-saving effort. The result was disastrous. Color television almost expired in the mid-1950s. Only when NBC finally "began broadcasting shows that were specifically made for color television"[56] were dramatic positive results realized.

When RCA began to explore videodiscs for prerecorded home use in the mid-1960s, its intent was to place movies on them. With an abundance of movies, "Repackaging" was the focus. By 1977 RCA had analyzed both optical videodiscs and pressure pick-up systems (such as TeD) for its videodiscs and players, but opted instead for capacitance technology, believing it to be less expensive and more reliable than the other systems. The format was called CED or Capacitance Electronic Disc. In many ways it was an extension of RCA's phonograph record foundation. During 1977 RCA also produced and tested over 200,000 of its own discs.[57]

The RCA videodisc system, SelectaVision, was released in 1981 amidst a $20 million promotion campaign. In the first five weeks 200,000 discs and 26,000 players were sold.

The discs were 12 inches in diameter, rotated at 450 rpm (NTSC) when read, with each rotation holding four frames, and contained spiral grooves that had video and dual-channel audio signals stored in shallow pits via an FM encoding method.[58,59] The electrical charges on the disc were read by an electrode-bearing stylus that was metal coated to complete the capacitor circuit. Such a system was not mechanical as is a phonograph stereo system. Rather, the stylus here, as a reading head, functioned in a way similar to the reading of a floppy diskette in a computer. The SelectaVision videodisc had a plastic base of polyvinyl chloride (PVC) that was covered with fine carbon particles for conductive purposes, then sprayed with a lubricant to prevent shorting out the electrical circuitry, and were readily mass replicated. With contact necessary between disc and reading head, and given the sensitive make-up of the disc itself, it was essential to keep the disc in a protective package or "caddy," which the disc player removed after insertion. Two hours of

Herb Schlosser, Division Vice President, RCA SelectaVision, with collection of titles for RCA's ill-fated CED videodisc player. (Courtesy The Videodisc Monitor)

playing time were offered on a double-sided disc, with a life expectancy greater than a phonograph record. In 1983 RCA introduced an interactive version of CED.

Sales for the SelectaVision system, however, were not as high as RCA expected. Complicating matters was the dramatic growth of the VCR industry. Following a Supreme Court decision, consumers were permitted to record television programs at home using a VCR. Videotape rentals elicited a significant and lively response from the motion picture industry, and home movies could be produced using portable videotape systems. VCRs clearly dominated and videodisc systems were basically ignored in the prerecorded home market.

On April 4, 1984, RCA announced its withdrawal from the videodisc field. It had produced about 1,200 movie titles on discs and manufactured about 550,000 videodisc recorders. It had also, over three years of operation, lost approximately $580 million.[60] RCA felt it had entered the market too late. What resulted, due to RCA's extensive promotion of the medium, was a major shock wave that continues to have an adverse effect on the acceptance and use of videodisc technology in general.

In 1986, General Electric Company "swallowed" RCA in what was, as High Technology Business reporter Herb Brody put it, "oil companies excluded, the largest corporate acquisition in the history of American business." Accordingly, ". . . RCA has ceased to exist as a corporation . . ." and "GE has stripped its new possession of many of its defining features."[61] In early 1987 GE/RCA's David Sarnoff Research Center introduced Digital Video Interactive (DVI) technology, which transforms personal computers into easily used personal interactive tools with the ability to deliver a combination of text, advanced graphics, full motion video and high quality audio through a variety of digital media—including CD-ROM.[62]

Shortly thereafter, GE donated this research center to SRI International and coupled that gift with a five-year, $250 million contract to continue work on DVI technology and other research initiatives. In October of 1988 Intel Corporation acquired the DVI Technology Venture from General Electric along with the 35-person DVI development team. Although no longer involved in consumer electronics manufacturing, GE remains committed to the DVI standard and is integrating the technology into several of its products.

JVC—VHD/AHD

In the spring of 1983, the Victor Company of Japan (JVC, which is an affiliate of Matsushita—the company that introduced Visc) unveiled a grooveless CED system that was similar to, but not compatible with, RCA's. This videodisc system is called VHD/AHD, for Video High-Density/Audio High-Density. The 10-inch disc is kept in a protective cover, holds two frames per track and 45,000 still frames per side, or a two-hour feature film (both sides) with two sound tracks. Because it has no grooves, accurate random access within three seconds per side is available with freeze-frame capability as well as slow, normal, or fast speeds in forward or reverse.

The videodisc rotates at 900 rpm with two frames per revolution, and is interactive. Notably, a pulse code modulation (PCM) unit that allows music to be recorded digitally is available for use with the VHD/AHD system. Life expectancy for the disc is up to 2,000 playing hours, which is made possible by a stylus 10 times larger than RCA's was—thus reducing wear on the disc.

The disc manufacturing process is similar to that of optical disc, which uses the laser, and the same player can be used for NTSC, PAL, or SECAM formats.[63] This system remains on the market, although it has never had a strong presence in this country.

Non-Contact Videodiscs[64]

Laser Optical Reflective Videodisc

The laser optical reflective videodisc, more commonly known as laser disc, is the most widely used videodisc today. It first emerged through the separate research and development efforts of NV Philips (a large European electronics firm) and MCA, Inc. (parent company of Universal Pictures).

NV Philips

In 1969 Philips' Research Laboratories initiated three parallel projects to explore and develop optical laser disc recording techniques for video, audio, and data.[65] Being consumer oriented, and given the advancing popularity of television at the time, Philips was attempting to develop a new system that would further promote sales of its television systems.

As hardware (player or drive) development progressed, the early software (videodisc) research was turned over to a subsidiary company, PolyGram, which Philips owned 50 percent of at the time. Phillips believed that PolyGram, a record-production company, was better suited to further develop the disc itself as well as replicating procedures. Some progress was made but eventually PolyGram, given its primary focus, lost interest in the videodisc project and gave it up. This left Philips with a rudimentary disc to play on the drive being developed and sent them in search of another organization with whom to pursue software development.

MCA

As television began to advance in popularity, cinema attendance began to subside. MCA, with some 11,000 titles in its film library, started to explore ways to reissue existing pictures as well as to realize a wider audience for new releases. The idea was to introduce them into the home environment.

Among the companies that MCA owned was Gauss ElectroPhysics, Inc. Its original co-owner, David Paul Gregg, had a varied background that included videotape recording experience at Ampex and participation in stereo record technology development as well as exposure to optical recording at Westrex. With such a foundation coupled with an inventive mind he became intrigued with using a record for movies. In March of 1958 Gregg announced his invention, which he called a "videodisk."[66] It was the first use of this term. "The optical videodisc was defined then as a plastic replica like a phonograph record that contains a video movie with full bandwidth and 30 images per second to conform to NTSC television signals, wherein the information could be read without a needle or other contact instrument."[67] By design the plastic material to be used was clear, rather than opaque, and the play side had a mirror-like appearance.

Putting this new concept into practice was no easy task. Unable to fund the project himself, Gregg turned to 3M's Mincom division, which in turn involved SRI. In the process the concept was changed from the rigid disc to photographic film. Gregg and several colleagues, wishing to advance the original focus on rigid plastic disc, parted with 3M and formed first Winston Research and then Gauss ElectroPhysics.

Numerous companies were interested in seeing their videodisc inventions in operation, including NV Philips (who purchased "high-speed duplication machines from Gauss to help launch their audio cassette technology"[68]) and MCA. The latter was so attracted that in late 1967 it purchased Gauss ElectroPhysics. MCA later coupled this subsidiary with several other acquisitions to form MCA Technology, Inc. MCA Technology became an electronics equipment manufacturing business, but in the late 1960s MCA decided to divest itself of that entity. To help evaluate the value of this entity, as well as to obtain recommendations for future direction with relevant technology, MCA procured the services of Kent D. Broadbent who came from Hughes Research Laboratories as a highly respected scientist. Broadbent picked up on the work done earlier by David Paul Gregg and Keith Johnson (co-owners of Gauss ElectroPhysics), and made recommendations for further development.

MCA then provided Broadbent with a secluded research facility and small staff to cultivate this technology in the late 1960s. In December of 1972, MCA demonstrated the first optical laser videodisc system with a replicated disc to most of the major electronic manufacturing companies from around the world. Six months earlier, Philips had demonstrated a similar system, developed independently, but had used the glass master disc to play, not a replicated one, as did MCA.

MCA, Broadbent explained, developed a 12-inch disc that rotated at 1800 rpm with one television frame per turn encoded with FM frequency modulation by an argon-ion laser that resulted in information being recorded in a series of microscopic holes. This early disc would play 20 minutes per side—which constituted 36,000 frames per side, and the track length was not fixed. It varied from inside to outside circumference. Freeze frame, with no wear on the disc since there was no physical contact, and instant replay were also possible, as were slow, normal and fast speeds in forward and reverse. To facilitate frame retrieval, the researchers developed a digitally encoded numbering (or index) process for each frame, and coupled it with coding and search programming, or logic. A videodisc of this type is called Constant Angular Velocity, or CAV. A low power helium-neon laser beam in the videodisc player was used to read and play back the disc.

To make the disc, 1/4-inch thick glass was optically polished to be as blemish free as possible, then coated with a thin photoresist film that was light sensitive in order to be encoded by the laser track by track, as the disc spun at 1800 rpm. The combined video and audio signals caused the laser to be alternately turned on and off to selectively incise the photoresist coating and thereby form pits or holes on the surface of the glass-based master. The mastering equipment, which takes any video, audio, and/or data information and records it in real time onto a master disc, is called a mastering bench. A high-power laser and computer are essential elements.

Once the glass master disc was developed[69] an electrical charge was put on it, after which it was electroplated with nickel. The metal plate master that was formed had a negative impression, once separated from the glass master. From it, a limited number of plastic replicas could be stamped out or otherwise formed, in much the same fashion as audio records were duplicated. This metal master plate, though, was somewhat fragile. For high volume runs it was reprocessed to create a positive metal disc, called a Mother disc. When the Mother disc was reprocessed, a number of additional metal discs with negative impressions were subsequently obtained from which multiple plastic replicas could be formed.

The mastering process described here was the one later used by DiscoVision Associates. Broadbent's earlier experimental method covered the glass disc with a thin film coating that the laser pitted. Next, a layer of light sensitive photoresist material was applied that was then exposed or polymerized with an ultraviolet light source through the information holes from the back side. Hardened bumps over the holes resulted, with the uncut areas not affected since the undisturbed film served as a protective shield. One of Broadbent's interests was in bubble memory. This method of raised bumps, however, was not further developed by MCA.

For replica material, Broadbent considered mylar, polyethylene terephthalate (which would have been a flexible disc), rigid plastic, polyvinyl chloride or PVC, as well as a transparent plastic (which will be discussed later). The rigid plastic replicas that were chosen were then metallicized with a reflective coating, in order to be read back by a low-power laser, and finally a protective coating of clear plastic was added to protect against handling and general exposure.

Broadbent was aware of numerous applications for this technology in addition to home entertainment.

> These include archival storage of documents and facsimiles; audiovisual encyclopedias, dictionaries, catalogs, etc., that may be accessed immediately on a frame address basis; teaching machine and educational applications which involve inter-active programming with addressable sub-routines and branching and many other applications where data, pictures, motion or general audio-video information must be stored inexpensively and accessed flexibly and rapidly.[70,71]

In this same article Broadbent mentions a longer playing (40 minutes per side) videodisc that had already been publicly demonstrated as well, but did not describe it. Further, he points out that the videodisc player was designed to be connected to any domestic color television receiver.

Given its past experience with MCA Technology, MCA did not want to go back into the electronics manufacturing business. Thus, MCA too began actively to seek a joint venture partner in order to further develop, manufacture and market this new technology—with their films encoded.

The search continued for almost two years, with several different possibilities seriously discussed. Finally, in September of 1974, MCA and NV Philips of Holland signed an agreement of cooperation, rather than one of joint venture. By combining their videodisc research and development work the two companies were able to select the best technology of both organizations and thereby eliminate differences in order to emerge with one system. MCA was to manufacture the discs and supply the films and Philips was to manufacture the hardware (drives). With one videodisc standard, which they hoped would stabilize the field, their intent was to focus on the home consumer market.

In December of 1977, the president of MCA announced that the MCA/Philips system would be introduced the following December. Surprisingly, MCA had at that time established no manufacturing plant for the videodisc. The product was still at the research stage of development. On December 15, 1978, at Rich's Department Store in Atlanta, Georgia, the first consumer laser optical videodisc system was introduced to an anxiously waiting public. NV Philips shipped the players under a Magnavox label (Magnavox was a subsidiary of North American Philips). Of the 50 titles that MCA brought, the disc quality—on a scale of 1 to 10, with 10 being the highest—ranked 3 or 4 at best.

Problems continued with the discs and the players, as well as with the interface and compatibility of the two. The technology was still underdeveloped. To further exacerbate matters, the working relationship was always somewhat strained between MCA and Philips—particularly given the cultural differences of Hollywood and Holland, coupled with the product orientation of each.

In 1976, MCA began to explore industrial applications for their own videodisc system. A model 700 drive was built. With a few sales to the U.S. government for research application to military training, it was determined that a market did exist and a model 7000 was developed. At this point, encouraged by negotiations with General Motors Corporation (GMC) regarding numerous videodisc systems, MCA turned to Pioneer Electronics and jointly set up the Universal Pioneer Corporation (UPC) in Japan. By design they planned to develop and build videodisc systems for the industrial market throughout the world.

Pioneer Electronics, Japan

Pioneer had saturated the audio market, both at home and abroad, realizing in the process a 40-percent growth in business every year since the 1950s. It was seeking a unique market to invest in, one that was related to the company's focus. When MCA asked for bids on the GMC project, Pioneer responded. From that emerged what seemed to be a desirable union. With its electronic expertise, Pioneer would enhance the existing drive for industrial application, and MCA would supply the discs and develop appropriate software.

With a concentration on the entertainment use of this technology for the domestic market, the Philips/MCA drive emerged with no controls to take advantage of interactive functions. Rather, it was a sequential or linear movie machine that could be activated or stopped. In contrast, UPC emphasized the importance of interactivity for education and training purposes, and Pioneer built remote controls into the model 7800 player to take advantage of those functions. From this emerged the 7820 model.

The first major industrial sale by MCA Videodisc—a newly formed subsidiary of MCA that owned 50 percent of UPC—was placed in late 1977 by GMC for 12,000 systems. GMC's objective was to use the system which consisted of a 7820 drive with discs, an inexpensive Zenith color television, and kiosk-type unit for introducing new cars in showrooms around the country, thus limiting inventory requirements. The player was tested extensively by GMC and found to be very durable. Dealers, however, had to purchase their own systems, and pay approximately $3,500 for each—which, at the time, would have purchased some of the new cars they had for sale.

New car secrecy was an issue, and consequently, original visual material was not received until the last minute by MCA Videodisc. Compounding production difficulties was the fact that separate car models needed separate treatment. Chevrolet alone needed 4–7 separate discs for its various models. Of course, GMC expected rapid turnaround.

Delivery took place during 1978 and 1979. With four separate handlers of system parts—player, discs, television, and cabinet—there were obvious complications including unmatched parts and slow deliveries, resulting in not the happiest of end-users in some places. To further aggravate this situation, the need to move into disc manufacturing so rapidly without perfecting the process in the laboratory necessitated copious production runs to get enough workable discs.

The same dilemma arose in the consumer market. Playing time had advanced to around 27 to 28 minutes per side on a CAV disc, but this meant that popular movies like "Jaws" or "The Sting" needed to be pressed (replicated) on four or five sides. If only one side were defective, it wreaked havoc on the entire movie. Manufacturing consistency was a sizable problem. Consequently, considerable numbers of discs were replicated in order to send acceptable products. Even so, both markets, domestic and industrial, returned many discs.

MCA Videodisc was running three shifts to keep up with the demand—while trying to adjust and perfect a method of working with plastic that had never been executed in large quantities before. The two did not mix well. Inventions are hard to schedule.

When the GMC project was concluding, MCA Videodisc, in pursuit of another likely user of its system, approached IBM—a large user of audiovisual equipment. After some deliberation, IBM indicated it was not interested in buying videodisc units. It was interested in buying MCA Videodisc.

IBM

Internally, IBM had a strong emphasis on employee training education. Service engineers who installed and maintained equipment were especially in need of product updating. Having them travel to select education centers was disruptive and expensive. In response to this problem, audiovisual and interactive programs using open-reel video and film, and other media were developed for use in branch offices in the field.

In 1976, IBM formed Project Castle to explore videodisc technology and interactive video, videodisc or videotape interfaced to a computer, in greater depth. Its belief and research strategy was that the personal computer probably could not be sold into the home directly. It was too expensive for most, and the business and game applications for it were limited. This conjecture was confirmed, and much of it seems to be accurate still today. IBM reasoned that if a videodisc unit was first placed in the home for entertainment purposes, it could then be augmented, gradually, with keyboard, floppy disk drives, expanded memory, better screen, and the like. In the end, a complete computer would reside in the home.

A consumer product division was envisioned for Project Castle. Among the prototype interactive programs developed were ones on the maintenance of sport bicycles, children's reading skills, art games, the care and breeding of dogs, and a travelogue. These were designed on videotape while the videodisc technology was being developed. In the process, a great deal of expertise was acquired pertinent to what constitutes effective and efficient interactivity. A major setback was experienced in their effort to encode video signals digitally. In the end they were unable to obtain pictures on the disc of the quality they had hoped for. Project Castle folded in 1979.

DVA

The technological development and the GMC contract at MCA Videodisc attracted the interest of IBM. In September of 1979, MCA Videodisc and IBM signed a partnership agreement and formed DiscoVision Associates (DVA). (Of note is that during the negotiations in July Kent Broadbent informed MCA Videodisc of his intent to retire at the end of the year. It came as a

Celebrating their agreement for DiscoVision Associates to custom press laserdiscs on the Paramount Home Video label are (left to right) Richard Childs, Vice President & Chief Operating Officer, Paramount Home Video; Jack Reilly, President, DiscoVision Associates; and Harry Tashjian, Vice President of Manufacturing & Development, DiscoVision Associates. (Courtesy The Videodisc Monitor)

shock to everyone.) MCA Videodisc put in its manufacturing plant in Carson, California, and 50-percent ownership of UPC. (Pioneer Electronics owned the other 50 percent of the Universal Pioneer Corporation.) All patents issued or applied for relating to videodisc technology, as well as MCA's technical expertise, and its agreement of cooperation with Philips were also placed in the DVA partnership. IBM put in a substantial amount of money, its videodisc-related patents, its technical know-how, and access to research personnel.

Jack Reilly, who came from an IBM marketing group to take over from James Fiedler as president of DVA on January 1, 1980, brought with him numerous IBM personnel, but very few from Project Castle. The only non-IBM person in a high executive position at DVA during the first two years was George R. Jones who was appointed vice president for manufacturing.

By design, DVA was to become a major company. An appropriate structure was located that had previously been a pharmaceutical facility. Video processing functions were established there, as was the headquarters. Later, a laboratory and pilot manufacturing line for quick turnarounds were included. The major manufacturing plant was kept in Carson, 35 miles away.

In attempting to run the organization like a big business, the reality that it was not was overlooked, although the number of employees more than doubled, reaching about 450 under DVA. Even though a great deal of money was expended, what IBM did not realize was how challenging this technology was and how much development was still needed. Both IBM and MCA were unaware of the need for a disc mastering and replication environment (clean room) more dust-free than most hospital operating rooms. With billions of bits of information contained on each side of the disc, the loss of a single piece of information can scramble an entire picture; thus dust, dirt, and scratches must be prevented from affecting the reflective layer that holds the information.[72] What they did have was a "class 1,000" clean room for the glass base mastering, photoresist development, and electro-plating processes. Laser optical disc mastering and replicating facilities today function in a "class 100" clean room—with fewer than 100 particles per cubic foot contained in the air.

The Sears Summer '81 Catalog was placed on videodisc, enhanced by sound and motion footage, for testing the concept of electronic retailing in both store and home locations. One thousand copies were distributed to home videodisc player owners. (Courtesy The Videodisc Monitor)

A Sears customer explores the company's 1981 Summer Catalog via videodisc. (Courtesy The Videodisc Monitor)

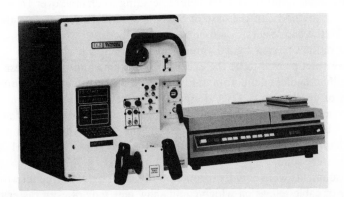

Perceptronics Tank Gunnery Trainer with DiscoVision Associates PR-7820 videodisc player. (Courtesy Perceptronics)

When Lynn Yeazel, who came from IBM to be the Manager of Program Development at DVA, visited the manufacturing plant on September 9, 1979, it was 101 degrees outside and 104 degrees in the plant with the skylights open to help ventilation. Phonograph records are duplicated much differently from videodiscs. It was an expensive lesson to learn, but then, unique and innovative products, particularly revolutionary ones, are frequently expensive to cultivate.

Other problems surfaced. Manufacturing costs for replicating discs were excessive due to a low disc yield. Also, customers—such as American Motors Corporation—wanted demonstrations with their models displayed, rather than GM's. It was not only an understandable and effective

Miles Pharmaceutical distributed 200 Learning Centers, comprised of DiscoVision Associates PR-7820 videodisc player and Sony monitor, to teaching hospitals and medical schools nationwide. (Courtesy The Videodisc Monitor)

marketing strategy, but a significant expense. Large corporations often required as long as one or two years of steady influencing from DVA before deciding to change over from their established delivery and training methods. In the case of Sears, a six-month test was conducted in approximately 50 stores. In the end, Sears would not even give the test results to DVA. (Unimaginably, DVA management did not have a signed agreement with them.)

The GMC contract proved to be the exception in volume and in their resolve to implement this technology without endless deliberation. Even so, the Sears disc was sophisticated for its time, and in the process of developing it, DVA designers became more aware of the limitations of the 7820 drive. In response, Gary Giddings, an IBM programmer, greatly expanded the function capability of the unit by eliminating the diagnostic-only function of the nine chips included, 1,000 bytes, and used them instead for added features and capabilities. The model 7820–3 emerged. Unfortunately, few were sold.

Other encroachments were equally formidable. Competing with free television seemed plausible until the rise of cable television which could show new movies even faster than DVA could, and do so with greater variety. Some theater owners began to complain about some of the movies being released on videodisc for which they felt they still had a market. Also, the U.S. economy in 1980 was somewhat tight, and the consumer market lagged more than expected.

Added to these was the ever-expanding popularity of videotape rentals as well as the use of VCR's to "steal" movies shown on television. MCA led the movie industry's fight against what they considered copyright infringement. All major motion picture companies were involved. They lost in the initial trial, and won on appeal but, in 1984, the U.S. Supreme Court found in favor of the consumer. In the end, videodiscs, as a read-only medium, could not compete head-on against videotape which permitted the consumer to erase and record information at will. This realization forced videodisc manufacturers to reposition the disc as an addition to tape and to focus on the disc's superior picture quality and unique programming and features to appeal to collectors and

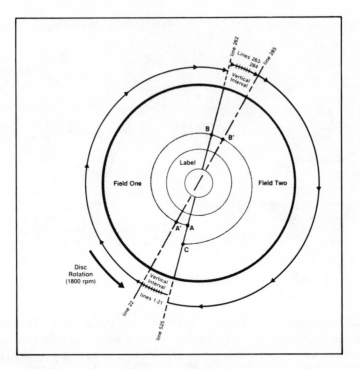

Figure 2.1. Format of a CAV Disc. (Courtesy 3M Optical Recording Department)

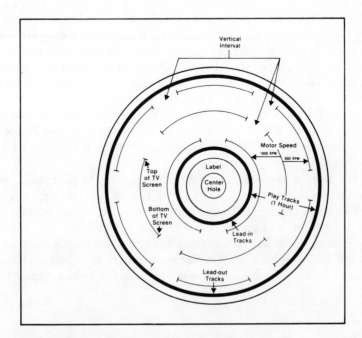

Figure 2.2. Format of a CLV Disc. (Courtesy 3M Optical Recording Department)

31

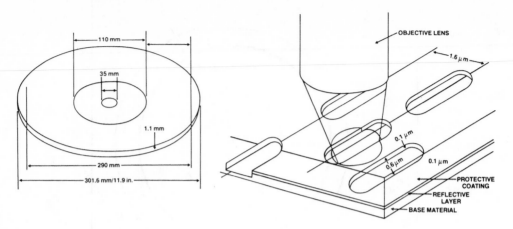

VIDEODISC DIMENSIONS   MAGNIFIED VIEW OF A VIDEODISC

Figure 2.3. Videodisc construction showing small size of information pits.

videophiles. These issues, taken as a whole and coupled with the inability to resolve the disc manufacturing problems, devastated DiscoVision Associates. (*Note:* The videodisc struggle to penetrate the consumer market continues today. By 1988, VCR sales had surpassed 50 million, making it "the fastest-selling domestic appliance in history."[73] Meanwhile, videodisc player sales were running a poor second at fewer than 400,000 units).

Prior to the establishment of the DVA partnership, UPC had established a pilot research plant in Kofu, Japan. MCA Videodisc had given Pioneer all the technical processes for manufacturing discs. Here, away from marketplace pressures, Pioneer methodically refined the disc manufacturing procedures. It also extended the playing time of the CAV disc to 30 minutes, as well as the duration of the longer playing disc that Broadbent and associates had developed for MCA. This latter disc, called constant linear velocity (CLV), had a fixed track rate with three frames contained on the outer circumference and one on the inner spiral. Whereas CAV discs rotated at a constant 1800 rpm, CLV discs started at 1800 rpm on the inner track but slowed to 600 rpm at circumference, the outer track. CLV was developed for movies only and Pioneer extended the playing time to 60 minutes per side. Intentionally, the interactive features on CLV are much less sophisticated than on CAV.

In 1980–1981 Pioneer expanded the Kofu plant beyond the pilot stage. When pressures mounted and problems would not abate, DVA began to send some disc manufacturing work to Japan. It became an escalating trend. The plant in Carson could not maintain quality control.

In May of 1980 Jones, vice president for manufacturing, had to have open heart bypass surgery. He was working seven days a week and the stress was simply overwhelming, with no respite close at hand. In December of 1981 senior management of MCA and IBM decided to stop all manufacturing at the Carson plant effective in March of 1982 when Pioneer took over.

As with MCA and Philips, there were strong cultural differences between the participating executives in DVA as well as with those at Pioneer who were involved through UPC. IBM had a more aggressive east coast, cosmopolitan deportment; MCA's demeanor was west coast, show-business oriented; and Pioneer brought an Asian perspective. Working together was difficult at times.

Under agreement, MCA took over the management responsibility of DVA and, in April of 1982, George R. Jones was appointed the third president. One of his unpleasant tasks was the reduction of personnel from approximately 150 people to 20. He also had to dispose of the manufacturing equipment and initiate DVA's amended focus which was to pursue the licensing of its patent portfolio.

Much smaller offices were required. Accordingly, the former headquarters, called the "black box" because of its color and shape, was vacated, and it reverted to a pharmaceutical operation. Ironically, on the back of this structure, etched in large letters, are the words, "He who has health has hope and he who has hope has everything."

As a videodisc manufacturing operation, DVA never was healthy. In the end that fact took its toll. Conversely, its insightful vision, coupled with a similar vision at Philips and Pioneer, was significantly ahead of its time. Struggling to achieve that vision was costly in innumerable ways.

Jones retired at the end of 1983 and James N. Fiedler became the fourth president of DVA, and director of its licensing operation. (Fiedler was also the first president of DVA.) In all, DVA had 400 issued patents (including ones dating back to the work of Gauss partners David Paul Gregg and Keith Johnson in the mid-1960s) and another 1,000 patent applications in various stages of process. They pertain to laser optical information storage and retrieval systems, and include disc mastering, replicating, playback units, and related processes. In effect, most aspects of the laser optical disc field are in some way related to patents they hold. Sony became a licensee with its compact disc (CD) audio business, and numerous others either are or will be licensees as well. MCA and IBM may, in the long run, have undertaken a very lucrative venture.

Pioneer Electronics USA

In March of 1982, Pioneer Video, Inc., officially took over the videodisc manufacturing operation of DVA. To do so, it leased the plant in Carson and kept key personnel, particularly from the video processing group, along with much equipment, such as the mastering bench. Pioneer later installed state of the art equipment and a class 100 clean room essential to disc mastering and replication. It took almost two years for the entire process to become profitable. To Pioneer's credit, the company endured extremely difficult times for videodisc technology and advanced its proficiency.

In 1982 the videodisc arcade market soared with games like Dragon's Lair, Bega's Battle, and Astron Belt. Pioneer had the greatest share of this game market,[74] but eventually the bottom fell out due to high prices and short life-spans of the laserdisc games. Another substantial investment has been Pioneer Artists, a continuing effort to both support and encourage the arts via the videodisc medium.

In December of 1985 Pioneer Video, Inc., was closed and the videodisc group folded into Pioneer Electronics USA. Its status went from that of a company to a division within a company. The company continues in the disc manufacturing business directed toward industry and the movie market.

Pioneer also continues to advance the technology. In late 1986 LaserDisc Corporation of America, the software division of Pioneer Electronics USA, announced a hybrid disc format that placed the entire audio portion of a compact disc onto a standard 12 inch laser videodisc.[75] This "Compact Laserdisc" with digital as well as analog tracks[76] plays on the Pioneer CLD-900, which was introduced in 1984 as the first combination drive that would play a videodisc and a compact audio disc. Its advanced version, the CLD-909, will also play the Compact Laserdisc.

Pioneer introduced the second generation of combination CD/CD-V/laser videodisc player with its CLD-1010, and then followed with model CLD-1030 which had improved audio and video quality plus additional programming features. Its commitment to this medium continues as does its flow of hardware for both the industrial and consumer markets. In mid-1988 the LD-W1 player was introduced which allows consumers to play both sides of two discs without turning the discs over. "This feat is accomplished by a single optical pickup mounted on a unique horseshoe-shaped optical track. The track allows the optical head to move around the edge of a disc to read the other side."[77]

With an expanding consumer awareness of and demand for laser videodiscs and CD-Video, coupled with a growing number of firms offering videodisc hardware, Pioneer Video Manufacturing in Carson, California doubled its capacity to 600,000 discs per month at the end of 1988. According to Tetsuro Kudo, president of Pioneer's LaserDisc Corporation of America (a software subsidiary of Pioneer Electronics USA) almost 90 percent of discs that are pressed in the US and Japan are movies. In the US, 80 percent of the purchasers of videodisc hardware and software are males that range in age from 30–45 years. In Japan, males are also the primary buyers, but the age range is 20–35 years old.[78]

For the education market, Pioneer commissioned and underwrote the production of a seven-minute videotape documentary on the use of videodisc in four representative schools. A free copy was then sent, in 1988, to the media coordinator at 26,000 selected K-12 schools throughout the US.[79] The LaserDisc Corporation of America has also begun to release its "Pioneer Special Interests" laser videodisc series. Sixteen titles were released in the summer and fall of 1988, including the eight-volume Encyclopedia of Animals with full motion video of over 700 species in their natural habitat. By design some of these discs will utilize and take full advantage of HyperCard software on the Apple Macintosh computer.[80]

North American Philips

Even though consumer videodisc player sales were not going well for Philips in the late 1970s and early 1980s, the company continued to exercise substantial and ongoing influence in the field. Originally, drives were manufactured in Holland using the Magnavox label of North American Philips for the players sent to the United States. (North American Philips—NAP—is independent, but related to NV Philips.) After a period of time, NAP managed its own videodisc market.

Negotiations were held with RCA (and NAP) to discuss standards cooperation, but no agreements were reached. In September of 1979 NAP and Sony agreed to exchange videodisc patents.[81] NAP also leased a mastering bench to 3M and arranged, in 1981, to have its disc mastering and replicating done there.[82,83] In retrospect, Messerschmitt, formerly president of Philips Subsystems and Peripherals, Inc., (a NAP company) felt that in the early years they all "underestimated how difficult it was to provide unique software for a unique new system."[84]

Simply put, the videodisc failed to immediately catch on as a consumer product, despite having a software library that built up to some 700 titles, most of which were motion pictures.[85] Promoting a movie machine proved ineffectual given the timing of its introduction and, consequently, the competition it then faced. The emphasis has since shifted to the interactive features of this medium, which are its foundation, as well as to the quality of the video and audio components. Emphasis is also placed on the essential requirement for high quality software. With

34

John Messerschmitt, Vice President of North American Philips Corporation, headed up company's US videodisc introduction in the early 1980s. (Courtesy The Videodisc Monitor)

Buckminster Fuller, Messerschmitt believes that "When we look back on the 20th century we will have to conclude that the marriage of the microcomputer and the optical videodisc will have been the most significant step in the century in terms of education and training."[86]

To that end, Optical Programming Associates (OPA) (comprised of executives from NAP, MCA and Pioneer interested in promoting interactive videodisc productions through funded projects) was formed and a number of interactive programs were developed including The First National Kidisc, Mazemania, Quest, and Timeframe. Its intent has been to select material that would have broad appeal, particularly since each costs between $150,000 to $200,000 to produce. In addition, NA Philips and NV Philips were responsible, in 1984, for developing the disc titled "Vincent Van Gogh: A Portrait in Two Parts," which cost approximately $400,000 to produce.

The original production run of this disc (approximately 1,000 copies) was sold out. But limited demand—resulting, in large part, from a small player (drive) population—caused the Van Gogh videodisc to be pulled from the market. Fortunately, Philips later reissued it. Even so, such meager initial marketplace response makes such high quality production and interactive designing very difficult to justify financially.

Perhaps the inference to be drawn is that videodisc projects such as this, as well as less ambitious ones, need to be initiated by those who have an application for it. Museums in general have been somewhat reticent to warmly embrace videodisc technology, though science and technology centers and history museums have been more receptive.[87] Understandably, art museums are concerned about inferior video images competing with original art, and are perhaps reluctant to emphasize gaps in particular collections. As electronic images improve, perhaps the response by museum art directors in general will be more positive.

In the meantime, technology has advanced for videodiscs,[88,89,90,91] but, more significantly, the demand for compact discs has increased the way many in the industry had hoped their predecessor would. Necessarily NAP has directed its attention to a technology that is selling, after investing so heavily and so consistently in one that, in terms of consumer sales, has been disheartening.

In August 1986 NAP opted for a lower profile in the videodisc industrial player market in order to place greater emphasis on the CD market.[92] Earlier, it had withdrawn quietly from the

35

consumer videodisc player and software markets. The action is indicative of the U.S. marketplace as well as the competition: Japan is leading the way. Philips' preference industrially has been to function as an original equipment manufacturer (OEM) to supply large system users.

Philips-DuPont Optical

Despite this specific down-scaling, NV Philips has continued its development efforts in CD-ROM and CD-I and entered into a joint venture with DuPont to manufacture and market optical laser discs. Europe's largest electronics company joined with the world's largest chemical company in this venture; together they invested $150 million for initial expenses. With headquarters in Delaware and several manufacturing plants (including one in Louviers, France, and another at Kings Mountain, North Carolina) the venture, by 1990, "is expected to have capital investment of more than $500 million, a $60 million annual research and development budget, and 3,500 employees world-wide."[93]

This commitment to supply the entire range of optical discs, spelled "disk," may well accelerate growth in all areas including videodiscs. Both are very optimistic as were two other resourceful and astute companies, MCA and IBM. Timing is important; and only time will tell how successful this venture will be.

Systems

Several interactive reflective videodisc hardware systems with drive and monitor controlled by a computer have had, or are currently having, a favorable impact on education and training. Digital Equipment Corporation's (DEC) made an early push in the education market with its IVIS (Interactive Video Information System). Introduced in January 1984, it was to be used internally for employee education, such as updating field service engineers, and then be marketed outside of the company, especially to academic institutions. Places like the Massachusetts Institute of Technology, Grove City College (Pennsylvania), the University of Pittsburgh, and numerous other colleges and universities have used it for interactive projects.

While enjoying great internal results from using the system, DEC had little success in marketing the system to others. A major drawback, for some, was its need for a DEC mainframe computer for courseware designing or "authoring" purposes. DEC subsequently scaled back its efforts for IVIS and is no longer offering it to outside buyers.

Sony's VIEW system (Visual Information Enhanced Workstation) was introduced in April 1985. It was the first integrated unit to be marketed with all components coming from a single vendor. The VIEW system has been subsequently upgraded several times and now includes an IBM-AT compatible Sony microcomputer and a choice of several Sony videodisc players. It remains one of the most comprehensive, readily available systems on the market today.

In June of 1986 IBM actively reentered this field with the introduction of its InfoWindow system. Like DEC, IBM is using its own system extensively for internal employee education and training.[94] Unlike the DEC system, however, IBM is enjoying broad market support for its unit. The IBM InfoWindow system is essentially a smart touch-screen monitor that incorporates the necessary computer cards for graphics overlay and videodisc control. It can be connected to any IBM-PC, -XT, or -AT compatible computer to complete the system.

Numerous other configurations are available and continue to emerge. In addition, with the rapid acceleration, and obvious potential, of compact disc read-only memory (CD-ROM) technology, systems like QuadVision have surfaced also. This compact work station, by Quadram Corporation and Comsell Inc., integrates a videodisc drive, a CD-ROM player, a color monitor, and an IBM PC-compatible computer.[95]

Sony LDP-1000 industrial videodisc player with built-in microprocessor for interactive user control. (Courtesy Sony)

Sony SMC-70 microcomputer combines with Sony LDP-1000 videodisc player to comprise a complete interactive video system. (Courtesy Sony)

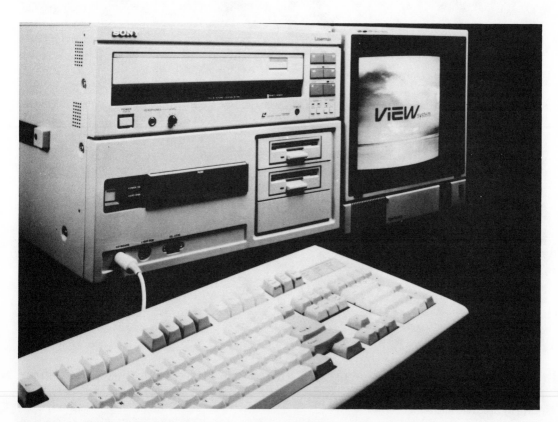

Sony Advanced VIEW system (Video Interactive Enhanced Workstation). (Courtesy Sony)

Students using IBM InfoWindow system with Pioneer LD-V6000 videodisc players at IBM Guided Learning Center. (Courtesy IBM Corporation)

A student interacts with "Exploring Computer Systems" course from Spectrum Interactive (formerly Interactive Training Systems) on an ITS-3100 system. (Courtesy Spectrum Interactive)

InteracTV system from NCR. (Courtesy The Videodisc Monitor)

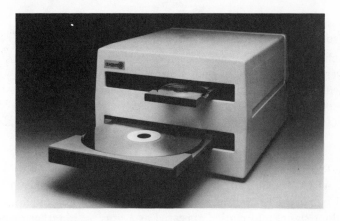

Prototype QuadVision system developed by Quadram and Comsell combines videodisc with CD-ROM. (Courtesy Comsell)

Transmissive Videodisc

Thomson-CSF (France)

In exploring the various materials to use for replicating videodiscs, Broadbent experimented with a transparent plastic that would permit optical reading of the record through the transparent back side.[96] This would obviate protective coatings.

Thomson-CSF, a French telecommunications company, expanded this concept and introduced a videodisc system in 1980 for the educational and industrial markets. Its flexible disc, made of a thin foil of plastic, was transmissive, as opposed to MCA's which was rigid and reflective. This disc permitted the playback laser to read both sides, via a refocusing process, without the need to turn the disc over. It had features similar to the CAV disc and was mastered in like fashion. Replication, without reflective and protective coatings, was a one-step stamping or molding process, and the disc was kept in a protective caddy.

Zenith developed a playback system to support this transmissive disc,[97] but, in 1981, Thomson halted production and has since redirected its interest to a recordable optical disc for the archival market. (Note: In 1987, General Electric "transferred control of all of its own and RCA's consumer-electronics businesses, including audio, video, and home telephones to France's government-owned Thomson."[98]

Film-Based Videodisc

i/o Metrics

In 1974 i/o Metrics, a Sunnyvale, California company founded by a group of former SRI researchers, demonstrated a film-based, silver halide system. It used "the raw video signal to modulate the intensity of a laser beam onto a sheet of photographic film, in much the same way that an optical sound track for film might be made."[99]

The master was created by simply developing the film using standard darkroom techniques, and replicas were made through ordinary contact printing methods.[100] It was possible to use either a laser for greater sophistication, i.e., random access and variable speed functions, or a conventional white light source such as a 25-watt bulb, with requisite but standard electronics to play back the disc, which rotated at 1800 rpm.

Multiple layers of the disc, with each storing additional information was proposed, and Thomson's work with focus adjustment was used experimentally. One outgrowth of their focus precision testing was the elimination of a protective caddy or coating. Prior to commercial development, i/o Metrics went out of business.

ARDEV

The Atlantic Richfield Company picked up on this photographic optical videodisc process. In February, 1978, ARCO established the ARDEV Company, Inc. to further develop its technical and commercial feasibility. The transmissive disc was mastered and duplicated much like the i/o Metrics disc; thus, signal information appeared as a gray scale rather than as pits or holes. Recording and playback could, if desired, involve the same disc. No special handling was required and the disc was read by a non-laser incandescent light source, had up to 54,000 tracks with random access, and offered compressed audio capability of up to 30 seconds per still frame. Digital and analog information could be processed in any combination. ARDEV also developed a unit for on-site recording,[101] which greatly enhanced their system. This particular feature, on-site table top recording (mastering) capability, has been one of—if not the—primary nemesis of laser optical reflective discs. In June of 1981 McDonnell Douglas Corporation purchased ARDEV to form its own videodisc division under the McDonnell Douglas Electronics Company.[102]

McDonnell Douglas Electronics Company—LaserFilm

LaserFilm incorporates several differences from standard rigid laserdiscs. Solid-state laser technology is used to both record and play this film disc, which is composed of mylar. Frame accurate random access to approximately 30,000 frames in less than 2 seconds is available with compressed audio, if desired, and the ability to manipulate analog and digital signals. In terms of quality, conventional pre-mastering is eliminated, which means the final product is one generation closer to the source, and the disc is kept in a protective cover. The player has an internal host computer and a remote control, but is also designed for computer control with an RS 232 interface and an IEEE-488 port. Perhaps most salient, the entire process from mastering through actual display can be governed by the designer/user.

McDonnell Douglas Electronics Company (MDEC) believed this to be the next generation videodisc system and in November, 1985 signed a large-scale production contract with Sansui Electric Company of Japan for Sansui to build MDEC LaserFilm videodisc players.[103]

LaserFilm got off to a roaring start in the commercial market when Innovative Business Associates (IBA), on April 20, 1986, announced its commitment "to purchase 20,000 such players during the next four to five years and has an exclusive agreement with McDonnell Douglas for the use of the system in real estate applications for the next 11 years."[104] This was the first announced application of MDEC's system, and the largest contract for a videodisc system to date.

IBA subsequently won a major contract to provide a real estate service in the San Fernando Valley of California and ran into numerous problems in implementing and marketing the application. The big purchase never materialized and MDEC dissolved the relationship and began buying back the players in mid-1988.

LaserFilm recording system from McDonnell Douglas.
(Courtesy The Videodisc Monitor)

Holographic Videodisc

Hitachi (Japan) has been conducting research and development of holographic storage on an optical videodisc since 1975. Using a 12-inch diameter disc that spins at 6 rpm and plays for 30 minutes, the method records an individual hologram with sound on each frame.[105] Further development can be expected in this area.

Magneto-Optic Recording

As videodisc competition with videotape so expensively demonstrated, on-site or in-home recordability is seen by many as a critical feature in any audio/video technology. With the information density of magnetic recording technology ". . . doubling every two to three years . . ." according to Mark H. Kryder of the Magnetics Technology Center at Carnegie Mellon University (CMU), magnetic recording "will clearly be the dominant storage technology for the next five to ten years. . . ."[106] To that end, digital audio tape (DAT) was introduced by the Japanese in 1987 with sound quality equivalent to a CD audio, which is non-recordable at this time.

DAT cassettes are about half the size of standard audio cassettes and the same digital technology used with compact discs is employed. However, instead of using a laser beam to detect the signal, DAT players use the magnetic-tape mechanics of a VCR to record and play back. Its advantages, particularly the ability to record near perfect clones of original material, has elicited fear and anger from American and European recording industry people, including CD manufacturers who have much to lose if compact discs do not realize a significant advantage through early market penetration.

The Recording Industry Association of America (RIAA) has been particularly active and pitted against the world's home electronics manufacturers, as they were in the 1970s over home video recordings. Even so, Sony Corporation of Japan and Philips Corporation of the Netherlands, along with other manufacturers, are working hard to strike a compromise.

While the data density of magnetic disks continues to increase, it is inherently limited by the difficulty of focusing a magnetic field on a single spot without affecting ajoining areas. Magneto-Optical Recording (MOR) technology tackles this problem by combining the recordability of magnetic media with the data density of laser optics. During MOR recording, a laser beam heats particular spot on a heat sensitive magnetic layer while applying a magnetic field and changing the polarity of the spot. These changes in polarity are then read by a less intense, lower-power laser. Data is erased or rewritten by reapplying the original laser and magnetic field—thus switching the polarity back to its initial direction.

Such technology, has been investigated since the 1960s[107] and worked on intensely by the Japanese since the 1970s through a coordinated effort involving industrial companies such as Matsushita, Sony, Hitachi, Toshiba, and Fujitsu, as well as governmental and university research organizations including Tohoku University and Kyushu University.

Through their concerted efforts, according to Kryder, "the Japanese firms dominate the video and audio recording markets, are challenging U.S. leadership in digital recording, and have assumed an early leadership position in the use of magnetic recording to replace photographic cameras—both still frame and motion pictures."[108] Of course, the Japanese are accelerating their magneto-optic work.

With the growth of magnetics technology in the United States seriously hampered by a lack of long-term research, CMU, in 1983, formed the Magnetics Technology Center (MTC) under the direction of Kryder. Its faculty, graduate students, and staff are "multidisciplinary, representing departments of electrical and computer engineering, physics, metallurgical engineering and materials science, mechanical engineering, mathematics, chemistry, chemical engineering, and the Mellon Institute." Among a number of areas of research it also focuses on magnetic recording and magneto-optic recording, and its funding comes primarily from industrial firms such as 3M and IBM, and from the U.S. government. "Money invested in the Center goes directly for support of research and students," with "approximately 85 percent" of the graduates going "to work for firms and agencies supporting the Center."[109] Such cooperative research, following the Japanese model, is already contributing substantially to this dynamic field, and MTC is currently expanding its efforts.[110]

Optical Recording Project/3M

Although 3M originally sought to develop a home videodisc system that was inexpensive

> by the mid-1970's, the original goal . . . had been superseded by (1) the quest to develop direct-read-after-write (DRAW) media, (2) an erasable medium that would operate similarly to magnetic recording, and (3) a simpler and higher quality replication process for all forms of optical discs—transmissive and reflective.[111]

The replication emphasis was encouraged by 3M's development of very durable plastic coatings that could be cast and rapidly cured. To test and evaluate these materials as well as other evolving ones for videodisc recording and replication, 3M built a number of experimental laser recorders. During this same period, 1975–76, 3M and MCA discussed a joint videodisc venture, but no agreement was reached. The Central Research Laboratories of 3M were also working with Thomson-CSF. Later, in 1978, 3M purchased laser equipment from the Zenith laboratory and in 1979 the magnetic audio-visual division provided the initial sponsorship and funding for the Optical Recording Project. Lloyd A. Troeltzsch was appointed director.

Early prototype videodisc player developed by 3M
Corporation circa 1962. (Courtesy The Videodisc
Monitor)

From the start, digital optical recording was seen as an area of development that would likely replace rigid computer discs. Too, the interactive potential of the CAV disc for education and training purposes was perceived as the most promising for videodiscs. With such a perspective, it was nonetheless necessary to pursue a circuitous route via the lead of its videodisc partners since 3M had no master recording bench or commercial players on which to play discs.

In the summer of 1979 the Optical Recording Project (ORP) signed a contract with Thomson-CSF. Thomson was to provide the players and 3M, having purchased a mastering bench from Thomson, would manufacture the transmissive discs and market the player in the U.S. and other parts of the world, excluding Europe.

Because transmissive disc recording and duplicating was not, seemingly, an expensive or overly complex procedure, the ORP felt that it could offer to interested users a desk-top replicator, built by another supplier, along with the necessary materials. A videodisc copier was envisioned that would function in somewhat similar fashion to other copiers that constituted a substantial business for 3M.

When DiscoVision was formed in September of 1979, the ORP realized that it would be a major force both in the marketplace and in developing the technology further. Accordingly, 3M began to explore reflective videodiscs to see if its materials and technology could be applied there as well. It could, and the company pursued the parallel path of developing laser optical reflective videodiscs.

In late 1979 Troeltzsch hired Frank M. Price as marketing and sales manager for the ORP to initiate and direct a market needs analysis and to cultivate a market for the products being developed in the laboratory, where the ORP still resided. The following summer Thomas L. Elmquist was hired, from another 3M area, to be the manufacturing manager for the ORP.

Almost a year earlier, in 1979, Troeltzsch had made contact with NA Philips. NAP wanted to sell drives and to compete with DVA. As a result of their ongoing discussions, the ORP purchased a mastering bench and related equipment from Philips, and, with Philips' expert assistance on such things as plant environment specifications, built a laser optical disc production facility in Menomonie, Wisconsin. Philips also supplied the ORP with glass master discs. As part of the arrangement, the ORP agreed that a certain amount of their disc production would be designated for Philips and its entertainment focus.

For the ORP replicating process, sheets of plastic were obtained from a plastic manufacturer and the appropriate disc diameters (such as a 12-inch videodisc), cut by a laser. The disc was then coated with a thin ultraviolet sensitive photopolymer and put in intimate contact with a plastic stamper that had been made from the glass master. Once embossed by the stamper, an ultraviolet light cured the polymer causing the information layer to become fixed on the duplicate disc. This disc was then coated with first a thin layer of reflective aluminum, then a protective coating on the information side. Finally, two halves, or discs processed on one side, were laminated together in fashion similar to DVA's.

In exploring other systems, the ORP looked at RCA's SelectaVision. The ORP went so far as to demonstrate that it could duplicate these discs, but felt they would not be a long-term viable product. Troeltzsch and others also went to Japan and talked with JVC, Pioneer, and others to learn about their work and to express a desire for cooperation. It was hoped that the ORP process could be established as the market standard. This effort proved unsuccessful.

Activity was also generated by 3M in relation to its videodisc player patents from the early 1960s. 3M's contention was that MCA Videodisc, DVA, and Pioneer were violating their patents. Eventually a settlement was reached in favor of 3M.

In the meantime, Thomson-CSF was having difficulty manufacturing players. Costs were too high in France, so the company arranged for its drives to be manufactured by Teac in Japan. This decision was very acceptable to the ORP and it in turn signed a new agreement with Thomson and Teac in 1981. The ORP, however, which had become a separate business entity within 3M operating somewhat like a mini-division, set certain requirements with a specified deadline for the product to demonstrate that it would be viable in the marketplace. When the criteria were not met, the ORP withdrew from the endeavor.

Troeltzsch requested the assistance of George R. Jones regarding how to package videodiscs and found him most helpful. Recognized and appreciated was the wealth of insight that Jones possessed, given his experience in having started the first manufacturing facility for laser optical videodiscs.

When Jones was disposing of DVA's manufacturing equipment in 1982, the ORP bought the pilot workbench, and placed it in its own pilot plant in Vadnais Heights, Minnesota. The intent was to understand the DVA process better, rather than use it for actual replication of discs for customers.

Like MCA Videodisc and DVA, the ORP experienced difficulties in starting up a laser optical disc manufacturing facility, in bringing the process under control, and in getting the disc yield high enough to make the operation profitable. As with their predecessors, there was a great deal of on-the-job learning, as well as a substantial amount of money invested in anticipated future returns. Technical problems were a sizeable nemesis as was the slow marketplace response. By late 1982 and early 1983, however, Elmquist and the group that he had hired began to solve the major manufacturing problems. Product yields began to increase dramatically.

In early 1983, 3M's DRAW disk for digital data storage was ready to move from the laboratory to the pilot plant. At that time, upper-level management believed that this product, as well as other laboratory developments yet to be introduced through the ORP, needed to be directed by a person with a stronger technical background. Accordingly, Troeltzsch was moved to director of distribution for the memory technology group, and Dave Davies, with a Ph.D. in physics, became the second director of the Optical Recording Project. The laboratory he was director of had developed the DRAW medium.

3M videodisc manufacturing facility in Menomonie, Wisconsin. (Courtesy 3M)

A 3M employee prepares a glass master. (Courtesy 3M)

A 3M employee examines one of many disc replicas being manufactured at 3M's Menomonie facility. (Courtesy 3M)

In 1986, Elmquist left 3M to join Philips-Dupont Optical as technical marketing manager. Also in 1986, the ORP/3M introduced an erasable optical disk for digital data storage that is changeable, easy to access, and uses magneto-optic technology. 3M also provides two read-only discs: CD ROM and OROM (optical read only memory), and maintains its commitment to the manufacturing of laser optical reflective videodiscs, especially for education and training via the interactive mode. 3M is today an industry leader in the laser optical disc/disk field, providing mastering and replication services directly to customers and on a private label basis to OEM [original equipment manufacturer] suppliers.[112]

Videodisc Trends: Present and Future

In 1983 Matsushita, under the Panasonic name, introduced a system that records and plays back a laser videodisc, the Optical Memory Disc Recorder.[113] This Direct Read After Write (DRAW) system employs an 8 inch disc that holds up to 24,000 color video frames. It is a record-only unit;, erasing and re-recording are, as yet, unavailable and discs are not compatible with other drives. In the fall of 1988 Panasonic released a 12 inch model Optical Memory Disc Recorder/Player with three record/playback modes - composite NTSC with 350 lines of resolution, component Y/C, and RGB with 450 lines. The 12 inch two-sided cartridge-held disc stores 54,000 frames per side in composite and component modes, and 36,000 in RGB. All of the functions on the 8 inch model (genlock, two-channel audio, software commands, phase controls) are also available on the 12 inch model.[114]

As recordable laser optical videodiscs continue to evolve, so too does digital encoding of analog information. What will emerge and have a significant impact is uncertain. Price writes:

> Industry analysts anticipate that integrated optical disc peripheral devices will soon be developed which are capable of satisfying all formats, including video, audio, digital read-only, write-once and erasable media. Such a system could incorporate music, television, video games, computer graphics, data and word processing, communication, message store and forward, education, training and mass storage in a single, low-cost package. The education, training, research and business potential for such a process is obvious, and it is clear that the implementation of laser optical recording is only beginning.[115]

In 1986, Philips demonstrated CD-Video (CD-V) which provides 5 minutes of analog video and 20 minutes of digital audio on a 4.75 inches optical disc. However, Sony, Philips' CD partner, expressed some opposition, pointing out that whereas a CD standard has been established worldwide, a video standard canot be so established due to the variations between countries, i.e., NTSC, PAL, SECAM.

In 1987 Pioneer was the first company to introduce a combination player that could accomodate videodiscs, CD-Audio discs and CD-V discs. CD-V software has been slow in coming but by mid-1988 several major record labels were producing for the format. More importantly, the advent of the combination player seems to have struck a chord with consumers who, having embraced the compact disc, are now re-discovering the videodisc. In Japan, where the consumer videodisc market topped 1.7 million players in mid-1988, the combination players account for over 80 percent of current sales. According to Rockley Miller, editor of The Videodisc Monitor, "It is anticipated that in the US, nearly all videodisc units to be imported after 1988 will offer a CD capability as well."

Possibly, the laser optical reflective videodisc is an interim technology to be incorporated into or even replaced by a new configuration that Philips[116] or Pioneer or some other organization will initiate. Magneto-optic videodiscs will likely have an impact, perhaps substantially so. Possible as well is that LaserFilm will develop further and have widespread appeal; or, Digital Video Interactive technology may become the next generation videodisc system, along with other, as yet unannounced, innovations. Whatever the direction, "the market for any type of interactive programming . . . is heavily dependent on the availability of high-quality software. Professional interactive disc programs require skilled video producers, art directors, computer programmers, and instructional designers."[117]

Panasonic Optical Memory Disc Recorder (OMDR) allows users to record their own videodiscs. (Courtesy The Videodisc Monitor)

The Enflex CD-ROM system from ERM Computer Services, Inc. offers a complete data base of environmental regulatory information. (Courtesy ERM Computer Services)

Magnavox CD Video combination player can accommodate 12-inch and 8-inch videodiscs as well as 4.75-inch compact audio discs (CDs) and CD Video discs. (Courtesy North American Philips)

Chronology of Videodisc Development[118]

Year	System and Developer	Type
1884	Paul Nipkow patent, Germany	Mechanical
1926	Phonovision, John Logie Baird, England (first functioning videodisc)	Mechanical
1958	David Paul Gregg develops concepts for optical videodisc recording and playback. Coins term "videodisk"	Optical
1960	Invention of the LASER, Theodore Maiman	
1961	Optical videodisc, 3M and Stanford Research Institute, USA	Optical
1963	3M demonstrates working videodisc player, USA	Optical
1963	Phonovid, Westinghouse Research Laboratories, USA	Mechanical
1969–72	University of Wisconsin Medical Center Project, Westinghouse Research Laboratories	Magnetic
1972	NV Philips demonstrates first glass master laser videodisc, Netherlands	Optical
1972	MCA, Music Corporation of America, demonstrates first replicated laser videodisc, USA	Optical
1972–74	Georgia educational television project, Westinghouse Research Laboratories	Magnetic
1974	Demonstration of film-based system, i/o Metrics, USA	Photographic
1974	Thomson/CSF demonstrates transparent system, France	Optical
1974	MCA and NV Philips announce agreement on videodisc format	Optical
1975	TeD, Teldec, Germany's AEG-Telefunken and Britain's Decca Record Company	Mechanical
1975	Holographic, Hitachi, Japan	Holographic
1978	Visc, Matsushita, Japan	Mechanical
1978	DVA, DiscoVision Associates, USA	Laser Optical Reflective
1978	ARDEV, Atlantic Richfield Company purchases i/o Metrics, USA	Photographic
1980	Transmissive, Thomson-CSF, France	Laser Optical Transparent
1980	3M and NV Philips sign agreement for 3M to manufacture videodiscs	Laser Optical Reflective
1981	SelectaVision, RCA, USA	Capacitance

1981	McDonnell Douglas purchases ARDEV, USA	Photographic
1982	3M/Optical Recording Project begins pressing videodiscs	Laser Optical Reflective
1983	VHD/AHD, Victor Company of Japan, JVC—an affiliate of Matsushita, Japan	Capacitance
1983	OMDR, Optical Memory Disc Recorder, Panasonic—an affiliate of Matsushita, Japan	Laser Optical DRAW
1984	3M offers same-day videodisc pressing	Laser Optical Reflective
1986	LaserFilm, McDonnell Douglas Corporation, USA	Photographic Laser Optical
1986	Sony, Japan, and NV Philips announce CD-I, Compact Disk—Interactive, digital format	Laser Optical Reflective
1986	Erasable Optical Disk, 3M	Magneto-Optic
1986	CD-Video, Compact Disk—Video, digital and analog format, NV Philips	Laser Optical Reflective
1987	DVI, Digital Video Interactive, General Electric/RCA, USA	Laser Optical Reflective +
1988	Read/Write/Erasable Disk, NeXT, Inc., USA	Magneto-Optic

Endnotes

1. Pat Hawker, "The Pioneers of Television," *Television: Journal of the Royal Television Society* 20,6 (November/December 1983): 273.
2. Michael DeBloois, Karen Clauson Maki and Arno Ferrin Hall, *Effectiveness of Interactive Videodisc Training: A Comprehensive Review* (Virginia: Future Systems Incorporated, The Videodisc Monitor, 1984), p. 13.
3. Stan Jarvis, "Videodiscs and Computers," *Byte* 9,7 (July, 1984), 187. Note: DeBloois, Maki and Hall incorrectly refer to Nipkow as Lupkow; and Jarvis refers to him as Gipkow.
4. Jarvis, "Videodiscs and Computers," p. 187.
5. Warren K. Agee, Phillip H. Ault and Edwin Emery, *Introduction to Mass Communications,* Sixth Edition (New York: Harper & Row, 1979), pp. 320–323.
6. John F. Ohles, "The Microcomputer: Don't Love It To Death," *T.H.E. Journal* 13,1 (August, 1985), 49.
7. Robert Heinich, Michael Molenda and James D. Russell, *Instructional Media and the New Technologies of Instruction* (New York: John Wiley and Sons, 1985), p. 201.
8. See Runes, *The Diary and Sundry Observations of Thomas Alva Edison,* pp. 64–65. Of note is that Edison "knew that in the phonograph he had hit upon a machine that could change the nature of communication. He foresaw it as an instrument of mass education that would put ordinary people in contact with the great teachers and speakers of the world. Its effect on the music and entertainment industries was only dimly forseen." See Efrem Sigel et al., *Video Discs: The Technology, the Applications and the Future* (New York: Van Nostrand Reinhold Company, 1980), p.2.
9. Albert Abramson, "Letters," *Television: Journal of the Royal Television Society* 21,2 (March/April 1984): 87–88. Several of Zworykin's patent numbers are included here.
10. Hawker, "The Pioneers of Television," pp. 274–5.
11. "Television Pioneering," *Broadcast Engineering* 21,5 (May 1979): 108.
12. Ibid.

13. Agee et al., *Introduction to Mass Communications,* p. 91.
14. M.H.I. Baird, "Letters," *Television: Journal of the Royal Television Society* 21,3 (May/June 1984): 131–132. Baird's son here draws from his father's memoirs.
15. "Developing Technology: Major Industry Milestones," *Broadcast Engineering* 21,5 (May 1979): 60.
16. Eric Parsloe, ed., *Interactive Video* (United Kingdom: Sigma Technical Press, 1983), p. 68.
17. Sigel et al., *Video Discs,* p. 9.
18. Pat Hawker, "Television's Spring Review of Books (The Secret Life of John Logie Baird by Tom McArthur and Peter Waddell)," *Television: Journal of the Royal Television Society* 23,2 (April 1986): 104–5.
19. Joshua Sieger, "Television's Spring Review of Books (The Secret Life of John Logie Baird by Tom McArthur and Peter Waddell)" *Television: Journal of the Royal Television Society* 23,2 (April 1986), p. 103.
20. Hawker, "Letters," *Television: Journal of the Royal Television Society* 23,3 (June 1986): 165.
21. Hawker, "The Pioneers of Television," p. 274. Hawker's selection of the four outstanding pioneers of television are: Swinton, Baird, Zworykin, and Alan Blumlein (p. 279).
22. Philip Rice and Richard F. Dubbe, "Development of the First Optical Videodisc," *SMPTE Journal* 91,3 (March 1982): 277. Note: Rice and Dubbe incorrectly refer to Baird as James rather than John as do Daynes and Butler, eds., *The Videodisc Book* (New York: John Wiley & Sons, Inc., 1984), p. 7.
23. Ibid., p. 9. In contrast, the National Television Systems Committee (NTSC) standard resolution in the United States today utilizes 525 horizonal scanning lines per frame that are displayed at the rate of 30 per second. Baird's early method was limited to a 30-line definition due to the limited bandwidth that could be broadcast over a medium-wave transmitting station.
24. Rice and Dubbe, "Development of the First Optical Videodisc," p. 277.
25. Rod Daynes and Beverly Butler, eds., *The Videodisc Book: A Guide and Directory* (New York: John Wiley and Sons, Inc., 1984), p. 7. "Historians of science and technology generally credit James Logie Baird with its invention."
26. Stan Jarvis, "1988: The 30th Anniversary of the Videodisc," *The Videodisc Monitor,* March 1988, page 15.
27. Parsloe, *Interactive Video,* p. 68.
28. Peter Waddell, "Letters," *Television: Journal of the Royal Television Society* 21,3 (May/June 1984): 133.
29. John Mullin, "Discovering Magnetic Tape," *Broadcast Engineering* 21,5 (May 1979): 80, 82, 105.
30. Sigel et al., *Video Discs,* p. 10.
31. Richard Ziff, "Magnetic Tape's Impact on Broadcasting," *Broadcast Engineering* 21,5 (May 1979): 78–79.
32. Mullin, "Discovering Magnetic Tape," p. 82.
33. For a retrospective account of Ampex's development of the VTR by its team leader, see Charles P. Ginsberg, "The Birth of the VTR," *Video Pro* 5,2 (March 1986): 22–26.
34. Hawker, "The Pioneers of Television," p. 279.
35. Parsloe, *Interactive Video,* pp. 98–99.
36. Alan Wurtzel, *Television Production,* Second Edition (New York: McGraw-Hill Book Company, 1983), p. 328.
37. Interview with Kenneth E. Farr, Westinghouse Research Laboratories (retired), Pittsburgh, Pennsylvania, 11 September 1986. Additional information was received from Michael E. Colbaugh and Douglas Howorth of the Advanced Systems Laboratory at Westinghouse's Research and Development Center. Further, a substantial amount of the material pertaining to John Logie Baird and early videodisc development was procured from Howorth, who came to Westinghouse from the BBC.
38. Kenneth E. Farr, "Phonovid—A System for Recording Television Pictures on Phonograph Records," *Journal of the Audio Engineering Society* 16,2 (April 1968): 163–167. With an M.S. in Electrical Engineering, Farr was, at the time of this project, Manager of Systems Development in the Communications, Display and Instructional Technologies Department.

39. Alan Wurtzel, *Television Production* (New York: McGraw-Hill, Inc., 1983), pp. 253, 267–269. See Sigel et al., *Video Discs,* p. 13. See also Bill Modoono, "NFL Unveils a Replay Official to End the Arguments Over Calls," *The Pittsburgh Press,* 7 September 1986, p. D8.

40. Rice and Dubbe, "Development of the First Optical Videodisc," pp. 277–8.

41. Ibid., p. 280.

42. Allen A. Boraiko, "LASERS: A Splendid Light," *National Geographic* 165,3 (March 1984): 335. Boraiko cites 1917 as the publication date of this document. It actually first appeared a year earlier. See M. Bertolotti, *Masers and Lasers: An Historical Approach* (Bristol, England: Adam Hilger Ltd., 1983), pp. 7, 28.

43. Schawlow was awarded the Nobel Prize for Physics in 1981 for his work with laser spectroscopy.

44. Bertolotti, *Masers and Lasers: An Historical Approach,* p. 111.

45. "Federal Judge Orders U.S. to Issue Patent to Man who Invented Laser," *Video Computing,* January/February 1986, p. 18.

46. Lee Hotz, "The Laser: CMU, Westinghouse Experts Beam as New Technology Spreads to All Fields," *The Pittsburgh Press,* 28 August 1983, p. E1.

47. Parsloe, *Interactive Video,* p. 68.

48. Bob Ingersoll, "Plastic Platters Vie for Role in Home TV Playback Battle," *Product Engineering,* August 17, 1970, pp. 49–50.

49. Ken Winslow, "Here Come the Home Video Discs," *Popular Electronics* 8,5 (November 1975): 39.

50. K.G. Thorne, "The Teldec Video Disc," *Television: Journal of the Royal Television Society* 9 (November/December 1972): 136.

51. Rolf W. Schiering, "The TeD Videodisk System" (a TeD presse information release. The unspecified date appears to be late 1975).

52. Parsloe, *Interactive Video,* pp. 69–70.

53. Sigel et al., *Video Discs,* pp. 15–18.

54. Agee et al., *Introduction to Mass Communications,* pp. 81–82.

55. Henry F. Ivey, "Optics at Westinghouse," *Applied Optics* 11,5 (May 1972): 985, 988.

56. Daynes and Butler, *The Videodisc Book,* p. 8.

57. W.C. Hittinger and R.W. Sonnenfeldt, the Foreword in *RCA Review* 39, 1 (March 1978): 3–5.

58. Sigel et al., *Video Discs,* pp. 19–23.

59. Parsloe, *Interactive Video,* pp. 82–3.

60. "RCA Offering Product Refunds," *The Pittsburgh Press,* 26 November 1984, p. B6. See also Paul Freiberger, "The Videodisc Connection," *Popular Computing* 3, 11 (September 1984): 67–69.

61. Herb Brody. "Picking Up the Pieces of RCA," *High Technology Business,* 8,5 (May 1988): 41–44.

62. "GE/RCA Puts Full Motion Video on CD," *The Videodisc Monitor* 5,4 (April 1987): 1.

63. Roger Wilson, "VHD - The United Kingdom Market Story," *Videodisc and Optical Disk* 5, 2 (March/April 1985): 148/155. See also Parsloe, *Interactive Video,* pp. 80–87; and Sigel et al., *Video Discs,* pp. 23–25.

64. Much of the information contained in this section came from the following sources: Interview with Thomas L. Elmquist, 3M Company, St. Paul, Minnesota, 12 June 1986; Interview with James N. Fiedler and George R. Jones, DiscoVision Associates, Costa Mesa, California, 13 June 1986; Interview with Donald J. Kerfeld, 3M Company, Vadnais Heights, Minnesota, 12 June 1986; Interview with John C. Messerschmitt, Philips Subsystems and Peripherals Inc., New York, New York, 11 June 1986; Interview with Frank M. Price and Lou L. Prudhon, 3M Company, St. Paul, Minnesota, 12 June 1986; Interview with Lloyd A. Troeltzsch, 3M Company, St. Paul, Minnesota, 12 June 1986; Interview with Lynn A. Yeazel, 3M Company, Airporter Inn, Costa Mesa, California, 13 June 1986.

65. "Philips in the Age of Optical Disc Media" (A report received from John Messerschmitt on 11 June 1986).

66. ". . . the term videodisc was originally spelled with a k. It was still spelled with a k in 1961 memos from 3M's Mincom division acknowledging Gregg's prior videodisk claims. The spelling evolved thereafter to videodisc since disc was the spelling in vogue with the audio record. TV disk also appears in the early 1960's, even though the term coined in the late 1950's was videodisk to call attention to its parallel relationship to videotape. Videodisk, however, was the dominant spelling choice through the 1960's." See Stan Jarvis and Steve Booth, "A Century of Optical Disc Development," *Videodisc News* (July-August 1982): 22.

67. Ibid., p.19.
68. C. Stan Jarvis, "1988: The 30th Anniversary of the Videodisc," *The Videodisc Monitor* 6, 5 (May 1988): 15.
69. For further, more recent, information on the process described here, see Parsloe, *Interactive Video*, pp. 71–74.
70. Kent D. Broadbent, "A Review of the MCA Disco-Vision System," *Journal of the SMPTE* 83,7 (July 1974): 559.
71. See also Junius L. Bennion and Edward W. Schneider "Interactive Videodisc Systems for Education," *Journal of the SMPTE* 84,12 (December 1975): 949–953. Bennion and Schneider refer to the above article by Broadbent while addressing more specifically the educational application of the videodisc (particularly for interactive instruction). Both, at the time of writing, were instructional scientists at Brigham Young University. Schneider was also a faculty member.
72. Alex van Someren, *Interactive Video Systems* (London: Century Communications Ltd., 1985), p. 30.
73. Harry F. Waters, "The Future of Television," *Newsweek* (October 17, 1988): 85.
74. Jill Ottenberg, "Discs Get Heavy Play in the Arcade," *Videography* 9,1 (January 1984): 23.
75. "Pioneer, LDCA Announce 'Compact Laserdisc' Format," *The Videodisc Monitor* 4,9 (September 1986): 5.
76. "Philips Shows CD-Video, Revives Laservision," *Television Digest with Consumer Electronics* 26,47 (24 November 1986): 10.
77. "Pioneer Offers New Player, Initiatives," *The Videodisc Monitor* 6, 5 (May 1988): 1.
78. "LDCA Optimistic on Consumer Market," *The Videodisc Monitor* 6, 8/9 (August/September 1988): 11.
79. "Pioneer Offers New Player, Initiatives," p. 1.
80. "Pioneer Releases 'Special Interests'," *The Videodisc Monitor* 6, 6 (June 1988): 6.
81. Sigel et al., *Video Discs*, pp. 34, 36. In October of 1979 Sony made the following announcement: "Sony believes that the video disc will not affect the consumer or industrial video tape recorder markets significantly. When the market conditions become suitable, Sony will be ready to take the lead in providing the necessary video disc hardware." Of note is that in 1981 Sony bid against DVA and won the Ford Motor Company contract for several thousand videodisc players (LDP-1000). See Daynes and Butler, The Videodisc Book, p. 13.
82. Rice and Dubbe, "Development of the First Optical Videodisc," p. 284.
83. "Conversations with John Messerschmitt," *Videography* 9,1 (January 1984): 55.
84. Ibid., p. 53.
85. Ibid., p. 55. In contrast, it was estimated in 1985 that Japan—where innovative consumer products tend to be accepted more readily than most other places—had a videodisc player market of 500,000 units. Of these, at least half were LaserVision drives, which is Philips' videodisc player. See "Philips in the Age of Optical Disc Media," pp. 4–5.
86. Ibid., p. 54.
87. Joan Cash, "Picture Power: Optical Discs and Video Computing Come of Age," *Museum News* 66, 6 (July/August 1988): 58–60; Joan Cash, "Spinning Toward the Future: The Museum on Laser Videodisc," *Museum News* (August 1985): 19–31. See also Roberta H. Binder, *Videodiscs in Museums: A Project and Resource Directory* (Falls Church, VA: Future Systems, Inc., 1988).
88. Leonard Laub, "The Evolution of Mass Storage," *BYTE* 11,5 (May 1986): 161–172.
89. Timothy Onosko, "Let There be Light," *Creative Computing* 11,9 (September 1985): 43–49.
90. Parsloe, *Interactive Video*, pp. 71–80.
91. Dale F. Rodesch, "Interleaving Multiple Channels on Videodisc for Rapid Interactivity," *The Videodisc Monitor* 4,3 (March 1986): IA- ID.
92. "N.A. Philips Scales Down U.S. Videodisc Efforts," *The Videodisc Monitor* 4,8 (August 1986): 5.
93. Alix M. Freedman and Richard L. Hudson, "DuPont and Philips Plan Joint Venture to Make, Market Laser-Disk Products," *The Wall Street Journal* 30 October 1985, p. 4.
94. Becky Hann, "IBM: Its Own Best Customer," *The Videodisc Monitor* 4,9 (September 1986): 18–19.
95. "Integrated CD-ROM, Videodisc System," *The Videodisc Monitor* 4,8 (August 1986): 3. For a directory of laser disc systems packages see Ed Schwartz, *The Educators' Handbook to Interactive Videodisc* (Washington, D.C.: Association for Educational Communications and Technology, 1985), pp. 41–46.
96. Broadbent, "A Review of the MCA Disco-Vision System," p. 556.

97. George W. Hrbek, "An Experimental Optical Videodisc Playback System," *Journal of the SMPTE* 83, 7 (July 1974): 580–582.
98. Herb Brody, "Picking Up the Pieces of RCA," *High Technology Business.* 8, 5 (May 1988): 44.
99. Sigel, et al., *Video Discs,* pp. 37.
100. Jonathan A. Jerome and Edward M. Kaczorowski, "Film-Based Videodisc System," *Journal of the SMPTE* 83,7 (July 1974): pp. 560–563.
101. "ARDEV Interactive Photographic Film Videodisc System" (Promotional release from ARDEV Company, Inc.).
102. Sigel et al., *Video Discs,* p. 39.
103. "Special Report: The Year in Review," *The Videodisc Monitor* 4,1 (January 1986): I-D.
104. "MDEC in First Major Application," *The Videodisc Monitor* 3,5 (May 1985): 1.
105. Sigel et al., *Video Discs,* p. 41.
106. Mark H. Kryder, The Magnetics Technology Center: Description and Proposal (Received from Mark H. Kryder 25 September 1986), pp. 11, 13.
107. R.N. Gardner, T.A. Rinehart, L.H. Johnson, R.P. Freese, and R.A. Lund, "Characteristics of a New High C/N Magneto-Optic Media," *Proceedings of SPIE—The International Society for Optical Engineering* 420 (Arlington, Virginia: June 1983), p. 242.
108. Mark H. Kryder, The Magnetics Technology Center: Description and Proposal, (Received from Mark H. Kryder 25 September 1986), p. 3.
109. Ibid., pp. 1, 5. Industrial funding is provided for contract research and is also given "in the form of outright gifts and fellowships for students". For more information on the work at the MTC, see Hotz, "The LASER: CMU, Westinghouse Experts Beam as New Technology Spreads to All Fields," p. E1.
110. Of note is that the MTC maintains a 4,000 square foot class 100 clean room.
111. Rice and Dubbe, "Development of the First Optical Videodisc," p. 283.
112. Frank Price, "Video: Disc Dynamics," *Audio-Visual Communications* 20,2 (February 1986): 42.
113. Parsloe, *Interactive Video,* p. 93.
114. "Panasonic Introduces 12" Optical Memory Disc Recorder," *The Videodisc Monitor* 6, 6 (June 1988): 6.
115. Price, "Video: Disc Dynamics," p. 43.
116. See "Philips Shows CD-Video, Revives Laservision," pp. 10–11.
117. Judith Paris Roth, "The Coming of the Interactive Compact Disc," *High Technology* 6,10 (October 1986): 46.
118. For a more complete videodisc chronology see George C. Kenney, "Special Report: A Time Line of Videodisc Milestones," *The Videodisc Monitor* (April 1985): IA-ID. See also the December issue of the Videodisc Monitor in each year subsequent to the above mentioned issue for a "Special Report: The Year in Review."

3

The Standards Dilemma
and the Research Data

The Standards Dilemma

Compact Discs

Optical laser reflective discs include videodisc, CD-Audio, CD ROM, CD-I, and CD-V. The compact discs all use digital recording and playback technology. Philips, the European and American technology giant, pioneered the development of the CD system, and then signed a cooperation agreement with Sony in order to set a world standard for this new medium that would ensure its acceptance and success.

Introduced in 1982, CD-Audio quickly became "the most successful consumer product ever launched."[1] In 1983 Philips and Sony introduced CD-ROM and were instrumental in establishing some universal standards for it as well. Not specified, though, were the types of information to store or how to store it. Also, there was no standard operating system environment designated to govern the logical file structure. Thus, CD-ROM information distributors were required to create a separate set of discs for each operating system environment. Fortunately, a group of vendors called the High Sierra Group[2] was formed and an agreement was reached on a standard logical file structure for CD-ROM. Its acceptance has enabled discs that follow this standard to be read as standard files universally—no matter what operating system is used.[3,4]

In 1986, Philips and Sony reached agreement in principle on specifications for a third compact disc to be called CD-I (compact disc - interactive). By December 1987 American Interactive Media (AIM) demonstrated the capabilities of the first CD-I disc. With a focus on entertainment, education and self-help applications, AIM is developing a multitude of CD-I programs that are scheduled for release to the consumer market in 1989. The goal, according to Philips, is "eventually to develop a worldwide standard in which one CD player will be compatible with any of the three CD formats."[5] These CDs represent an evolution in optical storage technology. The standards developed, as well as those being planned, were an outgrowth of lessons learned from the videodisc that preceded them and was a revolutionary form of optical storage. Having so stated, Miller continues on to emphasize that "it is always easier to take the next logical step than it is to participate in a revolution."[6] It is too soon to evaluate the educational impact of compact discs. They are, however, being explored and used in a growing number of learning environments.

Videodiscs

The videodisc, on the other hand, was introduced in 1978 amid much promotion and highly optimistic predictions. More than a few viewed intelligent videodisc systems as a milestone equivalent to Gutenberg's invention of the printing press. Many experts in videodisc technology still do.[7,8,9]

An interactive video system typically unites a video player, disc or tape, and monitor with a microcomputer that manages the information retrieval, storage, tabulation of results, and other functions as instructed by the user. The various components are integrated by way of an internal interface card, and external interface options such as keyboard, joy stick, track ball, light pen, mouse, and touch-sensitive monitor facilitate ease of use. As an instruction or training medium, it requires an active participation on the part of the user. Ideal as this sounds, it has, nonetheless, taken interactive videodisc almost a decade to find an effective and substantive niche in military and industrial training, and, to a lesser extent, in educational instructions.

A number of reasons exist for this moderate level of usage, principal of which has been the dearth of high quality software. High quality interactive videodisc programs require the input of skilled instructional designers, video producers, art directors, and computer programmers; and there has been a shortage of qualified development teams to produce such courseware. Added to these obviously high personnel expenses is the high cost of producing new master discs that are program specific. This medium is not inexpensive, which has been a formidable obstacle for many, especially educators. Also, when first introduced, disc and system unreliability were a hindrance. But this aspect has been resolved, and the technology is now very sophisticated and reliable.

What has not been resolved is the quandary of standards. While there is uniformity in videodisc size worldwide, this is not the case with analog video signals, which differ among countries and are not compatible.[10] Further complicating this quagmire is the escalating use of players governed by a variety of computers. Such a medley affects the way information is compiled as well as the types of information that can be stored. It also tends to keep system manufacturers as well as instructional designers in a state of flux, and, consequently, much less active than they would like to be. Such a state also keeps hardware prices high. "This tangled web of system configuration possibilities makes it extremely unlikely that system-level standards and compatibility will evolve beyond specific applications," according to Rockley Miller.[11]

The key issue of standards actually revolves around courseware portability, or the ability to take a course or program written for one hardware configuration and play it on another without modification. Some initiatives are underway to help resolve this issue. One recent trend comes from the hardware vendors who have begun incorporating emulation modes that allow their systems to pretend they are something different. Several systems now offer the ability to emulate IBM's InfoWindow system and thereby offer access to the entire InfoWindow catalog of nearly 400 courses.

Another initiative is coming from the Interactive Video Industry Association (IVIA). Formed in 1987, the IVIA is a trade association that was launched with over 100 companies aboard as founding members. Many of them are participating in and supporting the IVIA Compatibility Committee's efforts to develop recommended practices and public domain command structures that will facilitate courseware portability. This initiative has been endorsed by the Department of Defense which considers hardware compatibility a critical prerequisite to major system implementations.

Extensive Interactive Videodisc Applications: Governmental and Corporate

Specific applications are on the increase. Courses sponsored by the Pentagon and by corporations using interactive training and teaching, according to Rus Gant at the Massachusetts Institute of Technology, have indicated that "students learn two to three times faster than with books and retain nearly triple as much information."[12] In addition, laser videodiscs are easy to operate, offer reliability and superb image and sound quality, and require only a compact space.

The most common use of interactive videodisc technology has been in industrial and governmental training environments. Two of the largest industrial users are Ford and General Motors. Ford recently developed a system designed to convey the most recent information on automobile repair to its 40,000 widely strewn mechanics.[13] Using a light pen, the mechanic selects appropriate tools from one side of a split screen, transfers them to the other side, and then properly connects and adjusts the part displayed, such as a carburetor. The accompanying audio tracks reflect the work being done by emitting appropriate sounds. Beyond this particular and sophisticated application is the actuality that corporations in the United States spend approximately $60 billion to train people each year; and where interactive videodisc has been used, a substantial reduction in training time—25 to 50 percent—is reported.[14]

Within the federal government, the military is the largest user of this medium. A functional literacy program for Army field soldiers has been designed and placed onto a videodisc by the University of Maryland, as has training for the electrical maintenance of tracked and nontracked vehicles.[15] In the Army Training School system there are "projected expenditures of $100 million by 1990 for 20,000 interactive learning stations."[16] Included are peripherals, documentation, engineering drawings, and development tools. This Electronic Information Delivery System (EIDS) for the U.S. Army is an integrated videodisc and microcomputer unit with modem for telecommunications and touch-sensitive monitor for facile presentation of information. Excluding the monitor, all other components with portable carrying case collectively weigh less than 50 pounds. The initial contract for 1,985 systems was signed on November 4, 1986. Options allow the Army to purchase nearly 48,000 systems under the contract.[17,18]

Other branches of the U.S. armed services are expected to adopt this same standard with a commitment that could well result in over 50,000 such systems being obtained by the military over the next five years. EIDS is expected to become the standard system for delivery of both interactive video courses and computer-based training,"[19] for the military, and will greatly affect the U.S. market in general since such a plethora of training demands will necessitate the design and production of a tremendous volume of new videodiscs and computer programs, much of which will be contracted out to private firms. On June 20, 1986 a request for proposals was released for EIDS courseware (interactive videodisc) "for 11 different Army schools and representing over 3,600 hours of instruction under current programs of instruction. The contract will be awarded as a small business set-aside. . . ."[20]

Such application of technology-based education is clearly leading or directing the technology. It offers both an inspiration and a challenge to educators. A report submitted to the Congressional Office of Technology Assessment by the Human Resources Research Organization in 1982 accentuated that "because it has the needs, funds, and the conviction to develop and implement technology-based education, the military will probably play the leading role and be more effective in its development than marketplace, private sector entrepreneurship."[21]

Ford's Intelligent Video Learning System, using Sony equipment, provides technicians with individualized, self-paced, in-dealership courses that include a simulation of hands-on repair or diagnosis. (Courtesy Ford Motor Company)

Students participate in an interactive classroom using networked keyboards and videodisc courseware at a Winning Edge Learning Center in suburban Minneapolis. (Courtesy Winning Edge)

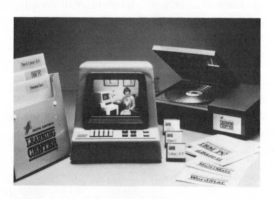

Digital Controls Learning Center (later acquired by Comsell) was one of the first dedicated videodisc training systems to be offered with a library of videodisc programs on popular personal computer software packages. (Courtesy Comsell)

Matrox Electronic Systems EIDS unit (Electronic Information Delivery System) supplied under contract to the US Army. The contract, issued in December 1986 allows the Army to purchase up to 47,900 units, making it the largest single videodisc application to date. (Courtesy Matrox Electronic Systems)

The Research Data

Interactive Video: General Perspective

Even though substantial development of interactive videodisc and delivery systems as an emerging educational tool is currently underway and a great deal is known about the engineering and hardware capabilities, much less is known about its teaching and learning effectiveness.[22,23,24] This is the case because relatively few academic environments are using and evaluating interactive videodiscs. There are, of course, exceptions, notably the University of Nebraska, the University of Maryland, Utah State University, Brigham Young University, the University of Georgia, the University of Delaware, Massachusetts Institute of Technology, Harvard University, Carnegie Mellon University, the University of Pittsburgh, Cornell University and a few others. The majority of academic institutions, however, have not attempted to experiment with the laser videodisc and ways to include it in their curricula. A corpus of research literature does exist, however, albeit diffused.

Interactive video currently uses both videodisc and videotape formats. A videotape system can be an effective way to be introduced to interactive video, and it has been and is being employed by a number of educators. Nicholas Iuppa believes that the only reason to use videotape in this way is due to economics. A "clean, efficient, and, therefore, effective operation"[25] is sacrificed in the process. Videotape wears and tears with use, is much slower retrieving visual information, and has a much reduced storage density and less still frame clarity than does a videodisc. Others recognize the drawbacks but have found videotape to be not just substantially more economic to use for many organizations, particularly in early efforts to develop interactive video programs, but also "a highly effective means of achieving cognitive and affective instructional objectives."[26] In addition—and unlike current videodiscs—visual information is easily added to or subtracted from a videotape. If required, this is a significant drawback to using videodiscs at the present time.

Visual-Based Instruction

The two primary educational components of interactive video are visual-based instruction and computer aided instruction. In a concise meta-analysis study[27], 1,400 references were sifted through and reduced to 74 studies that compared effects of visual-based instruction (VBI) to conventional teaching in college. The major applications of VBI were still projection, film, multimedia, closed-circuit television, educational television, use of video for observation, and use of video for feedback. (Feedback, as described here, represents videotaping or filming a demonstration or performance and then viewing it for learning purposes. The formatting of the tape is linear; that is, it progresses from the first scene straight through to the end without deviation, unless stopped.) In addition to comparisons of different types of VBI, the 74 studies also used various research designs, focused on different types of courses, and varied in terms of when conducted.

In retention, the correlation between aptitude and achievement, student ratings of their attitude toward medium used, and the likelihood of course completion, there was little difference between VBI and conventional methods of teaching. However, students learned slightly more from VBI than from conventional teaching. The average test score in the typical VBI class was 68.4 percent; in the conventional class the average was 66.9 percent. This 1.5 difference in percentage points represents a standard deviation of 4.5.

Regarding achievement, the most significant difference occurred when video was used as a source of feedback either for skill acquisition or for teacher training. There was an average percentage difference of 4.4. Though only five studies reported on this VBI, the results were consistent with a study cited by the authors that reviewed 350 instructional media comparisons.[28] That study found little difference when comparing televised instruction with face-to-face instruction. When videotapes were used to observe demonstration teaching, however, teachers in training benefited as much observing such video segments as from actual classroom visits. Further, when used to teach performance skills such as typing and athletics, video and film often produced a significant increase in learning and student attitudes improved also.

This meta-analysis included studies published up to 1977. Although authors Cohen, Ebeling, and Kulik do not understand why, their observation is that studies they reviewed that were published after 1970 had results more favorable to VBI, and studies published prior to 1960 showed little effect of visual-based methods. One possible explanation is that the production quality of VBI has steadily improved to emulate situations depicted rather than to serve as a parody of them.

Half of the studies focused on instructional television as the VBI that was compared to conventional instruction. The authors recommend more research on the use of videotape for purposes of feedback.

Nugent, Tipton, and Brooks[29] focus on presentation formats in television production. Previous research has been directed more toward presenting cognitive materials than considering learning characteristics. Clearly, some instructional models are more effective than others. Vignettes and dramatizations are more effective with children, while college students respond better to simple production techniques. The authors conclude that production techniques do make a difference when measuring the instructional effectiveness of television, even though one set of production guidelines will never be adequate, given the diversity of learners and learning objectives. Ongoing research is required for instructional designs that incorporate educational television.

In a related study, Morris asserts that most television research directed toward "attention and selective perception"[30] was conducted prior to the emergence of sophisticated technology and is thus limited.

He further emphasizes that studies conducted since 1960 to measure the effective use of instructional television have lacked substance. Morris' emphasis is on improving television instruction by enhancing production techniques. In this study, minor adjustments such as adding a few graphics and a dab of animation do increase student attention, but have a negligible effect on achievement. Sophisticated production improvements, however, do have an ameliorating effect on achievement. Requisite for academic significance is coupling enhancements such as instructional television development with "scientific" and "artistic" substance. In this medium, at its best, content quality unites with emotion to improve learning.

Nugent[31] explores the influence on learning that various media stimuli have and how to use them more effectively. Print, visual, and auditory presentations focused on television (film and video) were tested, and the results confirmed that the students learned equally well from each medium when the content was the same. The researchers recognized from the start that age is a critical factor in remembering and learning, especially from pictures. Students were able to transfer knowledge effectively from one symbol system to another, for example, from pictorial to print format. The research demonstrated that instructional presentation by two symbol systems—iconic and print or audio, for example—is superior to a solitary symbol presentation, confirming the hypothesis of one of the studies. "The combination of symbol systems evidently exploits the potential of each and promotes a synergistic interaction." An important distinction, though, is that instruction that combined iconic, pictorial, and linguistic symbol systems was superior to instruction that combined linguistic, print, and linguistic, audio, symbol systems. In addition, when information was nonredundant across the symbol systems, positive interaction was minimized.

According to Nugent, much more research attention is needed on how best to use each symbol system most effectively. With pictures, issues such as size, color, and positioning need to be explored in greater depth, as does their instructional objective and function, in relation to the needs of the individual learner. The amalgamating of symbol systems, too, needs a considerable amount of further research. Unfortunately, the paucity of sustained quality research and development focused on instructional television and instructional video that employ multiple symbol systems continues to hinder their beneficial use by many educators.

Computer-Aided Instruction

Microcomputers function in a similar milieu. By amplifying our intelligence and our ability to manipulate symbols, the microcomputer has the potential to become "the most civilizing influence that we have had to date."[32] Little published research exists, however, that perceives the computer as a symbolic technology, one that stores and dynamically manipulates symbols, which may well "serve as the currency of human thought."[33] With such a viewpoint, developing computer software as well as hardware begin to reflect recent advances in psychology, especially cognitive processes, to both expand and reorganize the structure and function of learning itself.

Bolt believes all benefit from computers should emanate from a "convivial" relationship between user and machine. As acting head of the Human-Machine Interface Group at the Massachusetts Institute of Technology's Media Laboratory, he has been working for more than ten years to achieve such a "pleasurable, even exhilarating" relationship. Unfortunately, such "supreme usability" is not yet available, and, as a result, according to Bolt, "the loudly trumpeted home-computer revolution seems to have stalled," not to be rekindled until computers provide "real help" and "good company."[34]

The computer "revolution" in U.S. businesses has also been delayed. Even though businesses have invested "hundreds of billions of dollars in computers and computer-aided communications,"[35] expected improvements in productivity have been far less than expected. Disappointment for some managers stems from their anticipation of immediate results from computer investments. This is not only unrealistic, but belies the fact that a learning process is involved which is time-consuming. Also, effective application of this technology is, in many instances, linked with changes in the way work is done.

Secondary and elementary school environments in the U.S. are also being inundated by computers. From the spring of 1983 to the spring of 1985, the number of computers in use expanded from 250,000 to over one million, according to a national survey conducted by Johns Hopkins University.[36] Virtually all secondary and elementary schools have begun to use computers in their instructional program. Even so, the typical school surveyed provided only one computer for every 40 students; a ratio that limits substantial computer time per student. At a minimum, one computer for every 12 students would be required if a school were to provide 30 minutes of computer time per day to each student. The same study cited above reported that as of the spring of 1985, such a favorable student-to-computer ratio was available at only 7 percent of the high schools, and roughly 2 percent of the elementary schools, and 3 percent of the middle schools in the country.

The common disparity in student-computer ratio will, no doubt, be ameliorated by the ever-widening conviction that computers will improve the instructional effectiveness of schools. As the educational computer revolution forges on, however, the primary issues continue to be quality, efficacy, and potential. The instructional effectiveness of computers has not been demonstrated for the typical school environment.

Several studies confirm the effect of computer-aided instruction on improving student learning (especially for older students), and in decreasing the amount of time required to learn.[37] However, extrapolating such findings to environments that have one computer per 40 students, or even per 12 students, is not valid despite the tendency to apply the favorable statistics. According to George Bear,

> the truth is that we have been sold on the process and not the product of microcomputer instruction, and few of us actually know if microcomputers are having any worthwhile impact on the effectiveness of schools in improving learning.[38]

Not surprising is that the producers and purveyors of the hardware and much of the software have been, for the most part, business entrepreneurs not too concerned with its educational quality.[39,40] In part, the uncertainty of the education market kept some early software developers from investing in the best possible product.[41] Generally speaking, the increasing numbers of computers in schools and universities have prompted similar growth in available software, that has, unfortunately, had quantity as its leitmotif, resulting in a massive amount of educational "garbage."[42] There are exceptions, notably Digital Equipment Corporation and IBM. Both are now investing substantial amounts of money for earnest curriculum development and others are beginning to do the same as they realize that the education market is growing more lucrative.

As with the business community, which itself has not as yet discerned how best to integrate the computer into the workplace, a learning lag is to be expected. Revolutionary innovations require persistence as well as patience. As outlined in the survey report from the Johns Hopkins University, of the teachers using computers with students during the 1984–85 school year, only 27 percent of the high school teachers were viewed as "expert" users; 21 percent of the middle school teachers and 10 percent of the elementary (K-6) teachers were so viewed.

Teachers, generally speaking, need much more familiarity with computers, and research data will be required to help determine which subject areas and which populations are best or least suited for computer-aided learning.[43] As Alfred Bork has pointed out, "the development of new courses is the heart of any successful use of the computer in improving our educational system."[44] Professional standards must be adhered to and multiple learning theories and approaches incorporated into the materials produced.

This process of effectively integrating the computer into the instructional environment will quite likely profoundly alter the organizational structure of the schools, and result in new and more dignified roles for teachers. For the student, it makes possible individualized mastery learning. Where computers are used effectively as learning tools students can have the means to direct their own learning and information management.

Michael Hannafin[45] has found that such transfer of instructional control is more effective if accompanied by "coaching"; he also has learned that age and learner ability are contributing factors. In the process, there is the potential for teachers and students to reorganize their mental function in a way that will, quite likely, change the way tasks are approached and undertaken. Symbolic technologies will help facilitate the realization of this potential.

The arduous journey conveying school environments from where they currently are to this dynamically restructured paradigm will require:

a. inspired leadership;
b. an openness to innovation and experimentation;
c. extensive and ongoing research and development of high-quality educational software that reflects developing learning theories and advancing cognition research;
d. effective implementation of hardware and software for teachers and by teachers; and
e. persistent and patient efforts by administrators, teachers, students, and support personnel.

One who shares this educational vision and who promotes it with evangelical enthusiasm is Steven Jobs, cofounder and former chairman of Apple Computer, Inc. With his development of the Macintosh, computer technology became much more convivial by offering an iconic oriented learning/work environment capable of storing and manipulating symbols. The addition of Apple Computer's HyperCard development system (created by Bill Atkinson) in August of 1987 greatly expanded this frontier.

By design this dynamic program (which has been given away with every Macintosh sold since HyperCard's introduction) makes the Macintosh's object (or component) oriented user interface—icons, graphics, flexible file structure, and sound—highly accessible to non-programmers. Users can create and customize a plethora of information from a HyperMedia environment that includes optical discs that store references or data such as printed text, graphics, motion picture clips, still photography and sound, for replay on video screens.

The organizing software, hypertext, then links all of this data and enables the user—non-sequentially and instantly—to summon whatever images, text or sound is desired. In addition, a particular inquiry or theme can be held or focused on while moving or searching about the various data or references. Vannevar Bush's vision that was described more than 40 years ago is finally coming to fruition, and a variety of educational environments are responding with enthusiasm.

One particularly creative application is at Dartmouth College where a student using a Macintosh in his/her room can communicate with the university's vast dormitory network, search the card catalog for any of the library's 1.5 million books, complete and send class assignments and projects, and use the electronic mail system with professors and other students. A vast array of information and data on Dartmouth's mainframe—such as a map of Europe that can be focused-down to specific towns, streets and gardens—can also be accessed.[46]

At Cornel University Medical College, an elaborate hypermedia environment enables students to use the system to review notes, inspect X-rays or examine color photographs of organs. "A student looking at a photograph of the liver can instantly summon up text describing liver disease, then compare that with slides of liver biopsies, all on the same screen."[47] Lowell High School in San Francisco worked with Apple Computer to develop a hypermedia/interactive videodisc accompaniment to John Steinbeck's "The Grapes of Wrath." Numerous aspects of life in America during the 1930s can be accessed including Depression-era radio programs, photographs, film footage and magazine articles. This "ultimate research tool for a generation raised on television and stereo systems" can watch and listen to Franklin Roosevelt deliver a fireside chat, hear a sampling of Woody Guthrie's songs and study agricultural conditions of that period.

Since leaving Apple Computer, Inc., in 1985, Jobs formed a new company, NeXT, Inc., and has developed a high-powered computer workstation that was unveiled in October 1988. Developed for use initially be researchers in university and college environments, it has revolutionary capabilities for graphics, simulation, and animation, in relation to research, teaching, and learning. The NeXT comes with a 17-inch screen, array processing for multiple task performance, and primary software, or operating system, that is largely object-oriented. Thus, components, or "objects", can be reused and built upon an infinite number of times. Potentially, productivity is enhanced for programmers and powerful computing capabilities are placed in the hands of non-technical users. NeXT is also the first personal computer to use higher-capacity (265 million-byte) erasable optical disk drives.

With an advisory board made up of representatives from 23 leading universities in the US, NeXT built its business plans and products to meet the needs of higher education. Coupled with its understanding of and commitment to higher education is the intent of NeXT to close the gap between current and ideal computer technology. Such development efforts for the education marketplace are focussed on innovative, personal, and affordable computer solutions for the 1990s and beyond. This collaborative initiative is both encouraging and inspiring for educators, as well as for hardware and software developers.[48,49,50]

Interactive Video: Specific Research Applications

Computer-aided instruction and visual-based instruction are currently at the inchoate level of efficacy for most school environments. A body of substantive research has yet to demonstrate that they can substantially improve instructional effectiveness for mass education. Potentially, however, as has been demonstrated in limited studies, they both have considerable educational contributions to make. In response to this potential and the challenge it poses—and in keeping pace with the rapid progression of technology—interactive video has emerged to unite these two components in a new medium that seems capable of transcending the limits of its separate entities.

With a variety of interactive videodisc systems and a range of software sophistication, the Nebraska Videodisc Design/Production Group in 1979 structured a gradation of "intelligence" or levels of sophistication for these systems. There are a number of other such classifications, but this model is still commonly used and includes:

Videodisc Systems—Levels of Interactivity

Level 0—a player designed for linear playback only (CLV and CAV).

Level 1—a player that can take advantage of the CAV functions such as instant replay and scanning capabilities, freeze frame, still frame, and variable speeds. Primarily a consumer model, it is not usually interfaced with a computer, although it probably could be. Level 0 is included.

Level 2—an upgraded industrial version of a Level 1 player with an internal microprocessor and a built-in port for external microprocessor interfacing.

Level 3—is Level 1 or 2 actually interfaced to and governed by an external computer.

Level 4—was not a part of this early classification. Daynes and Butler, writing several years later in The Videodisc Book[51], designated it "a theoretical domain in which all things are possible." At present, level 4 is minimally a level 3 system that is incremented by an artificial intelligence component relevant to the interactivity of the system.[52] Frequently, it is comprised of multiple systems or a variety of units interfaced together. It also is an open-ended configuration that is used primarily for research applications.

Interactive video, level 3, unites high-quality visual, audio, and computer information with rapid access of that information in myriad and interchangeable combinations. While its applications vary, this technology enables individual and group users to learn at their own pace and to access only those portions of a presentation that are relevant to their needs or interests. It also permits information or instruction to be presented and sequenced according to the user's response or interaction with the system; and, of course, an instructor may set a structured format if desired. Some measure of "coaching" or guidance is likely to be more effective for most learners. These unique features are made possible by connecting a videotape or videodisc player to a microcomputer and then programming or directing the system to present or access the information that it has stored. When programmed to do so, pertinent user data are gathered such as name, levels of learning, and others; questions are asked of the user to determine level of comprehension, corrections to questions asked are given by reviewing material already presented or by branching to feedback or remediation (additional information); encouragement is offered; and supplementary information stored in the system can be made available for advanced learners to access. Requisite statistical data can be compiled for users of the system, such as the number of right and wrong answers and the amount of time to answer questions as examples, and such data can further influence instructional decisions.

Understandably, given the standards dilemma, its recent entry into academia, the cost of producing a videodisc, as well as its unique features which, even with cursory observation, are far superior to its distinct elements, little empirical research of substantial quality has been published regarding the teaching or learning effectiveness of interactive video.[53] The following are somewhat representative of the interactive video research studies that have been completed. Of the 10 included, the first two focus on interactive videotape, a frequently ignored but beneficial medium; the subsequent four on videodisc-based training, level 2 systems; and the remainder on interactive videodisc instruction, level 3 systems. The organizations using this medium that are presented here represent the military, industry, higher education, and K-12 education. In addition to these, a capsular analysis of 28 evaluative studies, by James Bosco, is presented.

Middle School Science—Interactive Videotape

At a Texas middle school, a science teaacher divided the entire seventh grade—410 students—into three groups.[54] All watched a videotape program about the biological control of insects that was not particularly lively. The material had not been previously covered and, actually, belonged in a high school curriculum, not the seventh grade.

The video format for the first group was linear. The second group watched the same tape and then discussed the contents with their teacher. The third group had the program interactively adapted. That is, designated stop points were programmed throughout the tape to ask questions on material presented. Wrong answers would rewind the tape to the appropriate section so that it could be reviewed. Decisions as to right or wrong answers were based on class consensus and the videotape was controlled by the teacher. In a quiz the following day, almost all of the students that learned interactively scored at or above the 90th percentile, while those in the other two groups rarely exceeded the 80th percentile. Group one scored the lowest.

Besides being an excellent learning tool, the interactive videotape also elicited almost 100-percent participation, whereas the other two groups had only five or six participating. The science teacher who ran the trial now sees interactive video as a complement to teaching, where both teacher and students are compelled to participate and interact. The material presented can be worked with individually or in a group until the material has been understood. Although this study was innovative, it would have been helpful to know the basis on which the students were divided and to have had actual scores, or at least the means, cited.

Community Health—Interactive Videodisc

A more comprehensive comparison of noninteractive and interactive videotape instruction was conducted at a large urban Southwestern university, with 205 undergraduate students demographically representative of the enrollment. Levenson, Morrow, and Signer[55] designed this study to increase student knowledge about smokeless tobacco, an established hazard based on earlier research at the same university, as well as their inclination to dissuade family members and friends who were users.

The researchers designed and administered a questionnaire to the students at the end of the lesson, eliciting background information on age, sex, race, student status, and previous experience with a computer. Eighteen cognitive questions ascertained knowledge about smokeless tobacco. Additional questions to determine level of satisfaction with the lesson were also included, as was a "forced-choice question" in order to scrutinize how they would respond with a group of smokeless tobacco users.

Four groups were used:

1. a control group that simply completed the questionnaire and received no information;
2. an experimental group that viewed a linear videotape about smokeless tobacco as part of class (group) instruction. The tape included, at the beginning, a situation asking the learners to anticipate their response to smokeless users as well as group pressures;
3. an experimental group that viewed the same videotape, but did so individually; and
4. an experimental group that individually viewed an interactively adapted version of much of the same videotape segments. At key points of the lesson, however, the learner was asked questions and given appropriate feedback or remediation via computer generated text or branching to supplemental video and audio materials. At the end there was an alternative explanation of important facts, for those who missed more than four of the six review questions; and the interactive format enabled learners to rehearse different situational responses to smokeless tobacco prior to actually applying them.

Students were assigned to groups 1, 3, and 4 randomly. Subjects in group 2 were introduced to the videotape as part of a classroom discussion. The highest mean score, ranging from 7.4 to 15.1, and lowest standard deviation, ranging from 2.9 to 1.8, for the cognitive questions, were achieved by the interactive video group. According to the ANOVA analysis, the difference among the groups was significant. Through seven post hoc contrasts the researchers also determined that each of the groups differed significantly, and a chi square analysis, focused on the responses to the 18 cognitive questions by groups 3 and 4, showed significant difference on seven of them. The interactive group also indicated a strong proclivity to actively encourage others to stop using smokeless tobacco, in contrast to the other three groups, and expressed a desire to study other lessons in similar fashion.

Based on their findings, these researchers see interactive video as a highly effective means of achieving instructional objectives. They suggest that it may well be a supplement or even an alternative to film or videotape by itself. They also felt that by using branching capabilities more fully in the main menu that students could be given greater control of the lesson.

The novelty effect and its possible influence on this technology needs to be addressed by conducting studies over a period of time and thereby allowing the "newness" to wear off. Its effect here is unclear. Another fundamental issue is whether interactive video in this study, or any study, achieved the results it did due to instructional design superior to competing options. Also, was it the technology or the instructional design that motivated the subjects to learn more effectively? Obviously they work together. As a result, it makes the task of differentiating, even in experimental research, that much more difficult. Levenson, Morrow, and Signer affirm "that instructional design strategies need to be adapted to the unique features promised by new technologies rather than be developed only as extensions of existing efforts."

U.S. Army—Early Videodisc Explorative Study

Even though videotape is being used effectively primarily in school and university settings for instructional purposes, a far superior medium for the design and delivery of interactive video is the laser read videodisc. The primary strengths of videodisc are: its capability of storing up to 54,000 excellent quality still frames, such as slides, or 30 minutes of motion per side, in any desired arrangement; and, its ability to retrieve any frame per side in 1.5 seconds or less in any desired sequence or pace (individually, or at slow, regular, or fast motion—in forward or reverse). It also has dual audio tracks that encourage a variety of combinations; and, compressed audio can be used with single visual frames.

Shortly after the videodisc became available, the Army Communicative Technology Office decided to gather preliminary information on its delivery effectiveness, through the Fort Benning Field Unit (Georgia) of the Army Research Institute. The intent was to justify and to guide further research on this prototypic technology, rather than to evaluate its training effectiveness.[56]

This study was conducted through the Army Training Extension Course Program, whose function it was to upgrade job proficiency through instructional materials, 72 percent of which (as of December, 1978) were audiovisual programs. The standard half-hour program used super-8 mm visual frames coupled with audio cassette narration, and was designed for self-paced training.

For each lesson selected, two videodisc versions were made. The first was virtually a duplicate of the original. The second had visual frames added to the original material that gave the user the option to review material presented.

Subjects numbered 298 enlisted male soldiers selected for mandatory participation, but randomly assigned to one of four experimental conditions:

1. standard super-8 mm format (one-third of subjects)
2. unaltered videodisc (one-sixth of subjects)
3. modified videodisc with review capability (one-sixth of subjects).
4. Baseline condition receiving no instruction (one-third of subjects)

The reduced number of subjects for the videodisc conditions resulted from the limited number of players that could be made available by both MCA and Thomson-CSA. After the treatment, soldiers completed an attitude questionnaire and, the next day, a standard performance test on the lesson. The comparison between the mean for the super-8 mm format and the combined videodisc mean (both adjusted for the covariates) was not significant at the .05 level. The baseline mean was significantly less. Attitudes varied little between delivery methods. Given an option, soldiers chose to make little use of the review function.

No increase in effectiveness using the videodisc was demonstrated by this study. The experiment accomplished its objectives, but acknowledged its limitations. The researchers concluded that future studies needed to take greater advantage of the capabilities of interactive videodisc systems.

Elementary School Health—Interactive Videodisc

In a noncomparative study, Simon Fraser University in British Columbia, Canada designed and field tested an interactive videodisc with elementary school children, grades five through seven, titled "How Your Heart and Circulatory System Works."[57] The purpose was to discern the effectiveness of their experimental videodisc.

Following a two-month pilot study, field testing was conducted at another school with four teachers whose respective classes totaled 94 students. Separate and extensive inservice programs were conducted for both the teachers and the students in order to familiarize them with the operation of the videodisc player. In addition, the volunteer teachers, who had no prior experience in teaching the content matter, were themselves instructed in the knowledge and the teaching strategies of the Heart Unit. Each teacher was then asked to use the videodisc to structure a four-week heart unit for their students, according to his or her own teaching style.

Single videodisc players were set up in three separate learning carrels with a television monitor and a remote control unit to regulate the videodisc player. Usage was designed for individual or, at most, several students; every session was video recorded and later carefully evaluated to determine the operational proficiency of the students as well as to ascertain which parts of the videodisc were viewed the most.

At the conclusion of the four-week instructional program, teachers and students were asked to complete a questionnaire that evaluated the videodisc learning system. The teachers felt comfortable and technically competent with the medium and felt the videodisc to be an effective learning system with great potential.

The students responded very favorably also. A total of 75 percent indicated having no trouble operating the system, 94 percent felt they learned a lot from the material presented, and collectively they enjoyed taking the interactive test that was presented, as indicated by a mean score of 4.1 on a scale of 5. The test was non-threatening in design, in that no score was kept, and positive reinforcement accompanied each response. Also, where necessary, students were shown correct answers.

As a level 2 system, one not governed by an external micro-computer, but with built-in (internal) memory, the potential of the videodisc is significant. Students and teachers alike in this field study expressed a strong desire to continue using it. Examining the affective domain, which is well represented here, is essential to studies pertaining to a new medium, as are effective inservice programs. An accompanying cognitive design would have further strengthened this study.

U.S. Army Paramedical—Interactive Videodisc A more extensive level 2 research study was conducted at the U.S. Army Academy of Health Sciences, Fort Sam Houston, Texas.[58] Its Basic Medical Specialist Course trains approximately 12,000 soldiers per year to serve as combat medics, with 200 to 500 new students entering a six-week cycle every two weeks. Of the 120 tasks taught, the most stressful and most difficult, with a consistent 25-percent average initial failure rate, was the preparation and administration of intramuscular injection.

Traditionally, instructors trained students, had them practice, and then competency tested them by way of observation. Reteaching and retesting was taxing on instructors and expensive. To study the effectiveness, cost efficiency, and student reaction to a videodisc based system in this environment, the researchers randomly assigned 252 soldiers, 84 per group, to one of three groups:

1. traditionally taught control group;
2. instructor-controlled videodisc-based training group; or a
3. student-controlled videodisc-based training group.

The subjects were representative of the general population from which they were drawn, with no pretreatment differences in groups. The instructors were also selected randomly from qualified personnel, and trained on the new equipment. All groups received the same introduction and viewed a videotape covering all aspects of the process that had been in use for over four years. Instruction and practice followed. The information on the videodiscs was an exact duplicate of the introductory videotape, with the most difficult steps programmed for retrieval so that correct procedures could be reviewed.

Two days after the training a post-test was given to see if the students could prepare and properly administer an intramuscular injection. A chi square analysis determined no significant difference across all groups.

Fifteen days after the experiment a surprise delayed post-test was administered to those who had passed the initial test. Again a chi square analysis showed no significant difference across all groups for those who failed and those who passed. However, the teacher-controlled videodisc group took an average of 48 minutes less for training than the traditional method; and the student-controlled videodisc group took an average of 10 minutes less. The unsupervised students, it was surmised, were perhaps caught-up in the novelty of the equipment and would have benefited by the presence of an instructor, given the task at hand. In addition, students taught by videodisc rated their satisfaction significantly higher than traditionally taught students.

The substantial time savings with no reduction in achievement demonstrated that videodisc training with this high stress, sophisticated psychomotor task was potentially a more efficient method of instruction. Research that investigates multi-dimensional indicators of effectiveness and efficiency seems particular apropos to this medium and other emerging interactive technologies.

U.S. Army (Sequel to Preceding Study)

A sequel to this study under the auspices of the medical Information Technology Research Group was conducted by Balson et al.[59] Using the same environment and focus, they hypothesized that videodisc-based training with more complex programming, resulting in full access to the information contained, with more extensive performance (task) modeling, would be superior to the limited videodisc access of the previous study.

Access had been limited to nine of the most difficult aspects. Repetition of modeling with the videodisc system was always perfectly demonstrated and occurred ten to twenty times more frequently than with live instruction. These repetitive and "safe" exposures to plausible models also resulted in lower stress levels when approaching task performance, and influenced student attitude and motivation. Additionally, a number of prior research studies had indicated that instructor-directed training with videodisc-based programs was superior to fully interactive student regulated training modules. Thus, using the same selection format, 246 soldiers were randomly assigned to one of three groups:

1. standard instructor-based training control group;
2. limited-access videodisc experimental group with repetition permitted, but limited to nine particular sequences; and
3. full-access videodisc experimental group, with the instructor having full access to the entire program and able to augment training with anysequence at desired pace. The training of instructors for group 3 took three times longer than for group 2.

The two experimental groups demonstrated a 7 to 8 percent post-test superiority over the control group, as well as over 30 percent savings in training time. Notably, there was no significant difference between the limited-access and the full-access groups, even though the instructors for group 3 used the added features substantially.

In this instance, the more sophisticated application with the additional instructor training and videodisc programming required proved unmerited and excessively costly. Each learning task and student population, these evaluators stress, needs individualized research to first determine what the problem is, then how best to effectively and efficiently respond to it.

Corporate Training—Interactive Videodisc

When interfaced with an external microcomputer, the videodisc offers the designer unparalleled resources to amalgamate the still frames and motion sequences, dual aural channels, text, and graphics, for instructional purposes. The microcomputer stores its own material, as programmed, and manages all of the information available, as directed by the designer or user. The degree of interactivity is expanded considerably.

Such an interactive videodisc system, called level 3, was designed and extensively evaluated by Digital Equipment Corporation (DEC).[60] With over 15,000 field service engineers worldwide, whose job it is to maintain computer products and diagnose problems, DEC found traditional methods of keeping them abreast of new products and maintenance techniques inadequate. Periodically, the engineers were called to one of several training centers and instructed via lecture and lab courses coupled with self-paced instruction that employed books, linear videotapes, filmstrips, and lab exercises. Cost of training, absence from the field, varying quality of the training, and motivation were all mounting problems.

To address this problem, DEC developed the Interactive Video Information System (IVIS). Introduced in 1982, evaluation studies continued for over 15 months. One particular study randomly assigned a balanced distribution of male and female subjects who were field service engineers to one of two groups, each teaching essentially the same operation pertaining to the installation and repair of three company products. The groups for these three courses were:

1. traditional self-paced instruction, with hands-on experience; and
2. IVIS instruction, with presentation by simulation.

Having completed the training, all subjects were given a number of hardware problems that were scripted out, then timed as they attempted to solve them. A default time was used. No significant difference was detected between the groups. The IVIS courses, on average, however, were completed in 23.1 percent to 46.5 percent less time. For two of the courses, t-tests determined the difference was significant at the .001 level; for the third course at .05.

These results and similar studies from other DEC training centers, coupled with a student opinion questionnaire regarding IVIS which included a 5-point Likert scale for 22 statements, plus 3 completion questions, were highly favorable consistently. This research impelled DEC to use interactive videodisc as its primary educational delivery system. The intent was to have courses available at 515 learning centers throughout the world for field service engineers, and for software service and sales personnel.

More particular information from DEC's numerous evaluation studies would be helpful to review. Of note is that its application of interactive videodisc is akin to that of several in the automotive industry. Ford in particular, as was cited earlier, is taking full advantage of this technology.

Special Education—Interactive Video

An interactive videodisc educational delivery system has also been designed by a research team at Utah State University. Commonly, individualized special education instruction is thwarted in the classroom by the lack of independent work skills by some of the students. To address this problem, Friedman and Hofmeister[61] configured an interactive videodisc system that would work, rather than compete, with the teacher. The intent was to maximize the capabilities of each, thereby enhancing the learning environment.

One of the programs developed centered on telling time. The material used on the videodisc consisted of 11 instructional objectives and was adapted from a paper-and-pencil package produced by the Exceptional Child Center at Utah State University. The interactive videodisc system used a touch-screen monitor. Also, the disc included substantial reinforcing feedback and remediation, and a criterion-referenced test requiring 80-percent accuracy followed each of the objectives. The user determined the pacing of instruction.

The system was field-tested with four students ages 7–9, grades one and two. Three were learning disabled and one was educably mentally retarded. None of them could tell time at all, but they could identify written numbers 1–60 and count by ones and fives to 60.

They used the systems approximately 15 minutes per day, unobtrusively, in the back of the room, while the teacher worked with other students. Within six weeks, although the average was four weeks, they all mastered the task with 80 percent or better proficiency as demonstrated on several post-tests. Such rapid mastery is unusual, according to the researchers, for any child. The potential for individualized learning is encouraging, especially with the capability to accommodate a variety of entry levels, dissimilar instruction pacing, and these coupled with a tool such as the computer that maintains and processes user data including areas of weakness, length of session, correct and incorrect items which are an otherwise tedious chore for the instructor. This study emphasizes teacher and technology working together to address learner needs and specific subject matter.

Medical Students—Interactive Video

Matching the capabilities of interactive videodisc to a specific instructional need has also been effectively demonstrated by Blackman et al.[62] at the University of Iowa. Many health care professionals are not sufficiently trained in detecting motor development dysfunctions in infants. Traditionally, text and lectures are used in conjunction with viewing available infants. Texts are quite removed from actual encounters, however, and infants manifesting the various developmental disabilities are frequently unavailable during training periods. The severity and complications of many such dysfunctions could be reduced by early detection.

In an attempt to confront this instructional problem, the University of Iowa's Department of Pediatrics and Weeg Computing Center developed a computer-based videodisc program titled "Assessment of Neuromotor Dysfunction in Infants." It was designed to be an interactive self-instruction unit and included basic concepts, motor activities and assessments on 27 infants (some healthy, some with dysfunctions), and related material which was available but not required.

The program was tested on third-year medical students over a period of one year. As students cycled through their standard pediatrics clerkship, one six-week session would be assigned to an experimental group, the next to a control group. Of the 135 students so assigned, in quasi-random fashion, four experimental and four control groups resulted.

Program effectiveness was determined through a 10-item knowledge test coupled with a nine-item diagnostic skill test correlated to the children presented on a videotape. Both were part of the final exam. In addition, a 20-item attitude questionnaire was given. Preexisting differences were adjusted for and the results showed that the videodisc program increased the knowledge and diagnostic ability of these medical students regarding infant developmental dysfunctions. Between the experimental (N = 70) and control (N = 65) groups there was a statistically significant difference for both the knowledge test and the diagnostic skill test. The affective questionnaire responses were very positive also. All felt that this learning medium should be used regularly as part of pediatric instruction.

Student-recommended changes—primarily in the area of computer adjustments—have been made in the program. Although the students preferred this medium to traditional lectures and assigned readings, the researchers see its greatest strength as an aid or adjunct to teaching.

Based on the results of this study, this interactive videodisc program has been included in the medical and physical therapy curriculum at the University of Iowa.

High School Language — Interactive Videodisc

Such beneficial instructional development entwined with academic application is maturing in a cooperative project involving Brigham Young University (BYU) and the Provo City School District. Gale and Barksdale[63] have adapted an existing program from the British Broadcasting Corporation, "Digame," to interactive videodisc in order to teach basic Spanish in a first-year high school Spanish course. The original footage was intended to teach as well as expose the learner to the culture and the geography of central Spain.

At BYU, prior adaptations of films and videodiscs for teaching languages, history and other subjects via simulated experience had demonstrated that 40 to 60 percent less learning time was required, with 26 percent more content acquired when interactive videodisc was used in comparison to traditional methods. With the belief that foreign languages in particular are taught in rather archaic fashion, the College of Eduction at BYU established a partnership with Timpview High School to explore further the use of interactive video as a learning "set of tools."

A formative evaluation of the project was recently conducted to assist in development. The focus of the lesson presented was on listening comprehension. Subjects were students from two first year Spanish classes. All were pretested with the MLA-Cooperative Foreign Language Test. Three from each of the two classes representing high, average, and low performance were selected at random to receive treatment of personalized interactive videodisc (PIV). No additional support materials were used. The remainder of one class received classroom (group) interactive videodisc (CIV) instruction. Here the teacher controlled the instruction using the treatment as one component, coupled with lectures. Two support booklets were also prepared and used. The second class used traditional language instruction (TI) that was common in the school district and throughout much of the country. No computers or interactive video were involved. This class did, however, have higher average test scores than the group receiving CIV. All groups (N = 5–18) received five periods of instruction that were 54 minutes each. Given the circumstances, the subjects could not be randomly assigned.

At the end, all were tested with a listening comprehension exam. The means were significantly different, and the differences in performance, determined by comparing groups with their shifts in standard deviations, were notable. Clearly, interactive video dramatically enhanced learning in this environment.

Treatment	Mean	Treatment Comparisons	Performance Shift in Standard Deviation
PIV	45.8	PIV with TI	1.76
CIV	42.9	CIV with TI	1.11
TI	31.4	PIV with CIV	.45

In addition, the researchers altered the treatment given for four additional days of instruction, with the same post-test. They recognized the drawbacks of possible testing and treatment interaction but felt the results could be helpful. Four students with the lowest post-test scores that had received TI were given PIV treatment. Six groups were configured.

Initial Treatment	Mean	Follow-up Treatment	Mean	Improvement
TI	31.5	CIV	46.19	+14.7
TI	22.0	PIV	36.5	+14.5
CIV	28.5	PIV	39.0	+10.5
PIV	46.3	CIV	52.0	+5.7
CIV	40.8	TI	44.7	+3.8
PIV	45.0	TI	45.0	0

Surprising to the researchers was the strong performance demonstrated by CIV, as were the results of TI following CIV. This may have broad ramifications in the future for the use of CIV in public schools where one system per classroom is far more feasible than multiple systems. Such an educational design, whereby interactive video as a learning tool augments traditional instruction, promotes the model of a professional classroom environment. Attitudinal comments about CIV and PIV were, for the most part, very positive. The testing and development of this program are ongoing and PIV and CIV scores continue to improve. When completed, it will be integrated into the entire first year Spanish course at Timpview High School. Being refined as part of this project is a Spanish dictionary function, as well as an "automated authoring" system that the researchers have been developing to create interactive video programs more rapidly without programming skills.

For researchers Gale and Barksdale, "interactive video is a new way of thinking about instruction, a new way to perceive learning, a new way to view the roles of teacher and pupil." Lacking, however, are learning theories appropriate to the technology. More significant, particularly for language instruction, is the general inadequacy of learning theory and learning research that has been developed over the past 40 years in psychology, according to Gale and Brown.[64] The stimulus-response approach has segmented learning into manageable, but somewhat isolated, learning tasks. An "atomistic" approach has resulted. Schools of information processing, according to the authors, have done the same, and in addition are "guilty of positing all kinds of unobservable mental fictions that have the effect of cutting off inquiry." Helpful learning insights have accrued, but fundamental errors are inherent "in their account of human learning and the acquisition of knowledge."

Their expanded approach uses the "transparency theory" as a model, which "provides a kind of metatheoretical backdrop for the development of a broad theory of learning that is unified with other major areas of psychology such as perception, attention, and social psychology." The last aspect is particularly important in that the emphasis is on learning as a more functional and holistic social focus. The learning environment centers on climate and task, and teaching is viewed as a complex social process where "the best education is mutually edifying for teacher and student, and they grow together." Although this learning theory is in the process of development, Gale and Barksdale are testing it in the "Digame" project.

A "mechanical" environment has the potential, in this paradigm, to become heuristic and human. Speaking to a broader teaching and learning perspective, the authors believe that "nothing less than a total theory of learning that includes interpersonal dynamics and the search for meaning can have the kind of practical effects that are needed to transform our educational institutions." Vital to their vision is the integration of pedagogical tools (technology) into an evolving learning environment where they are implemented by wise and capable teachers. Albert Shanker is promoting a similar model for a professional teaching and learning environment.

Research Direction

Bosco[65] analyzed 28 evaluations of interactive video that involved the military, higher education, K-12 education, industry, and social services. Industry, which with the military is the largest producer of interactive video, had few studies publicly available due to proprietary concerns or, perhaps, to less emphasis placed on systematic evaluation. Overwhelmingly, the studies presented, coupled with the ones included in this chapter, with four in common, were oriented toward skill acquisition. This underscores an advantageous use of visual presentation as emphasized earlier by Cohen, Ebeling, and Kulik.

As a group, Bosco found that no categorical decision could be rendered regarding the effectiveness of interactive video in comparison to traditional instruction. Further, he found little difference between formative evaluation studies done in 1980 and those in 1985. This seems to indicate either little benefit is being realized from previous studies, or else that new areas are being pursued. Perhaps both are true.

Hannafin[66] recommends looking to the "parent technologies," computers and video, as a partial foundation for building a solid empirical perspective on interactive video effectiveness. In presenting numerous studies of computer-assisted instruction, programmed instruction, instructional video, and instructional television, he recognizes that interactive video is potentially a superior educational tool. There are similarities, however, particularly with the computer component, and empirical research needs to determine just how effective and how unique this medium is. Building upon related existing studies is, from Hannafin's viewpoint, more advantageous than proceeding from assumptions and intuitions that have prompted many to grant this technology "face validity." He would couple such a focus with learning and cognition research to form a research agenda for interactive video.

Bosco concludes that "it is not useful to think about interactive video as an approach but, rather, as a category designation for a wide array of approaches."[67] This offers some perspective to the variety of studies described. Even so, research that investigates multidimensional indicators of effectiveness and efficiency is essential to this medium. Attitudinal studies that give attention to the application and integration of interactive video into specific learning environments, coupled with instructional or training effectiveness, are all vital. As an emerging educational tool, the unique

John Talbot, Vice President of Pioneer subsidiary LaserDisc Corporation of America, demonstrates a Pioneer videodisc player and Grolier Knowledgedisc, containing the complete text of the Grolier Encyclopedia, to students in a junior high school reading program. (Courtesy Pioneer)

Optical Data Corporation has produced several series of interactive videodisc systems for earth, life and physical science education. The Earth Science series, seen here, features still images and movie clips from numerous U.S. space missions. (Courtesy of Optical Data Corporation)

potential of interactive video needs to be better explained to all users, including teachers. This medium also needs to be explored, evaluated, and cultivated over an extended period of time in a stable environment and in a way that complements, rather than threatens, the existing structure.

Meritorious, it would seem, is collaboration for mutual benefit. The various sectors have specific expertise, that, if shared, could strengthen the field. For example, Thompson has worked with the military, at Fort Sam Houston in Texas, while acting as chair of the department of education at Tulane University. Researchers and educators at Brigham Young University's McKay Institute and College of Education are currently pursuing, research and development of interactive video with the Provo City School District. That focus has also involved them with the BBC, the Department of Defense, and a number of major corporations. Such a synergistic union has the potential to greatly expand the beneficial use of this educational tool. If hardware standards become more stabilized, the field will be strengthened even more.

The timing and the extensiveness of these developments may be significant, given the need for schools and all teaching and learning environments to evolve and become more professional and more fecund. Generally, speaking, though, interactive video research is in need of a solid body of research, evaluation standards, more effective instructional designs, and substantive alternatives to interactive video instruction for comparative studies. A number of the studies presented in this chapter, particularly the more recent ones, demonstrated not only an awareness of these struggles, but offer insight as well as guidance. Much more research, development, and evaluation are needed.

Endnotes

1. Robert J. Moes, "The CD ROM/CD-I Puzzle: Where Do the Pieces Fit?" paper presented at the National Online Meeting, New York City, N.Y., 6–8 May 1986.
2. The High Sierra Group was so designated by the location of its initial meeting and its membership consists of: Apple, Digital Equipment Corporation, Hitachi, Laserdata, Microsoft, 3M, Philips, Reference Technology, TMS, Meridian Data, Xebec, and Yellick.
3. Moes, "The CD ROM/CD-I Puzzle: Where Do the Pieces Fit?" pp. 2–4.
4. Jeffrey Bairstow, "CD-ROM: Mass Storage for the Mass Market," *High Technology* 6,10 (October 1986): 45–47.
5. Robert van Eijk, quoted by Judith Paris Roth, "The Coming of the Interactive Compact Disc," *High Technology* 6,10 (October 1986): 46.
6. Rockley L. Miller, "CD ROM and Videodisc: Lessons to be Learned," in *CD ROM: The New Papyrus,* eds. Steve Lambert and Suzanne Ropiequet (Redmond, WA: Microsoft Press, 1986), p. 41. See also Steve Lambert and Jane Sallus, eds. *CDI and Interactive Videodisc Technology* (Indianapolis, IN: Howard W. Sams and Co., 1986).
7. Charles M. Reigeluth and Joanne M. Garfield, "Using Videodiscs in Instruction: Realizing Their Potential Through Instructional Design," *Videodisc and Optical Disk,* 4,3 (May-June 1984): 200.
8. Wiegand, "Interactive Here and Now: Keeping It Rolling on Tape," *Video Manager,* March 1986, p. 10.
9. R. Kent Wood, director of Utah State University's Videodisc Innovations Project, quoted in Larry McClain, "A Friendly Introduction to Videodiscs," *Popular Computing,* April 1983, p. 79.
10. Incompatible ways of composing and transmitting a television signal in various parts of the world have evolved primarily due to historical reasons. A group of American engineers developed the NTSC (National Television Systems Committee) standard which was approved by the FCC in 1953. Their hope was that it would be adopted worldwide. It was not, but it is used by the USA, Japan, Canada, Mexico, the Bahamas, and the Philippines. France developed SECAM (sequential couleur a memoire) which is also used in the USSR and some Middle Eastern and African countries. Another system, PAL (Phase Alternation Line), is a refinement of NTSC and was developed in West Germany and adopted by the United Kingdom and most of Europe, the Middle East, Africa, Australia, and South America. See Eric Parsloe, ed., *Interactive Video* (United Kingdom: Sigma Technical Press, 1983), pp. 43–53; Lynne Schafer Gross, *The New Television Technologies* (Dubuque, Iowa: Wm. C. Brown Company Publishers, 1983),

p. 150; and Rockley L. Miller et al., *Videodisc and Related Technologies: A Glossary of Terms* (Falls Church, Virginia: Future Systems, Incorporated, 1986), no page numbers listed.

11. Rockley L. Miller, "CD ROM and Videodisc: Lessons to be Learned," p. 38.

12. Rus Gant quoted in Harry F. Waters, et al., "The Age of Video," *Newsweek,* December 30, 1985, pp. 44–53. Gant (an artist, applications programmer, instructional designer and teacher at the Massachusetts Institute of Technology) is one of the foremost authorities on all aspects of interactive videodisc.

13. Harry F. Waters, et al., "Master Teacher" in "The Age of Video," *Newsweek,* December 30, 1985, p. 46.

14. Mark Patterson, quoted in "Firm Pushes High-Tech Training Video," *The Pittsburgh Press,* 11 August 1986, sec. B, pp. 4, 6. Patterson is the founder and president of MindBank, Inc.

15. Ron Thorkildsen and Susan Friedman, "Videodiscs in the Classroom," *T.H.E. Journal 11* (April 1984): 90–95.

16. Joan Cash, "Spinning Toward the Future: The Museum on Laser Videodisc," *Museum News,* August 1985, p. 20.

17. "Matrox Wins EIDS Contract," *The Videodisc Monitor* 4,11 (November 1986): Special Bulletin.

18. "Matrox Wins EIDS: Sony Protests," *The Videodisc Monitor* 4,12 (December 1986): 1.

19. Ric Getter, "Army to Purchase 400,000 Discs by 1990," *Video Manager,* March 1986, pp. 1, 12.

20. Rockley L. Miller and John H. Sayers, "EIDS Watch" and "Integrating Laserdisc Technology in Industry and Education," *The Videodisc Monitor* 4,8 (August 1986): 3, 18.

21. The report, titled "Information Technology Transfer from Military Research and Development to Civilian Education and Training," is cited in Sally Banks Zakariya, "Here's Why Most Schools Don't Use Videodiscs - Yet," *The American School Board Journal,* June 1984, p. 26.

22. Marjorie A. Cambre, "Interactive Video," *Instructional Innovator* 29, 6 (September/October 1984): 24–25.

23. Phyllis M. Levenson, James R. Morrow, and Barbara Signer, "A Comparison of Noninteractive and Interactive Video Instruction About Smokeless Tobacco," *Journal of Educational Technology Systems* 14,3 (1985–86): 194.

24. R. E. Halloway, "The Videodisc in Education: A Case for Gradualism," *Videodisc/Videotex* 11 (Spring 1982): 2.

25. Nicholas V. Iuppa, *A Practical Guide to Interactive Video Design* (White Plains, N.Y.): Knowledge Industry Publications, Inc., 1984, pp. 8–9.

26. Levenson, Morrow, and Signer, "A Comparison of Noninteractive and Interactive Video Instruction About Smokeless Tobacco," pp. 195, 200. See also Diane M. Gayeski, "Interactive Video: Integrating Design 'Levels' and Hardware 'Levels'," *Journal of Educational Technology Systems* 13,3 (1984–85): 146.

27. Peter A. Cohen, Barbara J. Ebeling, and James A. Kulik, "A Meta-Analysis of Outcome Studies of Visual-Based Instruction," *Educational Communication and Technology Journal* 29,1 (Spring 1981): 26–36.

28. J. C. Reid and D. W. MacLennon, Research in Instructional Television and Film (Washington, D.C.: U.S. Government Printing Office, 1967).

29. Gwen C. Nugent, Thomas J. Tipton, and David W. Brooks, "Task, Learner, and Presentation Interactions in Television Production," *Educational Communication and Technology Journal* 28,1 (Spring 1980): 30–38.

30. Jon D. Morris, "The Florida Study: Improvement in Student Achievement and Attitudes Through Variations in Instructional Television Production Values," *Journal of Educational Technology Systems* 12,4 (1983–84): 357–68. See also Jon D. Morris, "The Florida Study: Improving Achievement Through the Use of More Dynamics in TV Production," *T.H.E. Journal* 12,3 (October 1984): 104–107.

31. Gwen C. Nugent, "Pictures, Audio, and Print: Symbolic Representation and Effect on Learning," *Educational Communication and Technology Journal* 30,3 (Fall 1982): 163–174.

32. Gabriel D. Ofiesh, "The Seamless Carpet of Knowledge and Learning," in *CD ROM: The New Papyrus,* eds. Steve Lambert and Suzanne Ropiequet (Redmond, Wa: Microsoft Press, 1986), p.316.

33. Karen Block, "The Information Age in Education - Computer Aided Learning." See pp. 96–98 of this book.

34. Richard A. Bolt, "Conversing With Computers," *Technology Review,* February/March 1985, pp. 35–43

35. William J. Bowen, "The Puny Payoff from Office Computers," *Fortune,* May 26, 1986, pp. 20–24.

36. Henry Jay Becker, Instructional Uses of School Computers: Reports from the 1985 National Survey (The Johns Hopkins University: Center for Social Organization of Schools, June 1986), pp. 1–10. The data compiled in this report were collected in the Second National Survey of Instructional Uses of School Computers.

37. J. R. Kulik, R. L. Bangert, and G. W. Williams, "Effects of Computer-Based Teaching on Secondary School Students," *Journal of Educational Psychology* 75 (1983): 19–26; and M. Ragosta, P. W. Holland, and D. J. Jamison, Computer-Assisted Instruction and Compensatory Education: The ETS/LAUSD Study. Project Report Number 20 (Princeton, N.J.: Educational Testing Service [June 1982]).

38. George Bear, "Microcomputers and School Effectiveness," *Educational Technology* 24 (January 1984): p. 11.

39. Ibid., pp. 11–12.

40. Alfred Bork, "Education and Computers: The Situation Today and Some Possible Futures," *T.H.E. Journal* 12, 3 (October 1984): 92–95.

41. Isaac I. Bejar, "Videodiscs in Education: Integrating the Computer and Communication Technologies," *BYTE* 7,6 (June 1982): 78.

42. Alfred Bork, "Education and Computers: The Situation Today and Some Possible Futures," p. 93

43. William M. Bulkeley, "Computers Failing as Teaching Aids," *The Wall Street Journal,* 6 June 1988, sec. 2, p. 17.

44. Bork, "Education and Computers: The Situation Today and Some Possible Futures," pp. 96–97. Bork is the director of the Educational Technology Center at the University of California (Irvine). See also Maria Shao et al, "A Campus Groan: I've Got the Computer, So Where's the Software?," *Business Week,* October 24, 1988, p. 82.

45. Michael J. Hannafin, "Empirical Issues in the Study of Computer-Assisted Interactive Video," *Educational Communication and Technology Journal* 33,4 (Winter 1985): 237.

46. Shao, "A Campus Groan: I've Got the Computer, So Where's the Software?," p. 82

47. Michael Rogers, "Here Comes Hypermedia," *Newsweek,* October 3, 1988, pp. 44–45.

48. Katherine M. Hafner and Richard Brandt, "Steve Jobs: Can He Do It Again?," *Business Week,* October 24, 1988, pp. 74–80. See also John Schwartz et al, "Steve Jobs Comes Back," *Newsweek,* October 24, 1988, pp. 46–51; and Judith Axler Turner, "For Apple Computers Founder, Time for a New Vision." *Chronicle of Higher Education,* 10 June 1987. p. 19.

49. Michael Rogers and Richard Sandza, "Computers of the '90s: A Brave New World," *Newsweek,* October 24, 1988, pp. 52–57.

50. Richard Brandt, "A Chip That May Break All Sorts of Sound Barriers," *Newsweek,* October 24, 1988, p. 80.

51. Rod Daynes and Beverly Butler, *The Videodisc Book: A Guide and Directory.* (New York: John Wiley and Sons, Inc., 1984), p. 13.

52. This definition was procured from Omar K. Moore, University of Pittsburgh. John Vries utilizes a level 4 system at the University of Pittsburgh. A prospectus of his work on Medical Information Management at the University of Pittsburgh can be found in the Appendix.

53. D. Thompson Manning, Donald G. Ebner, Franklin R. Brooks, and Paul Balson, "Interactive Videodiscs: A Review of the Field," *Viewpoints in Teaching and Learning* 59, 2 (Spring 1983): 33. See also Hannafin, "Empirical Issues in the Study of Computer-Assisted Interactive Video," pp. 235, 236, 239, 245; and Levenson, Morrow, and Signer, "A Comparison of Noninteractive and Interactive Video Instruction About Smokeless Tobacco," p. 194.

54. "Interactive Video on a Shoestring," *Instructional Innovator* 29,6 (September/October 1984): 29, 40. The hardware used was a Panasonic interactive system.

55. Levenson, Morrow, and Signer, "A Comparison of Noninteractive and Interactive Video Instruction About Smokeless Tobacco," pp. 193–202. The hardware used for this study was selected according to availability and affordability for many organizations. They included a one disk drive Apple IIe microcomputer, a BCD interface card, and a Panasonic 8200 tape player.

56. J. E. Holmgren, F. N. Dyer, R. E. Hilligoss, and F. H. Heller, "The Effectiveness of Army Training Extension Course Lessons on Videodisc," *Journal of Educational Technology Systems* 8,3 (1979–80): 263–274. The hardware used were MCA videodisc players with RCA television monitors, and Thomson-CSA videodisc players with Sony monitors.

57. Glenn Kirchner, Don Martyn, and Chris Johnson, "Simon Fraser University Videodisc Project: Part Two: Field Testing an Experimental Videodisc with Elementary School Children," *Video Disc/Video Tex* 3,1 (Winter 1983): 45–58. The hardware used were: a PR 7820 videodisc player with internal programmable memory, a remote control unit, and a color television.

58. Paul M. Balson, D. Thompson Manning, Donald G. Ebner, and Franklin R. Brooks, "Instructor-Controlled Versus Student-Controlled Training in a Videodisc-Based Paramedical Program," *Journal of Educational Technology Systems* 13,2 (1984–85): 123–130. For the first analysis, in this series of three consecutive studies, see also Manning, Balson, Ebner, and Brooks, "Student Acceptance of Videodisk-Based Programs for Paramedical Training," *T.H.E. Journal* 11,3 (November 1983): 105–108. The hardware used were a Pioneer (DVA PR-7820), Model III—which had internal programmable memory, a color television monitor, and a remote control.

59. Paul M. Balson, Donald G. Ebner, James V. Mahoney, Henry T. Lippert, and Diane T. Manning, "Videodisc Instructional Strategies: Simple May Be Superior to Complex," *Journal of Educational Technology Systems* 14,4 (1985–86): 273–281.

60. Leslie Steven May, "Corporate Experience in Evaluating Interactive Video Information System Courses" (Bedford, Mass.: Digital Equipment Corporation, Educational Services, August 1984), pp. 1–9. The hardware used was an IVIS, comprised of a DEC professional 350 computer, a high resolution color monitor, and a videodisc player (probably a Sony LDP-1000).

61. Susan G. Friedman and Alan M. Hofmeister, "Matching Technology to Content and Learners: A Case Study," *Exceptional Children* 51,2 (October 1984): 130–134. The hardware used were a two disk drive Apple II microcomputer, a Discovision (7820–3) videodisc player, a Sony Trinitron color television monitor with touch-screen, and a dot matrix printer.

62. James A. Blackman, Mark A. Albanese, Jean Sustik Huntley, and Loretta K. Lough, "Use of Computer-Videodisc System to Train Medical Students in Developmental Disabilities," *Medical Teacher* 7,1 (November 1, 1985): 89–97. Hardware used were an IBM PC, Pioneer 7820–3 and Pioneer LD/V 1000 videodisc players, and two high resolution color monitors per system.

63. Larrie E. Gale and Karl Barksdale, "The Development and Formative Evaluation of 'Interactive Digame' Courseware: A Cooperative Project of Brigham Young University and the Provo City School District," report prepared at Brigham Young University, Provo, Utah, 13 June 1986. The hardware used were an IBM computer, a CRT monitor, a television monitor and videodisc player. *Note:* A similar process called "retrofitted" videodiscs has been experimented with at the Educational Technology Center of the Harvard Graduate School of Education.

64. Larrie E. Gale and Bruce L. Brown, "A Theory of Learning and Skill-Acquisition Applied to Interactive Video: Activities at the David O. McKay Institute, Brigham Young University," *Studies in Language Learning* 5,1 (Spring 1985): 105–114.

65. James Bosco, "An Analysis of Evaluations of Interactive Video," *Educational Technology*. May 1986, pp 7–17.

66. Hannafin, "Empirical Issues in the Study of Computer-Assisted Interactive Video," pp. 235–247.

67. Bosco, "An Analysis of Evaluations of Interactive Video," p. 15.

4

Dynamic Paradigms

Contemporary applications of interactive videodisc are proliferating, and interactive technology centers are being established. This chapter presents a chronicle of the evolving Future Centers in the Millcreek Township School District as a model for elementary-secondary schools. Several additional applications for the areas of education, training and information exchange are also delineated, along with a description of the developing interactive technology center at the Smithsonian Institute in Washington, D.C. Referenced here as well is the Medical Information Management research and development work of John K. Vries, M.D., at the University of Pittsburgh.

In the final section of this chapter, with support from Karen Block, a proposal for university-based regional interactive learning centers is put forth. Block, an associate professor of educational psychology, has researched and written in the area of relating instruction to the psychology knowledge base. Her publications address instructional issues concerning concept identification, strategies in computer-aided learning, writing with computer assistance, computer-aided learning in teaching spelling, reading programs and practices, and vocabulary concepts.

Educational Applications

Millcreek Township School District[1]

Millcreek Township School District (MTSD) in Erie, Pennsylvania, is comprised of seven elementary schools, two middle schools, and two high schools with approximately 390 teachers and a student enrollment of about 6,400. Excellence in all areas, especially in academics, created a demand that resulted in this school district becoming one of the first in Pennsylvania, and perhaps the U.S., to retain public school status while becoming a private preparatory school for students outside of its district. As an educational leader it has attracted national and international recognition. Educational technology has played a significant part in the district's achievements.

In January of 1978 MTSD hired Verel R. Salmon as director of public services to bring some technical education into the school system. At that time few school systems nationwide were doing much with computers.

The first microcomputers available to schools were just being introduced and in-house personnel qualified to use them were rare. At MTSD about a dozen students from the high school were bused to a regional vocational technical school outside of the district to learn data processing with key punch cards and the like. Within a relatively short time, Salmon was appointed to assistant superintendent for MTSD.

Salmon's background was in science education and educational administration. He had come from the Mentor Exempted Village School District (MEVSD) in the east suburbs of Cleveland where he had worked closely with the science and mathematics departments, particularly in the area of computers. MEVSD purchased one of the first Wang minicomputers available. It was at MEVSD that Salmon established a working relationship with corporations.

Shortly after Salmon's arrival at Millcreek, Radio Shack announced a microcomputer that was affordable (although not in volume) for most school districts. With that impetus, coupled with the then recent mandate by the state of Pennsylvania requiring gifted education programming in schools, Salmon purchased three Radio Shack computers and had three instructors traveling between the elementary and middle school buildings to work with gifted students. Radio Shack provided some training, but the teachers were mostly self-taught. The units are still in use today. Although not sophisticated, they are effective for the demonstration of computer concepts.

From the start, MTSD chose to build computer exposure into the system at the lower grade levels. Not only would that establish a firm foundation that would, in time, permeate the entire system, it was also felt that as students became more involved with computers they would lobby for greater sophistication in hardware as well as course offerings as they progressed academically, thereby further encouraging the entire process.

Due to the mandate as well as the limited hardware available, these computers were used initially for gifted students. However, MTSD viewed the computer as a powerful tool for all of its students, including the severely retarded. It would be used differently with students of different abilities.

A second and simultaneous initiative by Salmon was to work with local industry in an attempt to solicit donations of sophisticated computer equipment for use by the high school students. Salmon brought with him a dedication to the concept of "partnerships in education" and built it into his emphasis on using educational technology.

Through negotiations with Baldwin Brothers Real Estate, the largest real estate firm in Erie, MTSD received a corporate donation of an IBM 1130 mainframe computer system. It came equipped with the FORTRAN programming language. The math department structured a basic course in FORTRAN, and offered it during the 1978–1979 academic year. Advanced courses followed, which continue today.

As money permitted, more computers were purchased and distributed district-wide. When Nestar introduced its network system, around 1981, MTSD was the first school district east of the Mississippi River to have it. The common storage system that it used to serve multiple users introduced the district to a center and central concept. Subsequently, an Apple Center with multiple Apple computers was established in the intermediate high school.

To further implement his vision, Salmon early on set in motion several committees. The first was a Computer Advisory Council (CAC), which included a member of the board of education. Once approached for assistance in establishing a beginning program in technology for MTSD, a half-dozen major corporations in the area readily had one of their experts serve on the council. Several remain on the council today, and one member from General Telephone, who was an expert in telecommunications, steered them in that direction as well. Another early corporate member of the council went on to fill a seat on the board of education, and further assist the CAC in that capacity. From the start, these corporate advisors were essential to the implementation and use of computers and other technologies in MTSD.

Another committee was set in motion to promote a "teacher to teacher" concept. This teachers' committee initially drew a representative from each of the lower level schools, then expanded to include all schools. Inservice training for these representatives was provided on the computers being implemented. The representatives then were encouraged to interest the teachers they worked with in the technology.

An important lesson learned was that outside experts were usually not nearly as effective as using their own people, such as Gae Anderson Golembiewski, one of the early gifted teachers who acquired a great deal of expertise. Many hours of dedicated work were essential for such offerings to succeed. A couple of inservice sessions were simply inadequate.

As interest developed in particular schools, more computers were provided, and additional inservice programs were structured as teachers requested them. The enthusiasm became contagious. At no point was any teacher required to use computers with his or her courses; rather, computers succeeded because the teachers promoted them and used them. Of course, a catalyst or stimulus initiated the process. In time all disciplines got involved. The district is now adopting a computer curriculum that has emerged from the grassroots level.

This concept broadened to include many others. Secretaries got involved and filled some key leadership roles, and various administrators contributed also. Akin to drawing from the creative minds in the corporate sector, this process became one of involving all who were interested in extending and improving computer usage in the district. Offered talents were employed as needs arose. The emphasis was on a person-to-person, or professional-to-professional approach which further contributed to the school district as a whole working together for a common goal.

Still another project that Salmon took on was the upgrading of the television studio. The intermediate school, with assistance from a federal grant, had built a state-of-the-art black-and-white studio in the basement when the school was constructed in the early 1970s. By 1978, when Salmon arrived, the equipment was outdated. Because of the expense involved, improvements were gradual. As federal grants and district money could be designated or channeled to the cause, it became a state-of-the-art color studio, coupled with classrooms that were wired with coaxial cable. A satellite dish was also installed.

In 1979, Sam Petruso, a social studies teacher in one of the middle schools, became involved with audiovisual equipment for his building. A full-time audiovisual coordinator position was created for the district and he filled it while also helping with the growing computer use. His position grew into that of coordinator of computer services for the district, and in that capacity he has worked closely with Salmon.

Through this evolving use of technology in the school district, the board of education was both supportive and generous with funding. Around 1982 when it became necessary to purchase a new mainframe computer, the Board paid for a national consulting firm to come in and advise the district on what action to take. Teachers and others involved with computer use were interviewed in a thorough study. A VAX 750 was purchased, terminals installed in every building, with all networked together.

Following the recommendation of the study and the Computer Advisory Council, this computer was not purchased primarily for administrative services, with available time going to educational needs. Rather, its priority was direct service to students for counseling records, grading, and the like. In the second and third years, administrative services were gradually phased in.

About the same time, with computers and television equipment and course offerings well established, Salmon and Petruso began to think about the next step. Aware that they were preparing leaders for the twenty-first century, and that other technologies like interactive video, fiber optics, and robotics were emerging and would continue to do so, they decided to establish an innovation or catalyst center where teachers, students, and others in the district could "explore new technologies and learning tools of the future."[2] Two pilot Future Centers were established, one in a middle school, the other in the intermediate high school.

Having followed the developing field of interactive video, Salmon and Petruso decided to encourage its use in the district. Federal Chapter II funding enabled them to purchase an interactive videodisc system. A second unit was purchased a short time later. (Of note is that MTSD has several federal grant coordinators on the staff who constantly seek funding for the various needs of the district.)

At a conference that he attended, Salmon saw a demonstration of the Bio Sci Videodisc by its creator, Joe Clark—a former college professor of biology and founder of Videodiscovery, Inc. (Videodiscovery, a Seattle-based company creates and sells a range of videodiscs designed for use in the classroom.) With a strong educational focus, Clark created a general biology disc for secondary school and college level biology instruction. More than 6,000 images ranging from biochemistry to plant and animal diversity were included. Salmon bought the disc.

Anthony Ferralli, an audio and video engineer for Warren Radio in Erie at the time, had upgraded the television studio earlier. He and his wife, Kathryn, a former teacher and developer of interactive video programs for schools, agreed to offer a number of inservice training sessions.[3] Mike Andrae, a biology teacher, attended these sessions and became proficient himself. He interested the entire biology department and has become the primary inservice instructor for interactive video in the school district.

Inservice instructors are paid and teachers receive a small stipend for attending; in return, they are required to create a lesson using the system that can be implemented in their classes. This meaningful rather than generic approach is required of all inservice training where technology is involved.

Mostly general or generic videodiscs have been emphasized up to the present time, especially those with data bases that can be adapted to specific needs, such as the Bio Sci disc. However, through the efforts of Kathryn Ferralli especially, other methods have been explored. "Repurposing" is one such alternative that takes a videodisc originally designed for one application or purpose and adapts it to a specific educational need, through computer programming or some related method.[4,5,6] As meritorious as this method is, MTSD has reached the point where it is considering mastering its own discs for particular course offerings.

Millcreek has a commitment to developing technology and to encouraging participation by teachers, students, and staff. All new technologies are now channeled through the Future Centers. Evident throughout this process is the sense at they have not "arrived," that it is an ongoing process requiring much effort and professional collaboration.

The corporations remain very involved and equipment donations are not uncommon. Cash grants, however, are less frequent, except for special projects such as a student programming contest. The partnership that exists is commonly one of exchanging services, though some formal contracts and joint agreements have been undertaken. One such area that is of primary importance is that of software development. MTSD is involving corporations as it attempts to direct courseware development in order to be a force in moving computer education along, and thereby avoid being at the mercy of what is available on the market. In addition to local corporations, Digital Equipment Corporation (DEC) and Apple Computer, Inc. have also become involved at MTSD through grant offerings.

Salmon sees himself, in part, as an education broker orchestrating multiple resources involving the educational environment as well as the cooperating corporate and governmental sectors. Inspiring and drawing the most that he can from all simultaneously, enables the resource pool to remain substantial enough to keep up with the technology. Vital to it all, he believes, is the people networking and the coinciding respect for and cooperation among the multifarious talents and interests.

The joint efforts have enabled a nonprofit tax-exempt foundation to be established for research and development in all departments, including athletics. Throughout, excellence is pursued in the Millcreek Township School District. Technology is woven into all areas, but to the extent that it can truly augment the academic process being directed by the teacher. This elementary-secondary model of cooperation with the corporate community and governmental agencies in order to enhance the educational environment of MTSD is practicable for other school districts as well.

Other Educational Applications

Of necessity, many training programs are directed principally toward the proper or correct way to perform a task or function. In contrast, the ideal education or learning program extends the inquiry process while providing helpful and essential information. Interactive video is uniquely suited to accomplish this goal.

In 1975 Bennion and Schneider, of Brigham Young University, were two of the earliest educators to realize the educational applications of this medium.[7] A book followed in 1981 that further elaborated their interest and developing expertise.[8]

WICAT

In 1978 the World Institute for Computer-Assisted Teaching (WICAT), with funding from private and governmental organizations, developed what is considered to be the first videodisc program developed for individualized interactive instruction. This biology disc was based on a film by McGraw-Hill entitled "The Development of Living Things." A subsequent grant from the National Science Foundation enabled WICAT to evaluate and demonstrate the effectiveness of interactive videodisc technology as an instructional tool. (WICAT, based in Orem, Utah, currently offers interactive videodisc systems that include workstations, authoring software, and networking hardware.)

Nebraska Videodisc Design/Production Group

In 1978 also, the University of Nebraska, through research and development contracts from the Corporation for Public Broadcasting's Office of Science and Technology, established the Nebraska Videodisc Design/Production Group to explore and develop the full potential of the medium. With a seasoned staff of videodisc instructional designers, directors, producers, artists, computer experts, and technicians, the group has produced a wider variety of topics on videodisc than most all other comparable organizations. One of the more than 40 videodiscs that it has produced is "The Puzzle of the Tacoma Narrows Bridge Collapse" which interactively teaches college-level physics principles.[9] Working with both public and private sectors for educational and training applications, the group has, through its productions, annual conference, workshops, technical reports, and newsletters, had a vital influence on the field that continues today.

MIT

The most influential institution educationally, however, for interactive video and related educational technologies, is quite likely MIT[10]. In addition to projects already mentioned, in May of 1983 MIT announced the creation of Project Athena. Its objective is to assist the creative learning process across a wide range of academic disciplines via the integration of the computer and related communications capabilities. Grants from DEC and IBM amounting to almost $50 million over a five year span were awarded, and MIT committed itself to raising an additional $20 million for this project.[11] A number of projects have been developed in the area of linguistic studies.

Project Emperor-1

A special project worked on at the Athena Laboratory by Rus Gant, one of the foremost authorities on all aspects of interactive video, has been "Project Emperor-1: China's Treasure Revealed via Videodisc Technology." This was a joint project sponsored by the U.S. and China through the National Endowment for the Humanities and the People's Republic Ministry of Culture. In design it is intended to elucidate an important historical/archaeological period. (Though reigning only 15 years, the first Emperor of China realized major accomplishments in his efforts to modernize his empire, and around his tomb, replicated in life size, are all of the various elements of his culture. Individuals were sculptured in detail, and excavations have already uncovered in excess of 20,000 of these three dimensional artifacts, with the likelihood that excavations will continue for a long time. Gant, former senior applications programmer for MIT, notes that "In a sense he was able to emulate and execute one of the largest works of art that we know of from ancient times, and to use it to communicate what he saw as the nature of his world and to do that communication visually."[12]

The data base integrates visual, English and Chinese audio, and textual material, and is being used in the U.S. and in China. All of the material on the discs is readily accessible. It will, no doubt, be a valuable resource for libraries, Chinese studies departments, and many other applications.

The University of Georgia

The Department of Instructional Technology at The University of Georgia has been active in the development and evaluation of interactive videodisc for the past five years. In 1985–86, the Department collaborated with Dr. John Henry Martin and the International Business Machines Corporation to develop PALS, the Principle of the Alphabet Literacy System, which is currently being widely adopted for functional literacy training. Faculty and graduate students at Georgia have also designed interactive videodisc programs for the National Science Foundation, the National Science Center for Communications and Electronics, and Apple Computer, Inc. In addition, the Department has conducted in-depth evaluations of interactive training technologies for the U.S. Army, U.S. Navy, the National Library of Medicine, Apple Computer, and others.

The Record Group

In 1986, PolyGram, an NV Philips subsidiary, initiated and funded The Record Group (TRG) to develop software for CD-I. One CD-I program already developed is an interactive tour of London which can be journeyed through in any one of eight time periods including Roman days, Chaucer's era, or Shakespeare's time. The traveler can enter various buildings and view actual photographs or engravings of the period as desired. Similar programs are being developed for other European capitals.

Another of TRG's projects is "The Time Machine," a history of Western Civilization from 500 B.C. to the present. The learner can choose to listen to narration from any period while watching pertinent film excerpts, photographs, animations, and graphics.[13] TRG has also created an introductory course on the history of music—with digital audio sound accompanied by photographs of the composers, the instruments used, the original scores, and so forth. The Home Interactive Systems division of NV Philips is providing additional funding for The Record Group.

Authoring Systems

As MIT endeavors to devise a computer that is more user-friendly, a similar direction has been employed by a number of organizations that use the computer programming process to enable a videodisc to be used interactively for instruction. A number of high-level programming languages, such as BASIC, Pascal, or C, are employed in the instructional design of videodiscs. Gant used C to program the Project Emperor-1 videodiscs and it is his conviction that C and the UNIX operating system will become the predominate computer language for educational use. Even so, the considerable programming knowledge needed to efficiently use such high-level languages limits their use by many instructional designers and educators. To address this need, authoring languages and authoring systems were developed.

An authoring language is less complex than a structured programming language, and, consequently, less cumbersome to learn and use. While some power, flexibility, and processing speed are forfeited, much of the power indigenous to a programming language is retained. Authoring language software "is designed to interpret or translate a simple, English-like computer command into several lines of complex code understood by the computer."[14]

The result, for educators and instructional designers especially, is the ability to concentrate more on the content and instructional sequencing than on the arcane computer functions. PILOT (Programmed Inquiry, Learning, Or Training), which was developed by John Starkweather and associates at the University of California (San Francisco) in the late 1960s, is one of the most popular interactive video authoring languages along with its multiple versions, i.e., Apple SuperPILOT and others).[15]

As helpful as authoring languages are, those with little or no computer background often have difficulty with these languages. Accordingly, authoring systems emerged for their benefit and to assist with the complexities of instructional design logic as well.[16,17] As a prompt-driven creative tool, the ideal authoring system minimizes computer literacy and becomes a transparent aid to instructional designing.[18] This is accomplished by providing a series of menu-driven editors accompanied by a student management system and instructional templates.[19]

A convenient editing system enables an instructor to actually create and manipulate displays such as graphics, animation, and text on the screen that the student will use, and converts these creations to machine executable language. Ideally, a student management component keeps track of the responses of multiple users while enabling them to leave and re-enter the program at will, and also provides the instructor with a variety of summary analyses of pertinent user data, including means and standard deviations. There are also explicit templates (or format guides) included that facilitate the programmed presentation of information to the student via text frames, while making student input or responses to the information presented more facile by way of question frames.[20]

The problems associated with authoring languages, i.e., power, flexibility, and processing speed, are generally aggravated with authoring systems. Further, the templates used tend to constrict instructional models that are so vital to effective interactive videodisc designing. Two authoring systems with advanced instructional templates are PLATO and TICCIT.

Popular interactive videodisc authoring systems includ Video Nova,[21] Sony's Genesis system, and Allen Communication's Quest. At Brigham Young University, Gale and Barksdale are currently conducting formative evaluation on an intelligent system they are developing called "automated authoring." They recently reported that:

> Our automated authoring system is working well, is easy to use and requires minutes instead of hours to create an IV [interactive video] program. It reduces by at least a

factor of 8 the hours required to create, enter and debug IV lessons. Instead of 160 or even 80 hours to program, load data and debug one hour of courseware, our system required approximately 10 hours, from conceptualization to debugging, for each hour of instruction. Several intermediate steps are eliminated with our system and no data are manually loaded into the final run-time program. We hope to continue the development of additional authority tools and to make the present system even easier to use and understand.[22]

Even though PLATO and TICCIT were developed for computer-assisted instruction, their sophisticated instructional designs have ramifications for interactive video authoring systems as well. Macintosh's HyperCard, as described in Chapter 3, is having a dynamic impact on a variety of educational environments; and, the object-oriented advanced multitasking operating system of NeXT is expanding the hypermedia environment and ease of use by educators.

Select Training Applications

Educational authoring systems with abbreviated instructional design emanated from training programs that focused on equipment operation, repairs, and the like. Interactive program responses, by mechanics, field engineers, soldiers, and others, were usually either correct or incorrect; and mastery performance of a task or function was the goal. Many training programs today use these same principles, with variations depending on the application, as in the following examples:

CPR Learning System

Perhaps the best known interactive videodisc training program is the CPR Learning System which is certified by the American Heart Association. It was designed by David Hon,[23] to teach cardiopulmonary resuscitation effectively, efficiently, and consistently. The system has been further developed by Actronics, Inc., which is marketing it and other medically oriented training programs from its Pittsburgh, Pennsylvania, location.

Yankee Trader and Teacher

A developing program, Yankee Trader and Teacher, is being designed to couple international trade with entrepreneurial education. Intended as a private sector initiative, the aim is to introduce foreign markets to available U.S. tools and materials, which will be accompanied by appropriate vocational skills instruction. Interactive video will be used as the training delivery system.[24]

Interactive Still Video

Anthony and Katherine Ferralli, longtime advocates of videodisc repurposing, have developed interactive still video techniques. Images captured on a reusable two inch (2″) floppy diskette are combined with graphic overlays, menus, branching, authoring and other interactive elements, to permit the easy inhouse production of effective, inexpensive and immediately available interactive programs based on examples taken from the learner's own environment. These programs can function as standalone modules, or, in the repurposing mode, as relevant enhancements of generic interactive videodisc programs.[25]

The New York City Transit Authority uses a bus outfitted with interactive videodisc systems to bring training to its employees. (Courtesy NYCTA)

Inside the NYCTA training bus, employees brush up on their job skills. (Courtesy NYCTA)

Winthrop Pharmaceuticals offers mobile training using Sony VIEW systems aboard its Mobile Educational Resource Vehicle (MERV). (Courtesy Sony)

Laser Travel Network's Discovery system uses a Pioneer 8-inch videodisc player to bring both customer information and agent training right to the travel agent's desk. (Courtesy Laser Travel Network).

Select Information Applications

Interactive information systems vary substantially in degrees of sophistication. Most, however, are designed for the user's benefit even when a commercial product is promoted, and, consequently, are not learning or performance oriented in the instructional sense.

EPCOT Center, Disney World

One of the first visitors at the Westinghouse Research and Development Center interested in laser research in the 1960s was Walt Disney.[26] Understandably EPCOT Center is one of the largest exhibition users of videodisc systems. They have 83 different programs, of which some are

A bank customer using one of Spectrum Interactive
generic self-service banking applications. (Courtesy
Spectrum Interactive)

interactive but most are linear, that run on 272 players (Sony LDP-1000's) seven days a week, 24 hours a day. The laser positioning motors on each player, however, run only 16 to 18 hours a day. The linear programs used are short segments shown to visitors for entertainment purposes.

Examples of the interactive programs include the American Express Travelport which enables users to travel to various countries via videodisc and to preview vacation spots and get detailed information on the diverse services available. Of course, American Express is promoted. Another example is the World Key Information Service videodisc which employs 29 terminals throughout EPCOT for visitor use. Interactive information is available on every pavilion, as well as entertainment and special events schedules, and services available.[27] Noteworthy is the fact that the mean time between player failures is about 5,000 hours.[28]

Architecture Machine Group

Under the direction of Nicholas Negroponte, the Architecture Machine Group at the Massachusetts Institute of Technology (MIT) created "surrogate travel" around Aspen, Colorado on videodiscs. The entire town was organized on a visual data base, or, in other words, mapped from a driving perspective. The user decides which streets to travel on, what turns to make, and at what speed to journey with this interactive disc. Numerous buildings are compared photographically with how they looked 100 years earlier; and all four seasons are included for comparison or preferential selection.[29]

Maps

MIT also developed the Spatial Data Management System (SDMS)[30] that is commonly used today for videodisc based mapping. Although mostly used for military and intelligence gathering organizations, for whom it was created, Honda of Japan first announced such a system for automotive use, and Chrysler Corporation showed a prototype model at the 1984 World's Fair in New Orleans. This "in-car system is designed for use in trip planning, location identification and navigation."[31] It is not expected to be available to the public for several years.

An interactive retail system from Advanced Interactive Video offers coupons and information to customers at Woolworth Express. (Courtesy The Videodisc Monitor)

Merchandising Systems

Of note also is Advanced Touch Systems (ATS) of San Diego, California, which builds interactive videodisc systems with credit card readers for use by rental firms such as Budget Rent-a-Car.[32] Also supplied are directions to hotels and other notable attractions in the area. A somewhat similar system, the UniPort touch-screen terminal, was built by ByVideo of Sunnyvale, California, for the Balfour Company. This point-of-purchase (POP) system promotes and sells college class rings.[33] ByVideo has also developed a POP system for Florsheim Shoe Shops that is used nationwide. Another organization, Digital Techniques Inc., (DTI) of Boston, Massachusetts, has created a fully integrated Level III workstation with authoring system called Touchcom that is oriented toward the banking industry. DTI also develops information kiosk units.

Synergistic Direction: The National Demonstration Laboratory

The Smithsonian Institute, with its collections representing a vast spectrum of information, has joined with the Interactive Video Consortium of Public Broadcasting Stations to jointly establish a National Demonstration Laboratory in the spring of 1987 in order to strengthen the nation's educational system by promoting the understanding and use of interactive technologies. The center is an extension of the Smithsonian's interactive education programs, and an outgrowth

Visitors to Norway's Museum of Science and Technology can explore a variety of topics using an interactive videodisc exhibit called "Science at your Fingertips," developed by Scan-O-Vision of Oslo and Futuremedia Ltd. of London. (Courtesy The Videodisc Monitor)

of the Smithsonian's experiences with videodisc. The National Air and Space Museum, for example, has transferred all of its video programs to videodiscs. It is among the handful of museums that have begun to use discs for programming and administrative purposes.[34]

The National Demonstration Laboratory (NDL), located at the Smithsonian in Washington, D.C., was in its first year oriented primarily toward establishing a display and demonstration facility of "the latest interactive technologies [videodisc, CD-ROM, CD-I, and interactive videotape systems]. . . ."[35] With clear long-range plans, the goals of the NDL are:

a. to provide a nationally recognized center for the demonstration of educational applications of interactive video technologies;
b. to serve as a clearinghouse of information about interactive video technologies;
c. to promote the development of cooperative efforts among professionals in education, public broadcasting, museology, and public policy;
d. to provide a forum for setting research agendas and sharing research information related to educational applications of interactive video;
e. to provide a forum for discussion and research of technology equity issues among education, research, and public policy professionals.

Through seminars, workshops and the like educators, public broadcasters, museum personnel, and developers of software and hardware are brought together. Such a cooperative undertaking that demonstrates and encourages interactive technology explorations and development is a progressive, timely, and dynamic paradigm that numerous educators will benefit from.

Medical Information Management at the University of Pittsburgh

Another dynamic paradigm—an advanced level 4 interactive system—is currently being developed as part of a unified medical information system serving all of the institutions that make up the University Health Center of Pittsburgh. John K. Vries, M.D. is the principle investigator in developing this comprehensive database for the support of research, education, and clinical care. The system takes advantage of optical disc technology, microcomputers, fiber optic networking, artificial intelligence, and an expert system. Vries is a neurosurgeon, assistant vice-president for health sciences, and associate professor of neurosurgery at the University of Pittsburgh. His dynamic paradigm for medical information management at the University of Pittsburgh, from 1987–1992, is described in detail in the Appendix.

Synergistic Proposal for Interactive Learning Centers

Prominent academic and corporate organizations, including both public and private institutions, frequently have similar goals but often have difficulty working together for mutual benefit. All wish to serve their constituencies as best they can in the present while designing and preparing for the future. Most are also involved in disseminating either knowledge or product and are concerned with the expense involved in doing so. Commonly, a research component is needed as well as the effective testing and practical implementation of the knowledge or product developed. With related interests, particularly in the area of educational (teaching, learning, training) technology where there are frequent innovations and expenses can be high, it is time for academic institutions, corporations, and governmental agencies to work together.

During the winter of 1986, under the sponsorship of the School of Education and the Regional Computer Resource Center at the University of Pittsburgh, this author designed an Interactive Learning Forum (ILF) to bring together regional representatives from academic institutions, corporations, and governmental agencies who were either actively involved or seriously interested in becoming involved with videodisc and related interactive technologies.

At the first meeting in May of 1986, the objectives were three-fold:

1. for all present to become more familiar with the research and development being done in and around Pittsburgh in the field of interactive laser optical media;
2. to explore possible ways that we as a group might better work together for mutual benefit;
3. to serve as stimulus for an ongoing Interactive Learning Forum.

The participants numbered over 100, representing 27 organizations. The group accomplished all of the objectives.

Pitt remained the host site for the ILF until March of 1987, when the Interactive Learning Forum came under the aegis of the Center for Design of Educational Computing (CDEC) at Carnegie Mellon University (CMU). With a primary focus on improving learning and teaching in higher education through well designed applications of advanced technology, CDEC develops and extends applications for advanced-function workstations. Accordingly, it is both a service organization and a research and development center. In the latter capacity CDEC became interested in interactive video.

Its PROJECT THEORIA—Testing Hypotheses in Ethics/Esthetics: Observation, Reality, Imagination, and Affect—encompasses strategies for teaching ethics and esthetics. The vision that CDEC has is one of employing interactive video to better elucidate the process of ethical reasoning, and, in doing so, to demonstrate more cogently the potential of this technology for the humanities.

With sponsorship and guidance from CMU, the ILF has received a central location, administrative assistance, a place to house reference and resource materials (literature, courseware, discs, and the like), and a place for Forum meetings and workshops. This commitment on the part of Carnegie Mellon is part of the university's larger vision of the future of education and it provides tangible evidence of its support for the promise of laser optical media for education. An expanded objective of the ILF is to bring to the area leading representatives and innovators in the field of interactive laser optical media. Over the past year-and-a-half the Forum has hosted presentations by John Messerschmitt (formerly vice president of North American Philips), Robert Hurst (from RCA's DVI technology), Rus Gant (from MIT's Project Athena), Rockley Miller (from The Videodisc Monitor), Danny Cassidy (Chairman of Actronics, Inc.), and Tom Reeves (from the University of Georgia). Forum participants now number over 200 and represent some 30 organizations.

A proposed expansion of the ILF would establish an interdisciplinary Interactive Learning Center (ILC) that would house a resource library and focus primarily on research and development of interactive educational technology. Academic, corporate, and governmental sectors would collaborate on projects within the Center.

The Interactive Learning Center would be a resource center with a research and instructional design base coupled with broadcast-quality television production facilities. Ideally, it would be comprised of the organizations participating in the ILF.

The ILC's major objectives would include research and instructional design, seminars, forums, conferences, and publications.

1. Resource Center

There is no one location in Pittsburgh that contains a good collection of books, journals, articles and related materials relevant to interactive video and optical laser technology. There are a number of isolated "libraries" specific to particular interests, especially in the corporate sector, but these are not available to outside parties. This Center would establish and maintain an excellent interactive technologies library. In addition, optical laser discs, including videodisc and CD ROM, could be acquired relevant to topics of interest, and a more extensive cataloging of available discs could be maintained. Data on people and organizations with skills specific to this medium could also be compiled for quick reference, and organizations so included could display products, hardware and software, at the Center.

2. Research and Instructional Design Center

When the Educational Technology Center (ETC) was established by the National Institute of Education at the Harvard Graduate School of Education in 1983, it was designed as a consortium.[36] Its stated mission was to "find ways of using the computer and other information technologies to teach science, mathematics, and computing more effectively."[37] Accordingly, several research grouus were formed that focused, relevant to interest and expertise, on content or subject matter, students' thinking and learning, teaching, and technology. In a collaborative way, the members of each group then sought to identify and define the essence of core concepts and skills in its area of focus; to better illuminate the difficulties students experience in coming to understand the subject matter and master the skills; to develop teaching strategies that promote understanding and mastery; and to find dynamic ways of using information technologies in support of these strategies.[38] An additional and significant component of their work is the belief "that the emerging technologies have the potential to transform the way all of us learn. . . ."

94

As a research center ETC did not intend to develop or evaluate software, to offer a service, or to develop curriculum. Rather, it focused on the advancement of theory and the improvement of practice for the areas specified. In the process of going about their work, however, ETC staff realized that the work itself was requiring them to become educational technologists in spite of themselves. Accordingly, they have decided to make teaching their primary focus—teaching with the use of technology. They have also found it necessary to develop their own prototype software. In doing so they have begun to realize a better balance between theory and practice.

The proposed Center, as at Harvard, would have as primary research direction the advancement of theory and the improvement of practice in relation to teaching and learning. The content areas would be determined by available personnel and by the needs of the interdisciplinary participants.

The use of educational technology would, however, receive the primary emphasis, especially interactive video and related technology such as CD-ROM. Rockley Miller, president of Future Systems, Inc., and editor and publisher of the Videodisc Monitor, sees both media having a bright future. They both have many similarities, including high data density, excellent durability, and the capacity to randomly access high-quality information almost instantly. CD ROM is just entering the market and has evolved from the videodisc which is finally beginning to realize its potential after years of "unbridled optimism" followed by a period of "pessimistic depression." In Miller's words, "Too many entrepreneurs tried to sell the videodisc rather than a solution to a specific problem. Nobody buys technology. People buy what it can do for them."[39]

Despite the expanding popularity of interactive video, particularly within industry and the federal government for training, there is little data that substantiates its effectiveness. Much essential research will be forthcoming in this area.[40] Another area ripe for research and development is electronic publishing and database publishing on CD ROM.

Encyclopedias, documents, books, as well as numerous reference works will soon be stored on this medium for the reasons cited above as well as for storage conservation. Quality research and application, of course, need to be underscored. When coupled with one effective way of using innovative technology, the resulting synergy may well revolutionize the way we communicate and learn. In the words of Omar Moore:

> I think educators are well advised to be careful of technological innovations that are over-promised, oversold and sometimes disappointing. But I think this particular complex of innovations (interactive optical laser discs) is really quite different because it integrates and synthesizes many things that we have all been dealing with. The trouble with past innovations is that they were one-shot affairs. This kind of technology has a kind of holistic quality that depends much on the user and the user's imagination. I think this is one that is going to help pull together the diverse technological developments and hence really is important in a way that individual innovations that are faddish are not.[41]

Instructional Design and Project Application

Another obvious and related focus is instructional design. Much of the software on the market today, for both interactive video and CAI, is rather poor. This is the case because heretofore most designers were not educators. Creative instructional designers are needed and every phase of their work needs ongoing research and development. This includes: analysis, design, development, production, authoring, implementation and evaluation (both formative and summative). One outstanding institution that can be looked to for guidance in these areas is MIT, especially its Project Athena, which is educationally oriented.

There is also an MIT Industrial Liaison Program which offers symposia, reports on research in progress, and related support offerings. Some of these projects, once developed, could perhaps be available for testing and application in Pittsburgh. The Center would also design, develop, and produce instructional videodisc, CD ROM and CAI programs, courseware, and data bases for particular needs. Where effective, existing material would be used, as in the "repurposing" of videodiscs on the market, generic or otherwise, for particular applications. Another process, one that is being explored by Harvard University and Brigham Young University, is that of "retrofitted" videodiscs. Production costs and developmental time are minimized by using existing broadcast quality video segments with an authoring system to create a new disc. At the Center, accessible videodiscs coupled with videos and films available at the schools and universities as well as those either stored at or available through WQED would be an avenue well worth exploring for particular educational applications. The content design and editing of material for the new or "retrofitted" disc would be the largest expenses outside of the disc mastering. The production of new material, video and film, for optical laser discs would also be pursued.

The Information Age in Education—
Computer Aided Learning
by Karen Block

Computers and Change in Education

Much has been written about the profound pedagogical potential of computers and related information technologies. Many believe it will be possible to reverse the deteriorating quality of elementary and secondary education by adequate employment of computer aided education.

Certainly, the intellectual excitement is there. One need only read the burgeoning discussions among educators and psychologists who have new visions of the cognitive benefits of computers.[42]

What exactly does this technology offer the processes of education? Many leaders in the field would claim that it offers the opportunity to redefine the possibilities of education. Computers are commonly believed to change how effectively we do traditional tasks, amplifying or extending our capabilities, with the assumption that these tasks stay fundamentally the same. More recently emerging trends highlight a quite different primary role emphasizing reorganized cognitive functioning.

This new role for the computer in education is to change the tasks we do by reorganizing our mental functioning, not only by amplifying it. The underlying notion is that computers are universal machines for storing and dynamically manipulating symbols, which appear to serve as the currency of human thought.[43] Symbolic technologies can therefore qualitatively change the structure and function of mental activities such as problem solving or memory. This restructuring capacity has led researchers to focus on and study in detail cases in which software has qualitatively changed both the content and flow of the cognitive processes involved in human problem solving.

Reorganized Cognition in Instruction

Several prototypes exist, but possibly the best known come from the area of mathematics education. In the area of algebra, the use of selected microcomputer programs permits complex equation solving, including solution of numerical and literal equations, factoring of polynomial expressions, evaluation of integrals, etc. A student using these programs spends time primarily in algorithm design and search of appropriate operators, rather than acting as a mechanic for calculating numerical expressions. Search is not a central concept in algebra instruction today, but a central insight of cognitive science research is that learning problem solving skills in math fundamentally involves search, that is knowledge about when to select what subgoals, in what sequence. In most classroom instruction, the teacher selects the operator to be applied in an equation (e.g., to add to both sides) and the student carries out the arithmetic. Thus, students are not being explicitly taught what they need to know to solve problems effectively.

In one program, Algebra Land, a search space window records solution steps the student took, and the search space is represented graphically as a search tree that displays solution paths with all the backtracking points and problem solving moves made while trying to solve the equation. The computer environment of this program emphasizes a procedure diametrically opposed to traditional instruction, where the teacher chooses the operators. Here, the student chooses the operators, and the computer carries out the mechanical procedures to transform the equation. Learning effective search skills in algebra equation solving is not an easy task. This computer program reorganizes learning and presents a tangible record of it so as to highlight more fundamental skills involved—emphasizing the mathematical thinking, rather than the rote calculation of arithmetic operations.

Other software exists which reflects a similar re-orientation for the objectives of mathematics education. Within English and Humanities education, computer based writing technologies have appeared recently which assist the exteriorization and revision of thinking processes that written language allows. These writing tools include "outlining" programs—where users report more experimentation with alternate organizational schemes, and more attention during revision to how the details of the text contribute to the purpose of the whole. Other programs allow bottom-up discovery and definition of relationships between ideas, which do not yield easily to the top-down outline approach to composition. Through cycles of reorganizing separate ideas into different categories, one can discover idea structures during writing. These writing technologies provide the possibility for reorganizing one's writing processes and trying out different activities during writing. They thus appear to have deep qualitative effects on how problem solving in writing occurs, which are not captured within the usual processes of writing education.

Implications for Education

How is education responding to these developments? Some would argue that education is not keeping pace with these transformations of the student's world, and of these new cognitive objectives for education. Some claim education has assimilated the computer to its "earlier, fact-oriented" agenda.[44] Although there are good educational reasons for today's fact oriented computer assisted instruction, we cannot let current models of CAI curtail our thinking about what is possible. With fact-oriented curricula, we are not preparing students for lifelong learning that the information age requires. We need to work to help students to learn for themselves, how to seek out, organize and use information for different purposes. Students must become able to control their own learning and information management. Thus, our curricula must refocus emphasis upon cognitive skills including problem solving that permit such management and control.

Given the above, what we in education need are tools to achieve new aims for information age education. We first need to acquire the significant educational software prototypes discussed in the artificial intelligence, cognitive science oriented educational technology literature. We also need to acquire a library of software tools used by adults in such disciplines as business, history, math and science—software for graphing, data base management, word processing, and spread sheet software. Overall, we want software currently available to determine how it may be usefully adapted for use with public school students.

Research Objectives and Teacher Education

In this effort, we require the participation of experienced subject matter teachers and University faculty. The basic first step would be to examine in some detail what the software does, and what it teaches, and what effects, positive or negative, can be empirically examined, reshaped, reassessed and debated. We need to know whether and in what ways hands-on experience with programs influences the stated objectives and instructional strategies of current public school teachers.

We already know that teachers depend greatly on curriculum guides, and upon other teachers for advice about how to teach. We also know for selected areas of the curriculum that instructional strategies which appear in texts and other places do not pay attention to what research has discovered about the psychological processes involved. Thus, we can expect that some programs will appear novel to these teachers. Although to their developers they express powerful ideas, what teachers derive from them will have to be developed under well structured instructional conditions of workshops. These workshops should explore the specific and the general instructional implications of the prototype computer aided learning programs.

Research questions the workshops should address include:
a. Do teachers ever spontaneously use objectives or strategies embodied in the computer programs? How do computer aided and human aided instruction compare for similar instructional objectives?
b. What skills do teachers think the computer programs teach? How would they evaluate their (computer programs) learning effects?
c. Do the teachers think the pedagogy employed is of good quality?
d. When asked to plan how to implement a program into a regular classroom, how would teachers do this? Who would get the program, and why?
e. Is any additional instruction needed to make sure students learn what is claimed to be taught by the program?
f. What other pedagogical purposes can be served by this program in what subject matter domains?
g. Who learns best from this program, and why?
h. What other instructional ideas have been stimulated by exposure to the programs?

From this research, it will be possible to determine the instructional effects upon teachers that exposure to such prototype programs permits. There is every possibility that teachers might refocus their efforts on teaching the kinds of objectives highlighted in the program. However, it is also possible that because of constraints in the actual classroom and school setting, less dramatic results may be obtained. The research proposed should also let us better understand the implementation context into which such programs must fit, paving the way for better designed field tryouts. Such research would take place at the Interactive Learning Center. Additionally, other interactive media and their potential for educational environments would be explored at the Center.

HyperCard software, now bundled with all Apple Macintosh Computers, offers interactive control of videodisc players. (Courtesy The Videodisc Monitor)

3. Seminars

Specialized seminars and workshops would be offered regularly for the interdisciplinary members of the Interactive Learning Center. They would focus on the research and development work of the Center. In addition, workshops and seminars would be designed and offered for specific interests such as those outlined in the Computer Aided Learning and Creativity sections above.

4. Forums

The Interactive Learning Forum would continue. Besides five to six general meetings per year, separate sections for industry and for education would meet more frequently to discuss and to explore topics of interest to them. The focus, as stated from the start, would be on working together for mutual benefit. The Center would both offer and receive direction from the forum participants.

5. Conferences

A regional conference would be structured annually. Recognized researchers, producers, and instructional designers of videodiscs and related interactive educational technologies would be invited to participate. Faculty, students, and staff from the various schools and universities would be able to describe and demonstrate their work, as would other organizations involved with the Center.

6. Publications

Every project worked on at the Interactive Learning Center would be written up in a technical report. These could be made available to participating organizations and individuals, as occurs with the MIT Industrial Liaison Program.

In addition, some type of publication would emanate from the Center. Minimally it would be a newsletter, but it could well advance to a scholarly journal.

The National Demonstration Laboratory (NDL) will give greater visibility to interactive technologies and will be of direct assistance to some educators. For many others it will not be very accessible, other than through publications, and these media need more than a few hands-on demonstrations if they are to be effectively and efficiently used.

Accordingly, why cannot such a paradigm be expanded for educational purposes and established as regional centers across the country? Perhaps the NDL could serve as the parent center.

Of course, a wise approach is to build such structures in deliberate fashion as interest and need dictate. Such direction by the Interactive Learning Forum in Pittsburgh which, at its best, is a cooperative and synergistic initiative that draws from multidisciplinary inspiration (as interactive video must) and across a variety of sectors has already been very influential in this region. Ideally, as the Forum develops, a more comprehensive Interactive Learning Center that is university-based will evolve, similar to what is described above.

Endnotes

1. Unless otherwise specified, the information in this section was obtained from the following sources. Interview with Anthony Ferralli and Kathryn Ferralli, Erie, Pennsylvania, 29 April 1986. Anthony Ferralli, an audio, video, and systems engineer with more than 20 years of experience, is director of research and engineering at The Ferralli Group in Erie; Kathryn Ferralli, a former teacher, is director of resource development at The Ferralli Group. Interview with Sam P. Petruso, Millcreek Education Center, Erie, 29 April 1986. Petruso is coordinator of computer services for MTSD. Interview with Verel R. Salmon, Millcreek Education Center, Erie, 29 April 1986. Salmon is assistant superintendent for MTSD.
2. Anthony and Kathryn Ferralli, "Interactive Video in Education: A New Approach," *The Videodisc Monitor* 3,6 (June 1985): 14.
3. The Ferrallis had devoted much of their available time and resources to developing expertise in interactive video and were the foremost authorities in the Erie area at the time.
4. Kathryn Ferralli is presently compiling an extensive data base of existing videodiscs. Daynes and Butler's book has an extensive listing of videodiscs as well.
5. For a directory of videodisc software see Ed Schwartz, *The Educators' Handbook to Interactive Videodisc* (Washington, D.C.: Association for Educational Communications and Technology, 1985), pp. 47–81.
6. Starship Industries in Great Falls, Virginia regularly updates its Laser Video Disc Catalog which lists mostly movies, but some CAV discs are included. All are for sale.
7. Junius L. Bennion and Edward W. Schneider, "Interactive Videodisc Systems for Education," *Journal of the SMPTE* 84,12 (December 1975): 949–953.
8. Edward W. Schneider and Junius L. Bennion, *Videodiscs* (Englewood Cliffs, New Jersey: Educational Technology Publications, 1981).
9. Diane M. Gayeski and David V. Williams, "Interactive Video in Higher Education" in *Video in Higher Education,* ed. Ortrun Zuber-Skerritt (New York: Nichols Publishing Company, 1984), p. 67.
10. Steward Brand. *The Media Lab: Inventing the Future at MIT*. New York. Viking Penguin Inc. 1987.
11. Edward E. Balkovich et al., "Project Athena: An Introduction (Project Athena prospectus, Massachusetts Institute of Technology, 1983).
12. Rus Gant, "Introducing Interactive Video Information Systems into the Educational Environment" (Transcription of presentation at the Seminar on Interactive Video and Laser Disc Technology, University of Pittsburgh, 31 May 1985), p. 18. Gant pioneered the use of interactive video in archeology. On this project he was responsible for on-site filming, audio data collection, processing of the database onto the videodisc, and for directing courseware development.
13. Judith Paris Roth, "The Coming of the Interactive Compact Disc," *High Technology* 6,10 (October 1986): 46. Roth incorrectly states that The Record Group is a subsidiary of Warner Brothers. The president of TRG, Stan Cornyn, came from Warner Brothers.
14. R. Scott Grabinger, "An Evaluation of Three Authoring-Language Software Packages," *Tech Trends* 30,4 (May/June 1985): p20
15. For a directory of interactive authoring languages see Schwartz, *The Educators' Handbook to Interactive Videodisc,* pp. 84–85. See also Gerald A. Souter, *The DISConnection: How to Interface Computers and Video* (White Plains, NY: Knowledge Industry Publications, Inc., 1988); and Nicholas V. Iuppa and Karl Anderson, *Advanced Interactive Video Design: New Techniques and Applications* (White Plains, NY: Knowledge Industry Publications, Inc., 1988).
16. Michael J. Hannafin, "Options for Authoring Instructional Interactive Video," *Journal of Computer-Based Instruction*, 13 (Summer 1984): 98.
17. Richard E. Pogue, "Authoring Systems: The Key to Lesson Development," *Journal of Educational Technology* Systems 13,2 (1984–1985): 75–81.

18. Dennis Sinnett and Sheila Edwards, "Authoring Systems: The Key to Widespread Use of Interactive Videodisc Technology," *Library Hi Tech* 2,4 (Issue 8, 1984): 42.

19. M. David Merrill, "Peter Dean Lecture: Where is the Authoring in Authoring Systems?" *Journal of Computer-Based Instruction* 12,4 (August 1985): 92.

20. Ibid., pp. 93–94.

21. Sinnett and Edwards, "Authoring Systems: The Key to Widespread Use of Interactive Videodisc," pp. 39–50. Video Nova, Inc. is located in Detroit, Michigan.

22. Larrie E. Gale and Karl Barksdale, "The Development and Formative Evaluation of 'Interactive Digame' Courseware: A Cooperative Project of Brigham Young University and the Provo City School District," report prepared at Brigham Young University, Provo, Utah, 13 June 1986, p. 10.

23. David Hon, "Interactive Training in Cardiopulmonary Resuscitation," *BYTE* 7,6 (June 1982): 108–120, 130–138.

24. "Videodisc Sails the World," *The Videodisc Monitor* 4,9 (September 1986): 1,3.

25. Through Interactive Still Video technology it is now possible for numerous instructors to have immediate and sophisticated control over their interactive instructional resources. The Ferrallis work extensively with educational and corporate environments.

26. Lee Hotz, "The LASER: CMU, Westinghouse Experts Beam as New Technology Spreads to All Fields," *The Pittsburgh Press,* 28 August 1983, p. E1.

27. Ken Christie, "One Year in the Life," *The Videodisc Monitor* 2,1 (January 1984): 12–14. Christie is a former unit director of the Nebraska Videodisc Design/Production Group and currently has his own videodisc design and production company—Silver Platter Productions, Inc. He was responsible for the development of these discs for the EPCOT Center.

28. "Practical Advice from a Videodisc Designer: An Interview with Ken Christie," *Museum News,* August 1985, p. 33.

29. Rod Daynes and Beverly Butler, eds., *The Videodisc Book: A Guide and Directory* (New York: John Wiley & Sons, Inc., 1984), pp. 14–15.

30. This work was directed by Nicholas Negroponte and funded by the Cybernetics Technology Office of the U.S. Defense Advanced Research Projects Agency. See Sigel et al., *Video Discs,* pp. 87–88.

31. Linda Helgerson, "Videodisc for the Storage of Maps," *International Television* 3,4 (April 1985): 44.

32. "Grapevine," *The Videodisc Monitor* 4,9 (September 1986): 6.

33. "Balfour Rolls Out ByVideo Kiosks for Colleges," *The Videodisc Monitor* 4,10 (October 1986): 3.

34. Joan Cash, "Spinning Toward the Future: The Museum on Laser Videodisc," *Museum News,* August 1985, p. 21. Cash writes (p. 19) that "there is no accurate measure of how many museums are using videodiscs now or will be in the near future . . . a reasonable estimate is that three percent of American museums are either using videodiscs or are in the first stages of project development."

35. "Smithsonian and IVC Establish National Demonstration Laboratory," *The Videodisc Monitor* 4,8 (August 1986): 1.

36. The consortium that operates the ETC is comprised of: Harvard Graduate School of Education, Cambridge Public Schools, Children's Television Workshop, Educational Collaborative for Greater Boston, Education Development Center, Educational Testing Service, Interactive Training Systems, Newton Public Schools, Ware Public Schools, Watertown Public Schools, WGBH Educational Foundation, and the ETC Rhode Island Satellite, based at Brown University.

37. ETC Targets 3,3 (Educational Technology Center, Cambridge, MA, Fall 1986).

38. "Educational Technology Center, Second Year Report" (Harvard Graduate School of Education, November 1985).

39. Rockley L. Miller, "CD ROM and Videodisc: Lessons to be Learned," in *CD ROM: The New Papyrus,* eds., Steve Lambert and Suzanne Ropiequet (Redmond, WA: Microsoft Press, 1986), pp. 37–41.

40. An excellent starting place for such research in the ILC would be with the work of James L. Bosco, Director of the Tate Research Center at Western Michigan University. James Bosco, "An Analysis of Evaluations of Interactive Video," *Educational Technology,* May 1986, pp. 7–17.

41. Omar K. Moore's presentation at the Interactive Learning Forum, University of Pittsburgh, May 1986, quoted in George R. Haynes, "Actively Interactive in Pittsburgh," *Video Computing* (September/October 1986), pp. 8, 12.

42. See R. D. Pea, "Beyond Amplification: Using the Computer to Reorganize Mental Functioning," *Educational Psychologist* 20,4 (1985): 167–182.

43. J. G. Greeno and H. A. Simon. "Problem Solving and Reasoning," in *Stevens' Handbook of Experimental Psychology, Revised Edition,* eds., R. C. Atkinson, R. Herrnstein, G. Lindzey, and R. D. Luce (New York: Wiley, 1987).

44. Pea, "Beyond Amplification: Using the Computer to Reorganize Mental Functioning."

5

Summary

"Tribal men everywhere regard themselves as integral parts of nature. They belong to a seamless web of kinship & responsibility. They merge the individual with the whole society. They're involved with life: they experience a *participation mystique*. This experience is one in which people are eager to merge with cosmic powers.

Beginning with the phonetic alphabet & the Greeks, there came a habit of detachment & noninvolvement, a kind of uncooperative gesture toward the universe. From this refusal to be involved in the world he lived in, literate man derived detachment & objectivity. He became alienated from his environment, even from his body. He believed there was an elegance in detachment. He valued the isolated, delimited self, especially the mind. He became an island, complete unto himself.

Today we've entered a relatively dim, resonating tribal world in which the electronic extensions of everybody's nerves involve him deeply in all other lives. Where writing & print technology tore man out of the group, creating the great misery of psychic alienation, suddenly & without warning the electronic media hasten him back into the embrace of the group. Electricity binds the entire human community into a single tribe, with much resulting erosion of individualism.

While this threatens the sense of identity of many people, it can also heighten our awareness of the shape & meaning of our lives to the level of extreme sensitivity: Eliot's to "understand what it is to be awake, to be living on several planes at once."[1]

When television pioneer John Logie Baird was persistently promoting his inventive insights in the 1920s and 1930s, he acquired the reputation of being a lonely and shy individual. Some people found him to be a difficult and uncooperative. Even so, without the constant pressure and incessant publicity that he generated, the United Kingdom would no doubt never have had an advanced high-definition TV service on the air by 1936. Home entertainment on a videodisc (mechanical) system was not a success for him, nor was it for its laser optical promoters 50 years later. Many who influenced the videodisc field in the late 1970s and early 1980s attempted with considerable effort to drive the market with their agenda. As was Baird's original interest, commercial success was their objective. Underdeveloped technology and timing worked against them all. Yet, out of their visionary tenacity has emerged a revolutionary medium.

Hindsight has promoted an altered application of the videodisc system so as to augment educational and training use which is in keeping with the most advantageous use of the medium. Included with this encouraging leitmotif is a vigorous emphasis on cooperation among hardware manufacturers, software suppliers including disc replicators, instructional designers, and publishers. American Interactive Media, Inc., for example, a joint venture of Philips and PolyGram, employs professional educators currently involved in developing high quality software for all academic levels that will accompany CD-I when it is introduced. IBM is coordinating videodisc development projects among a consortium of medical schools, and Allen Communication is providing it authoring system, Quest, to interested schools to promote the development of student authoring skills.

Taking advantage of this synergistic paradigm seems to be in the best interest of educators as well. The Magnetics Technology Center at Carnegie Mellon University, in reflecting the Japanese model, unites university research with industrial and governmental interests for the mutual benefit of all. Such structuring is one that sophisticated and expensive technology, with equally sophisticated intellectual inquiry, requires. Laser and computer developments would have been hampered significantly without governmental and corporate sponsorship. CMU, MIT, Cornell, Harvard, and a number of other universities actively pursue such joint ventures—especially in the fields of science and technology.

It is time for broader application of such a concerted multidisciplinary union. The research-oriented consortium at Harvard's Graduate School of Education is focused on teaching with the use of technology in science, mathematics, and computer education for the advancement of theory and the improvement of practice in relation to teaching and learning in these areas. Faculty members in the College of Education at Brigham Young University (BYU) have similar goals but are focused on linguistics. The Harvard and BYU avant-garde explorations will likely have significant ramifications for other educational environments that are aware of their work.

The developing paradigm at Millcreek Township School District is exemplary, as is what is evolving in the Rochester, New York school district which has forged a model for educational reform by working with business and community leaders. Their quest, like Shanker's, is for a revolutionary redesigning of contemporary education, elementary and secondary education particularly, with professional teachers in professional environments offering quality education to all students. Dewey had comparable objectives in his efforts to improve the intelligence of all students, rather than the elite few. This concern with inequality is also addressed by Rogers: "One important role for diffusion research in the future is to explore more effective strategies for creating a greater degree of equality among the members of social systems. This is a new, difficult, and promising role for diffusion scholars."[2] In the same vein, Gale and Brown of BYU emphasize that "the best education is mutually edifying for teacher and student, and they grow together. Nothing less than a total theory of learning that includes interpersonal dynamics and the search for meaning can have the kind of practical effects that are needed to transform our educational institutions."[3]

Quality education that is democratic and holistic needs the auxiliary support of interactive technologies. Interactive video in particular is a synthesis of diverse technological developments that transcends its individual parts. It has emerged as a revolutionary medium and has spawned the compact discs. Even so, their educational potential remains largely untapped. Electronic publishing of encyclopedias and other, innumerable, reference works on optical and magneto-optic discs has an immediate library application and dynamic potential in hypermedia environments.

Innovative classroom use of interactive technologies has the potential to augment standard pedagogy and to advance individualized and mastery learning as well. In the process, the best teachers would be empowered to draw from a wide range of materials to expeditiously arrange or instructionally design that information according to their perspective. Local electronic publishing will likely increase substantially, as well. The use of textbooks may indeed recede, as Thomas Edison predicted.

This technology is no longer underdeveloped. It is now highly sophisticated and readily available. Lacking is educational software that is of high quality and creatively designed. The use of and benefit to be derived from these interactive laser discs is indeed dependent upon the imagination of program designers and users themselves.

The National Demonstration Laboratory at the Smithsonian Institute will give greater visibility to this medium and will be of more direct assistance to some. Much more practical and very timely are the establishment of numerous multidisciplinary interactive learning and creativity centers, uniquely positioned to serve regional interests. Unlike medical doctors, professional educators tend not to be scientifically or technologically oriented. In fact, keeping high quality technical people in educational institutions, at all levels, is an obvious problem. This academic chasm is further exacerbated by the fact that the implementation and diffusion of innovation is significantly affected by the amount and the quality of assistance received.

In the proposed Interactive Learning Centers, requisite experts from the various disciplines could unify their efforts while focusing primarily on research, development, and evaluation of interactive educational technologies (hardware and software) and creativity for teaching, training, learning, thinking, problem solving, and leadership. Academic, corporate, and governmental sectors (both public and private) would all be served. Such a relationship, if wisely and efficaciously established and managed, would enable the educators and academic researchers to lead the technology rather than being led by it—which has been a perpetual nemesis for many academics. Carnegie Mellon University has demonstrated the feasibility and real benefit of such a nexus, notably through the Magnetics Technology Center and by supplying the genesis for NeXT, Inc. Cornell University has established the Interactive Media Center with support from International Business Machines Corporation, and Minnesota has established a statewide task-force focused on integrating videodiscs throughout the educational system. In doing so, they established a partnership between higher education, k–12 schools, businesses and industry, and the state department of education.

Educational institutions have here an opportunity to assume a vital new role in society and in the process to be the agent of change, the catalyst of innovation. The academic community and the rest of society have a real need for better communication, as Kingman Brewster advised the college presidents assembled in 1986 at a meeting convened by the Association of American Universities to discuss the future of college education. Brewster, formerly president of Yale University and U.S. ambassador to the United Kingdom, was also master of the University College at Oxford. Wesley Posvar, president of the University of Pittsburgh, further asserts that "we've [the university] got to take this action because nobody else can do it. . . . Government can't do it alone. Industry can't do it alone because it's linked to the bottom line, and besides, industry just doesn't have the impulses to reach out and experiment. Major research universities must do it, in cooperation with government and industry."[4] Working together as a catalyst for creative innovation, they have the potential to advance master teaching as well as individualized and democratized learning.

Endnotes

1. Edmund Carpenter, "The Tribe that Swallowed the Private 'I'," in *They Became What They Beheld* (New York: Ballantine Books, Inc., 1970), no page numbers used.
2. Everett M. Rogers, *Diffusion of Innovations, Third Edition* (New York: The Free Press, 1983), p. 413.
3. Gale and Brown, "A Theory of Learning and Skill-Acquisition Applied to Interactive Video: Activities at the David O. McKay Institute, Brigham Young University," *Studies in Language Learning* 5,1 (Spring 1985): 109.
4. Wesley W. Posvar quoted in Tim Ziaukas, "200 Years and Counting," *Pittsburgh Magazine,* October 1986, p. 48.

Appendix

Medical Information Management
at the
University of Pittsburgh

Developmental Plans
1987–1992

John K. Vries, M.D.
Assistant Vice President for Health Sciences
(Biomedical Informatics)

Gina D. Carlos
Andrew S. Latchaw
Bernadette S. Marshalek
Ken L. Mitchum
Stephen W. Pfeiffer
Bernadette A. Reddy
C. Gray Watson, Jr.
Russell J. Yount

Office of Biomedical Informatics
University of Pittsburgh

February 1, 1988

Medical Information Management

1. Specific Aims

The goal of the Office of Biomedical Informatics is to develop a medical archival system. This system, which has been christened MARS (Medical Archival System), is to provide access to a comprehensive biomedical database containing all of the patient and reference information needed in the course of clinical care, medical research, and education. MARS will be one of the integrating elements in a unified medical information system serving all of the institutions that make up the University Health Center of Pittsburgh.

MARS is being designed to meet the five criteria listed below:

1. MARS must provide interactive access with acceptable response time to all information generated by the health care process for 1,000 simultaneous users. The patient care information to be archived includes text, images, laboratory data, and physiologic data.
2. MARS must provide access to relevant external medical databases, such as MEDLINE or DRUGDEX, and the capability of searching them.
3. MARS must provide adequate computational power to allow 100 simultaneous users to perform interactive research using the medical records archive. The archive is expected to accrue up to 500,000 medical records over 10 years; the system must allow retrospective application of the scientific method in epidemiological, clinical, or statistical analyses of this database.
4. MARS must be able to assist clinical decision making with intelligent decision support programs.
5. MARS must be cost-effective.

To achieve these goals, MARS utilizes a distributed parallel processing environment, optical disk storage and broadband fiberoptic data transmission, and asynchronous switching networks.

2. The Need for Medical Archival Systems

2.1. The Problem

The explosion in medical information that has taken place over the last decade has generated the need for new approaches to information management. Traditional hospital information systems have only supported fiscal and administrative operations. Typical systems process thousands of transactions per hour, but have no capability to deal with clinical information. This information is relegated to paper based medical records that often number in the hundreds of thousands. The only way to retrieve this information is through tedious manual searches. Information in external databases is also hard to acquire. Online searches are expensive and aren't available at the sites where clinical care is rendered. In 1982, Matheson and Cooper published a landmark report entitled "Academic Information Management in the Academic Health Sciences Center". The report documented that the quantity of biomedical information doubled every decade, while the useful half-life for biomedical facts had dropped to 5–7 years. In 1985, over 100,000 biomedical journal titles were published. Health care professionals cannot cope with this information overload without automation.

2.2. A Solution Applying Available Technology

The technology to gather, store, and distribute the information generated by a modern health center already exists. Optical disks the size of a phonograph record with the capacity to store millions of pages of printed text can be purchased off the shelf. Jukeboxes containing hundreds of these disks have recently become available. Such devices could store all of the textual records, laboratory data, and diagnostic images generated by a large health center over a twenty year period of time as well as the information in external databases such as MEDLINE. Advances in fiberoptic networking have made it possible to gather and distribute large amounts of data throughout an institutional complex at low cost and at speeds that permit effectively unlimited simultaneous sessions between end users and computers. The largest fiberoptic network in an academic environment is already in place at the University of Pittsburgh as a result of the "Campus of the Future" initiative. New concepts from the field of artificial intelligence have made it possible to construct natural language interfaces for communicating with computer systems, and automatic indexers for classifying textual information. It has also been possible to build functional models of the reasoning behavior of medical experts and decision makers. Microcomputers now available operate at up to 1 MIP (millions of instructions executed per second) and can be equipped with laser disk storage devices that can hold 1 gigabyte (billion bytes) on each interchangeable laser disk.

Most of these technologies are already in use in MARS modules that are running in the laboratory or that are undergoing field testing in the University Health Center. If the completed system performs according to expectations, it will be integrated with enhanced hospital information systems that are being installed in the hospitals of the University Health Center. These enhanced HIS systems are described in the next section.

2.3. State of the Art Hospital Information Systems

The traditional services provided by hospital information systems include registration, admission-discharge-transfer (ADT) processing, census control, utilization review, billing, scheduling, inventory control, cost accounting, and financial management. Over the last decade these services have been augmented by independent information systems geared to the needs of specific departments. Such departments include radiology, clinical and anatomic pathology, microbiology, pharmacy, nursing, and nutrition. Medical software vendors have recently begun to integrate these independent modules with core hospital systems by means of data dictionaries and master patient indices. The newer systems also support order entry and results reporting for all of the integrated modules. Strategic plans have been formulated by Presbyterian-University Hospital, Falk Clinic, Eye and Ear Hospital, and Western Psychiatric Institute and Clinic to upgrade existing hospital information systems to these levels of service. The process will begin in 1988–89. The expanded services for Presbyterian-University Hospital will be delivered from an IBM 3081-GX mainframe. The expanded Falk Clinic services will be organized around a VAX 8200 complex. Hardware decisions for the other hospitals and the clinical laboratory systems are pending.

3. The MARS System: Overview and Operation

Figure 4.1 illustrates MARS operation in overview. Briefly, information of varied types is gathered into the MARS system through interfaces to the HIS systems of the University Health Center and through direct interfaces to such devices as CT and MRI scanners and the central word processing operation of the Medical Records Office. Broad-band fiberoptics will provide the medium for much of the data collection. The links to HIS systems will use TCP/IP - SNA bridges or other network links.

Once it has been gathered, data is stored in a MARS-format database that can contain all types of data-textual, pictorial, or numeric-in a single, universal database structure. The MARS database exploits the fact that all data is either textual or is associated with text (radiologic images with radiology reports, for example). By manipulating textual components, all data can be automatically indexed, classified as to data type, encapsulated in the database, and retrieved with excellent precision and recall using bibliographic searching techniques. Low-level object-oriented I/O routines, using data type classifications, allow higher-level software to treat all types of data as interchangeable objects. Asynchronous additions to the database can be consolidated with parent medical or other records before final archiving to speed retrieval of information.

Physically, the MARS database will be stored online on optical disks. A 100 to 200 gigabyte (billion byte) optical disk jukebox will soon be installed, and will be used to begin providing MARS electronic medical record and other services for textual and laboratory data. When images are added to electronic medical records, a 4 to 8 terabyte (trillion byte) optical disk jukebox will be required.

To distribute information, three layers of MARS computers work together in a distributed parallel-processing network. Traffic will flow through fiberoptic and other links in an asynchronous switching network under completely automatic control.

The computers of the top layer, (the central data processing layer), maintain a central "gold standard" archive. They also manage the network, making decisions about how to allocate network resources.

The computers of the next layer, (the local server layer), satisfy user requests for information. These local server processors are each configured with a subset of the "gold standard" archive and with retrieval software specialized for working with that subset of the archive. The central data processors configure the local servers on the basis of decisions on how to allocate network resources.

In the bottom, end user layer, microcomputers interpret user requests for information and pass them up to the appropriate local server computer. Users are automatically connected to the local server that has the subset of the database that they wish to access. Requests for information that cross database subsets are passed up to the central data processors, which redirect them to the appropriate local servers. Connections between the layers are asynchronous. The many high-traffic links between local server and end user computers will be through the University's fiberoptic network and ancillary Starlan networks.

By distributing processing between central database/network managers, local servers, and end user workstations, the MARS network as a whole is expected to perform at speeds far exceeding the capabilities of current supercomputers. The expected performance levels are shown at the right side of the figure in MIPS (millions of instructions executed per second). MARS is expected to achieve these performance levels at 20 to 30% of the cost of an equivalent mainframe-based system.

Control of the MARS network will be automated. The ARIADNE and JANUS expert systems, shown at the left side of the illustration, will control information gathering and distribution. The ARIADNE system will manage the asynchronous flow of information into MARS, and will allocate resources for distributing information. Multiple instances of the JANUS expert system will carry out the resource allocation decisions made by ARIADNE. Key mechanisms of these expert systems are currently in operation in the MARS central data processing facility.

111

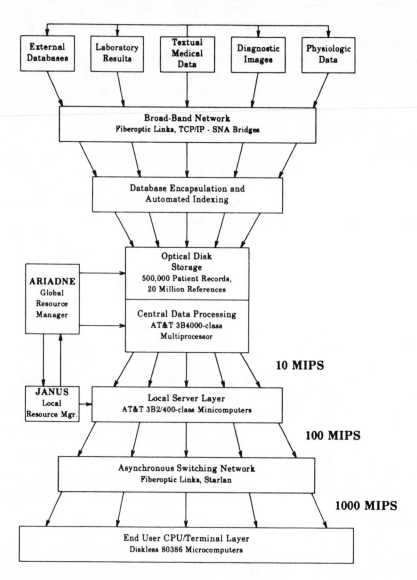

Figure 4.1. MARS Operation in Overview.

In the sections that follow Figure 4.1, we will describe in greater detail how the MARS system gathers, stores, and distributes information. We will also describe our plans for automating management of the MARS network and for providing standard MARS workstations that can be affordably deployed in the University Health Center and other locations.

3.1. Gathering

As Figure 4.1 illustrates, the MARS system will gather five different types of data. An electronic medical record may contain up to four of these: textual medical records; images from such sources as the CT or MRI scanners; real-time physiologic data from EEGs and other monitoring

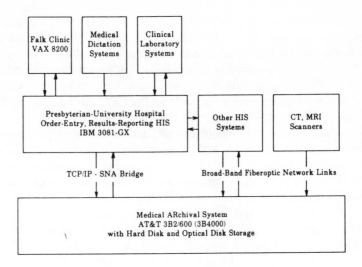

Figure 4.2. Information-Gathering Links.

equipment; and laboratory results. External databases that may be archived in MARS range from large textual collections such as MEDLINE to specialized databases containing a variety of textual and non-textual data types. These external data-bases are supplied to MARS in a variety of physical and logical formats.

The volume of information that must be gathered is enormous. It is estimated that MARS will have archived 500,000 patient records within 10 years of full operation. Together with images and data from external sources, those records will represent 20 million items of data and will require several trillion bytes of storage.

The physical medium for much of MARS data collection will be the University's fiberoptic network. The broad-band transmission capabilities of this network will enable it to accept large amounts of MARS traffic without adversely affecting other communications. Collection of a digital representation of a single slice from a CT scan will require transmission of almost half a megabyte (million bytes) over the network.

Figure 4.2 illustrates the data collection network that will be put in place in the University Health Center. Initially, the primary network interface for MARS will be be an AT&T 3B2/600; however, a larger computer of the AT&T 3B4000 class may be installed when MARS is fully deployed.

Most of the interfaces shown in Figure 4.2 are already in operation in MARS. The textual portions of patient medical records can currently be read from the stand-alone word processors on which these records are transcribed from hand-written or dictated notes. Text also will be digitized directly from type-written records using an optical character reader at the Office of Biomedical Informatics. Images can be read directly from the digital output of the CT and MRI scanners that serve the University Health Center. The Office of Biomedical Informatics can also digitize images from film, if required. A neuroradiology teaching collection is being computerized using a high-resolution video camera and the AT&T TARGA digital/analog image processing system. An image on film can be digitized in 1/30 of a second into a 512 × 512 pixel image in 32,768 shades of gray. A TCP/IP - SNA link, similar to the one that will be installed between the Presbyterian-University Hospital HIS system and MARS, has already been established elsewhere in the University. Links to additional HIS systems, such as the AT&T 3B2/400 in the University of Pittsburgh Epilepsy Center, will be established as necessary. Additional device interfaces will also be added to collect lab or physiologic data that is not available from the HIS systems. The EEG module, for example, will digitize analog output from the EEG machines of the Epilepsy Center and will incorporate EEG tracings in a patient's electronic medical record.

To define the information that should be collected in the MARS archive, the Office of Biomedical Informatics is leading the IAIMS planning effort at the University of Pittsburgh. The IAIMS Medical Records/Clinical Facilities Task Force has been created to define the constituent parts of an electronic medical record. The members of this task force include the heads of medical records, nursing services, and the hospital information systems of the Presbyterian-University Hospital, Falk Clinic, Eye and Ear Hospital, and the Western Psychiatric Institute and Clinic. The task force also includes clinicians representing a cross section of the medical specialties practicing in these institutions. An additional task force, the Legal and Ethical Issues Task Force, has been created to advise on patient confidentiality and on other legal and ethical issues involving electronic medical records and the use of medical archives.

The Medical Records Task Force, Technology Task Force, and Falk Library Advisory Committee will advise on resources, such as national medical databases, that are needed in medical care, research, and education and which should be made available through MARS. These task forces will also oversee the integration of the MARS system with the University's HIS systems and fiberoptic network to form the comprehensive medical information management system envisioned by the IAIMS process.

3.2. Storage

As indicated in Figure 4.1, MARS ultimately will archive some 500,000 electronic medical records comprised of text, images, laboratory test results, and physiologic data. In total, several terabytes (trillion bytes) of online storage will be required. MARS will utilize optical disk technology to provide the required storage capacity. Through a corporate grant, a prototype optical disk jukebox will be installed in early 1988. This jukebox will contain 100 to 200 gigabytes (billion bytes) of storage. With this storage capacity, MARS will be able to provide textual medical information services, beginning with beta test electronic medical records services for the Medical Records Department of the Presbyterian-University Hospital and for the University of Pittsburgh Epilepsy Center. The jukebox will be able to archive all textual medical information in the University Health Center's records as well as textual databases like MEDLINE. When images and physiologic data are included in archived medical records, it will be necessary to acquire the 4 to 8 terabyte optical disk jukebox described earlier in this report.

The MARS database software is based on a single fundamental concept: since all medical information is either text or is associated with text, all medical information can be manipulated by manipulating text. For example, a diagnostic image is always associated with a radiology report. The image can be indexed according to the demographic and diagnostic information in the radiology report and can be retrieved by searching for the text with which it was indexed. Based on this concept, the MARS database has evolved into a single database structure that can contain all types of medical data. A single set of MARS utilities can store and retrieve any type of data in this database structure.

Because of the volume and variety of format of medical data, the MARS database strategy also incorporates an automated indexing system and concepts from object-oriented programming. LEXX, the automated indexing expert system, produces a list of highly specific indexing terms which can be used as keywords when the data is encapsulated in the MARS database. LEXX also functions as a natural language interface, mapping free English user requests into appropriate, specific medical terms that can be used to search for data. To perform its indexing and natural language translations, LEXX expands input terms along narrower-than links in a semantic network. Four such semantic networks-actually, specially constructed thesauri of domain-specific terms—are being constructed. A procedure for automating thesaurus construction also has been devised.

The object-oriented programming strategies embedded in the database software simplify the manipulation of data of different types. Essentially, the database software classifies data according to type—diagnostic image or text, for example. Intelligence is built into the low-level storage and retrieval routines of the database software so that different types of data are automatically handled correctly. Based on the type identification associated with an image, for example, the software knows that the data should be sent to a video display adapter. The advantage is that higher-level database software can manage all data in the MARS archive as interchangeable objects. The database software as a whole is less complex, more efficient, and easier to modify and maintain.

Figure 4.3 illustrates the process by which data is encapsulated in the MARS database. At the top of the illustration, textual medical data arrives from interfaces to the word processors used to transcribe medical records and to other devices, such as the HIS systems. The MARS system has a generalized parsing routine that can be configured to read free text or database records in any consistent record format. The parsing routine extracts three types of data from incoming records. Firstly, it finds out what type of data is contained in a record. This "tag type" identifies the data to the object-oriented, low-level data management routines. Secondly, the parsing routine extracts demographic identifiers, such as patient name and id number, which are incorporated in record headers in the MARS database. These identifiers are among the fields that can be searched with the MARS database retrieval utilities. Lastly, it identifies the data fields in an incoming record.

After parsing, the data can be encapsulated—physically stored—in an ASCII database. The MARS database uses a variant of the MARC header format, used in OCLC databases, for the MARS database. Demographic, tag type, and other information is stored in a header in each record. All external data that is not already in the MARS format, such as MEDLINE, is converted as it is read in so that a single set of retrieval routines can access all data. Because information relating to the same patient or other entity arrives asynchronously, condensation routines are run against the database periodically. These routines consolidate related information into one record. Pictorial or other non-textual data is read directly into the database and is included in records by reference, through pointers to files containing the images.

To allow data retrieval, the ASCII database is processed with file inversion routines producing a single hash table containing field and whole-text entries. This all-inclusive hash table format minimizes storage requirements and provides rapid access to data in the ASCII database.

Initially, only selected text will be indexed with the LEXX automated indexing expert system. As more thesauri are completed, more text will be indexed with LEXX. Eventually, all data will be indexed.

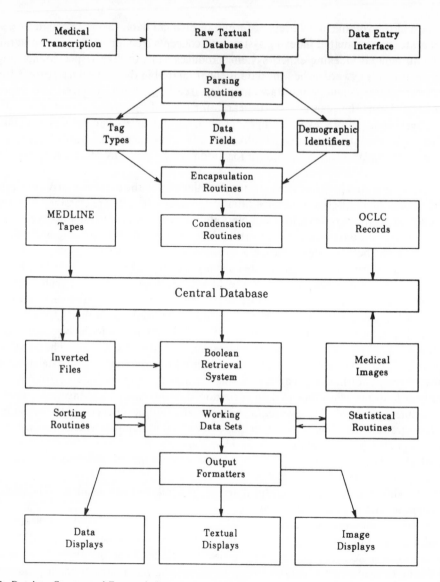

Figure 4.3. Database Storage and Encapsulation.

All information retrieval is carried out through a set of Boolean retrieval utilities: AND, OR, and NOT searches are supported on full text, filtered full text, or specific fields in records, with distance operators. Searches can be carried out on the full database or on the saved results of previous searches (labeled as "Working Data Sets" in the figure). A Boolean search language that allows relational queries of a database also has been implemented. This language allows searches across data fields in the unitary MARS hash table using any logically-valid combination of search terms and Boolean operators.

When it is used as a natural language interface, the LEXX expert system uses the Boolean search routines to carry out user requests for information. LEXX maps free English input into appropriate keywords and uses those keywords as input to the Boolean search routines. Both the LEXX system and the Boolean search utilities use a data dictionary to translate keywords from alphanumerics into integers. All natural language processing and inverted file reference is done by manipulating these integers; no alphanumeric string operations have to be performed. Because of the efficiency of this technique, interactive natural language processing and Boolean searching can be successfully performed on a microcomputer.

Later in MARS development, sorting and statistical routines will be added to the database retrieval routines to provide specialized searching capabilities. Data may also be mapped into formats that can be used by statistical analysis software packages that are in use in the University Health Center, as desirable.

At the bottom of Figure 4.3, the tag type of retrieved data is used to route the data to an appropriate output formatting routine. Textual and image displays currently are operating; graphic routines for charting physiologic data are in plan as part of the LAB module (described later in this report).

3.3. Distributing

The MARS data distribution strategy relies upon distributed processing. MARS will distribute information to users through a three-layer network of processors that will share the burden of providing large amounts of data to a large number of simultaneous users.

The distributed processing strategy is based on the recognition that most of the time, most users will reference only a portion of the MARS central database. A neurologist, for example, will reference primarily medical records and medical literature from that subset of the MARS database that pertains to neurological diagnoses. This fact means that subsets of the database and specialized software for accessing each subset can be run in parallel on relatively small machines to serve the needs of particular sets of users.

To implement this distributed processing strategy, the MARS database and user audience will be divided into approximately 25 logical subsets. Electronic medical records will be divided according to diagnostic criteria. Data from external databases such as MEDLINE will be divided in the same way, and the resulting subsets will be associated with the appropriate portion of the electronic medical records database. Clinical care-givers, the largest portion of the MARS audience, will be divided into logical groups according to the diagnoses of the patients for whom they normally provide care. The database subsets will be downloaded to minicomputers in the MARS "Local Server Layer" (shown in Figure 4.1). Users at microcomputer work stations will be mapped to the appropriate local server under automated control by the ARIADNE and JANUS expert systems.

Figure 4.4 shows how the layers of the MARS network will work together to achieve greater than supercomputer performance at relatively low cost. At the top of the pyramid, the MARS central data processor, an AT&T 3B4000-class multiprocessor, provides 10 MIPS (million instructions executed per second) for central database management and network management. The middle layer of the pyramid will consist of approximately 25 AT&T 3B2/400-class minicomputers equipped with 500 megabytes of disk storage. Each local server will manage a database of 10,000 to 50,000 objects (medical records and references) and will service requests for data from 30 to 50 users. At the bottom of the pyramid are the 1,000 workstations that will be distributed throughout the University Health Center. These machines, running at about 1 MIP, will perform much of the processing required for the MARS interface, such as LEXX natural language processing.

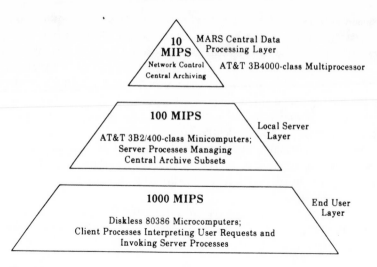

Figure 4.4. Distributed Processing.

Most of the time, most MARS users will interact only with their "home" local server: the local server with which they are connected when they log in. Most of the time, therefore, the 25 local servers will run in parallel, satisfying user requests from the database subsets immediately available to them. In this situation, the aggregate of the local servers and the central CPU will equal the power of a supercomputer (100 MIPS) at a fraction of the cost of a supercomputer. Since most interface processing is done in parallel in the work station layer, the power of the network as a whole is equivalent to the power of many supercomputers.

When a local server does not have the information requested by a user, it refers the request to the central processor for redirection to the appropriate server. We expect, however, that parallel processing mode will prevail about 90% of the time if the associations between database subsets and user groups are correctly defined.

It seems likely that only a distributed processing solution such as the one we envision can meet the goals of the MARS system: distributing data from a 4 to 8 terabyte repository to up to 1000 simultaneous users. For example, it would not be possible to serve many simultaneous users if all data were provided directly from the optical disk storage facility. While complete medical records or other units of information can be assembled at will from the storage facility, the process is too slow to serve many simultaneous users. Subdividing the database and distributing it from servers eliminates the storage facility as a bottleneck. Also, the cost of providing sufficient mainframe processing power to support MARS users at dumb terminals, in the traditional mainframe configuration, would probably be prohibitive for the MARS project. The computers that will make up the MARS network, however, are relatively inexpensive; we expect to deliver MARS for 20% to 30% of the cost of a mainframe configuration of equivalent power. Additionally, the distributed MARS network will limit the effects of a failure in any one processor. Most requests for data will continue to be satisfied, even if the failure is in the MARS central processor. We expect, as well, that the distributed network will prove to be efficient for carrying out epidemiologic or statistical studies that transcend the logical database subsets. Such large database queries would be carried out by a group of local server computers running in parallel, satisfying the request many times faster than would be possible in a conventional mainframe.

3.3.1. MARS Workstations

Two kinds of work station have been developed for use with the MARS system. For distribution in the hospitals and clinics of the University Health Center, we have emphasized low cost and data security. The prototypical system would be a 80386 microcomputer equipped with a hard disk but without any drive that uses removable media. Ensuring the confidentiality of patient records will be much easier if there is no way to write records to any easily concealable medium. MARS programs and programs for other purposes, such as word processing, can be downloaded to the hard disk over the network. Where it is desirable to display images as well as text, the work station will be equipped with a second, high-resolution monitor and an AT&T TARGA video display adapter board. Currently, diagnostic images in 512×512 pixel digital form can be displayed in approximately 4 seconds in 32,768 shades of gray or 4096 simultaneous colors. Though the configuration described above would be best for clinical settings, MARS can also be used from most existing microcomputers and terminals. The AT&T TARGA adapter can be used with most IBM-compatible microcomputers.

We have also been exploring a free-standing work station that could be used to deliver subsets of MARS data without necessarily being connected to MARS. This work station uses an inexpensive optical disk drive to hold data and binaries. Currently, the disks can store about 1/4 of a gigabyte (billion bytes). However, our drives can soon be enhanced to quadruple that storage capacity, to a full gigabyte of storage. With MARS software and the optical disk drive, enormous amounts of medical information could be made available anywhere that a microcomputer can be run. For example, the entire MEDLINE database could be stored on 9 of the enhanced optical disks. The MARS natural language interface (LEXX) and Boolean search utilities can be used on a free-standing work station to perform interactive full-text or field-specific searches on the MEDLINE references and abstracts. This capability has already been demonstrated on our current configuration, an AT&T 6300+ with an AT&T TARGA video display adapter and an NHance 244 megabyte optical disk drive. A similar Zenith work station, with hard disk storage instead of optical storage, will soon be deployed in the libraries of several Pennsylvania mental health facilities to allow local searching of the holdings of the Library of the Western Psychiatric Institute and Clinic.

In a variation on this concept, two clusters of AT&T and Zenith 80286 microcomputers have been installed in the Falk Library of the Health Sciences and the Library of the Western Psychiatric Institute and Clinic. These clusters will use Starlan local area networks to share data locally on optical disk drives. The LANs will also be connected to the MARS central systems through Starlan.

3.4. Network Management

Managing a distributed network is complex, but involves only a few basic tasks. These tasks are (1) allocating resources correctly to meet demand, and (2) managing local servers—down-loading the appropriate database subset and mapping users to the appropriate "home" local server. We are currently developing a pair of expert systems that will work together to perform these tasks. Figure 4.5 shows how these systems—ARIADNE, the Intelligent system Controller and JANUS, the network resource manager—will interact.

The ARIADNE expert system will run in the MARS central processor and will govern both the gathering and the distribution operations. In data collection, its primary responsibility will be to schedule and carry out communication with the various devices from which MARS data will come. In distribution, its responsibility will be to allocate network resources.

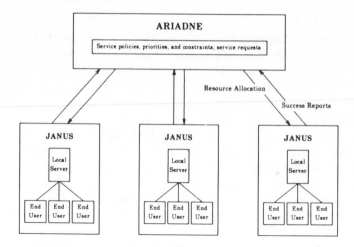

Figure 4.5. Automated Network Control.

ARIADNE will base its resource allocation decisions on two data streams. The first, relatively static stream will be composed of top-down considerations for network management. We expect, for example, to include University service priorities and policies, University Health Center subunit priorities and policies, financial and physical constraints, and specific requests for scheduled services in this data stream. The second stream will be composed of bottom-up utilization information: reports from JANUS processes on the success or failure of current resource allocations.

JANUS processes will be invoked by the ARIADNE system to carry out specific allocations of resources. A JANUS process will configure local servers and work stations with appropriate database subsets and MARS software, and it will connect users with the local server that has been designated to serve them. JANUS processes will also have the intelligence to carry out resource reallocation within the limited resources assigned to them. For example, we want a JANUS process to be able to correct a situation in which 52 users have been connected to one local server, while another server that has the same or a related database subset has fewer than average users. JANUS processes will report asynchronously to the ARIADNE system on their success or failure in carrying out a resource allocation and on utilization levels.

The two underlying objectives of ARIADNE and JANUS development are, first, largely to automate the management of the complex, parallel-processing MARS network, removing the need for an elaborate central monitoring effort by human operators. Secondly, ARIADNE and JANUS are to provide the MARS system with flexibility by allowing rapid reallocation of resources in the network. As top down service policies and constraints change or bottom-up utilization data comes in, the network will automatically respond with changes in resource allocations.

In preparation for ARIADNE and JANUS, we are configuring all of the various UNIX systems in our network to present a single-system image; our intelligent controller will not have to sense differences between one system and another. Tools have been provided that allow a user on one system to remotely execute commands on another. These tools are currently used to strip and then reconfigure our systems for tests or demonstrations of MARS components. Using network links to download and execute binaries does not take significantly longer than it would to load and execute a program from local disk storage.

120

We are also working on a technique for providing automatic multi-threading across systems in MARS processes. In effect, this software will make the MARS network operate as if it were a single very large multiprocessor. A process running in one system will be able to invoke a server process in another system that has a resource needed by the first process. ARIADNE and JANUS will control where resources are located, and hence, which constellation of systems will be used by a multi-threading process. The C code that implements this technique has already been written and tested. Converting existing MARS programs to use the multi-threading code will not be difficult; essentially, it will only be necessary to recompile the programs with the new multi-threading library. To make optimal use of this technology, the subgoal and subtask structure of our software will have to be evaluated and fully specified.

4. Implementing MARS

MARS is currently moving from laboratory systems into its initial deployment. Electronic medical records service, initially emphasizing textual information, is about to begin for the Medical Records Office of the Presbyterian-University Hospital and the University of Pittsburgh Epilepsy Center. A new central processor and an optical disk jukebox will soon be installed. This section describes the hardware and software configurations of the MARS system and reviews medium- and long-term plans for deploying MARS.

4.1. Physical Configuration

Figures 4.6 and 4.7 show the physical environment in which the MARS system will be prototyped. Figure 4.6 illustrates the central data processing network of the MARS system as it will appear when our AT&T 3B2/600 is installed (installation is expected to be completed by early 1988). This central data processing configuration will satisfy MARS requirements for about 3 years. At the end of that time, the final MARS configuration will be brought online. The final configuration will employ orders of magnitude more optical storage and possibly a larger MARS computer, replacing the AT&T 3B2/600 shown in the illustration. Figure 4.7 illustrates the Starlan networks in which we will test the distributed processing techniques to be used in the full MARS network. As Figure 4.6 shows, two Starlan networks—comprised of up to 32 microcomputers—will be running in the near future.

4.2. The MARS Central Data Processing Network

The architecture of the MARS central data processing network is shown in Figure 4.6, on the next page. When the "MARS" AT&T 3B2/600 is installed (within the next two months), the network will consist of nine UNIX systems in a TCP/IP network. As the figure shows, there are several satellites of the main system, including Starlan networks of AT&T and Zenith microcomputers in the Falk and WPIC libraries. Up to 32 microcomputers may be linked to the central network through Starlan local area networks and/or fiberoptic network links. (The final number of microcomputers in the Starlan networks depends on purchasing decisions that are still being made.)

The network will be organized around a central file server which will provide 5 gigabytes of hard disk storage. That storage will soon be augmented by the 100 to 200 gigabyte optical disk jukebox discussed in previous sections.

The 3B2/600 will perform most data collection, indexing, and encapsulation. The other systems in the network will be used flexibly to assist the 3B2/600, to support software development

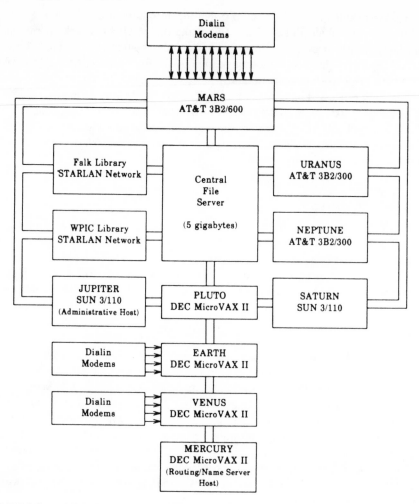

Figure 4.6. MARS Central Data Processing Network.

and thesaurus construction, and to support services such as the electronic mail service provided by the Office of Biomedical Informatics.

The MARS central network as it is now constituted can support initial phases of MARS deployment. There is sufficient computational power to archive the entire daily information output of the University Health Center and to distribute textual information to a significant number of simultaneous users. The network is robust; service to users can continue even if a system fails. Because of the redundancy of systems in the network many functions and hardware resources of a failed system can be switched to another of the same type. There will be sufficient storage, when the 200 gigabyte optical disk jukebox is added, to hold all textual information that will be delivered by MARS. As importantly, the present central network provides a very good test bed for the distributed processing and automated network control strategies upon which full MARS deployment depends.

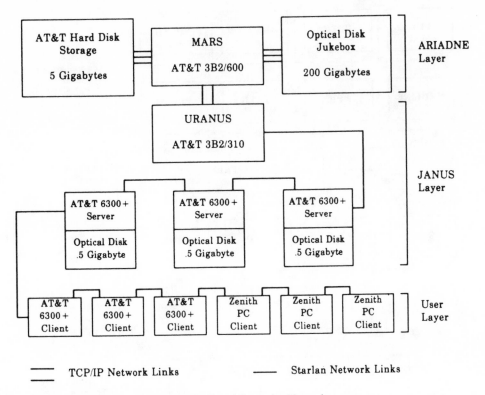

Figure 4.7. Test Configuration for the MARS Distributed Processing Network.

Figure 4.7 illustrates the configuration with which we will test the MARS distributed processing software and hardware. The local server and end user layers of the MARS network will be simulated in a Starlan network. Under the control of ARIADNE and JANUS processes running in MARS central data processors, appropriate retrieval software will be loaded from optical disk storage into Starlan server microcomputers. Users at client microcomputers will be mapped into the correct server using the multi-threading software described earlier in this report.

4.3. MARS Software

4.3.1. Overview

Figure 4.8 lists the twenty MARS modules by type. Since ARIADNE and JANUS, the resource management modules, have been described in earlier sections, this portion of the Plan will focus on current applications of the MARS database software, on the MARS query modules, and on the expert systems that will be integrated into MARS.

More than half of the MARS modules shown in the figure are either already in beta test or will soon be in beta test at sites in the University Health Center.

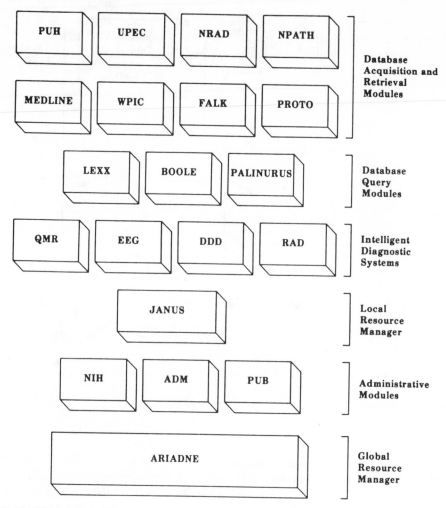

Figure 4.8. MARS Modules by Type.

Briefly, the "Database Acquisition and Retrieval Modules" are the eight current applications of the MARS database software. The applications fall into three major categories:

1. Electronic medical records databases (PUH, UPEC, and PROTO). These modules, for managing Presbyterian-University Hospital records, University of Pittsburgh Epilepsy Center records, and the Epilepsy Center surgical database, respectively, are the initial instantiations of the electronic medical records portion of the MARS archive.
2. Bibliographic databases (WPIC and FALK online card catalogs, local MEDLINE retrieval). The WPIC module will shortly be exported to several area mental health institutions to provide local searching of the holdings of the WPIC Library. The MEDLINE module will shortly be deployed to supplement and eventually replace the costly dial-up MEDLINE services currently used by the University Health Center libraries.

or ISN links or through the TCP/IP - SNA bridge to the Presbyterian-University Hospital HIS computer. Some records, notably some recent discharge summaries, will be digitized by the Office of Biomedical Informatics. Records will be parsed with the generalized parsing utility of the MARS database software. This utility can be configured to accept any consistent record format used by the word processing departments.

The PUH module also provides routines for managing laboratory results obtained from the HIS systems of the University Health Center. Display utilities for this data currently allow the user to select up to six lab values for simultaneous numeric display. The utilities also allow the user to step backward and forward through "snapshots" of the selected lab values. For example, a user could step through displays of lab values obtained within the same six hour periods to review changes in values over time.

Lab and physiologic data will be collected across the TCP/IP - SNA bridge as enhanced order-entry, results-reporting HIS systems come online. Both the IBM 3081-GX system maintained by Presbyterian-University Hospital, and the VAX 8200 system maintained by Falk Clinic will be used for order entry and results reporting. Laboratory data and information from management modules, such as pharmacy and nursing, will be obtained from these systems by emulating IBM remote job entry sites and results reporting terminals. Software simulating a standing order for all results will be developed. This information will be encapsulated in the MARS database structures as it arrives.

Software will be developed to generate PUH electronic medical records in a format that can be read by the HIS systems. This software will enable MARS to provide archive retrieval services to users of the HIS systems as well as to users in the MARS network.

The UPEC module, which will be in use in early 1988, is an electronic medical record program for the University of Pittsburgh Epilepsy Center (UPEC). All UPEC patients are evaluated according to well defined protocols. Extensive databases consisting of textual reports, data, and diagnostic images are collected on every patient. This database is ideal for defining the form of electronic medical records because it contains examples of all types of medical information. Furthermore, portions of the database are already stored on hard disk in the Decision Systems Laboratory. Electronic medical records in formats defined by the Medical Records/Clinical Facilities Task Force will be written to optical disk cassettes. These records will contain digital images as well as text and data, and will be accessed from personal computers equipped with optical disk drives located in the UPEC clinic.

The PROTO module provides specialized software for maintaining and displaying data in keyword databases such as the Epilepsy Center's surgical database.

4.3.2.2. NPATH and NRAD: Electronic Textbooks

Three teaching collections are being computerized as part of the MARS project. These collections will function as a form of online reference that might best be termed an electronic textbook.

The first, labeled NPATH, is the neuroanatomy collection of Dr. John Moossy. A total of 16,000 slides of gross and microscopic neuroanatomy have been pressed on a videodisk. The MARS database management software is being used to annotate and access the images on this videodisk. Dr. Moossy and staff members of the Office of Biomedical Informatics are editing the collection, using MARS utilities to associate indexing keywords, extensive commentaries, and literature references with each image.

The second, labeled NRAD, is the neuroradiology collection of Dr. Richard Latchaw. The 20,000 images in this collection are being recorded digitally in the Office of Biomedical Informatics. We are using a high-resolution video camera and the AT&T TARGA digital recording adapter to capture images directly from film. The TARGA adapter, running in an AT&T 6300+ microcomputer, is able to digitize an image at 512×512 pixels in 1/30 of a second. As the images are entered, MARS utilities are being used to associate demographic and diagnostic information and teaching commentary with the images.

TARGA technology will be used to computerize a third collection as well, the pathology collection of Dr. Robert Lee. Dr. Howard Seltman will prepare this collection for use as course material for pathology. We will use a free-standing microcomputer equipped with an optical disk reader to deliver this collection at a site that is convenient for the pathology students and faculty.

Before the collections are put in service, natural language search capabilities will be added. Concurrently with the mastering of the collections, we have been developing neuropathology and neuroradiology thesauri. These thesauri each have about 8,000 terms and 40,000 semantic links at this time. They will allow us to use the LEXX expert system to index the collections, and end users will be able to use LEXX as a natural language interface to the collections.

Additionally, we plan to associate images in the collections with the original medical records from which they were extracted as our electronic medical records processing comes on line. Removing identifying information from the records so that they can be included in the collections will be straightforward. Similarly, subsets of the MEDLINE database can be associated with the collections.

4.3.2.3. WPIC, FALK, and MEDLINE: Bibliographic Reference Modules

The WPIC and FALK modules use the MARS software to make online card catalogs available in the Falk Library of the Health Sciences and the Library of the Western Psychiatric Institute and Clinic (WPIC). FALK has more than 220,000 books in its collection, and receives 2,500 current Periodicals. The WPIC library is noted as one of the finest psychiatric libraries in the nation. Data for these modules is obtained directly from digital tapes of the library holdings, so the database can be refreshed periodically.

WPIC has a support relationship with several state mental health institutions in Pennsylvania. Microcomputers are being purchased so that the WPIC system can be made available in the libraries of these institutions. The system will be used to provide a low-cost, convenient way for these institutions to search the holdings of the WPIC library.

The MEDLINE project is designed for the dual purpose of field testing major components of the MARS system, and providing local MEDLINE services for the University. The MEDLINE tapes will be leased from the National Library of Medicine. A large subset of the tapes will be mounted on optical disk drives, and delivered to users through Starlan networks. The database management software of the MARS system will be used for searching the database. At the same time, the MEDLINE database will be divided into logical groups of approximately 20–50,000 references. These data subsets will be associated with classes of users, as described earlier in this report. The reference sets will be prepared for delivery on personal computers using either hard disks or optical cassettes. If successful, this will provide users with instant access to 20–50,000 medical references from personal computers. With a set of optical cassettes, a single personal computer could provide access to hundreds of thousands of bibliographic references.

4.3.3. The MARS Query System: LEXX, BOOLE, and PALINURUS Modules

LEXX, as described in previous sections, has double duty in the MARS system. It automatically indexes incoming medical data. It also provides a natural language interface, capable of mapping free English requests into appropriate keywords from a controlled vocabulary.

LEXX is based upon a natural language processing system developed by Peretz Shoval in his 1981 doctoral dissertation. The key property of the system designed by Shoval is that concepts expressed in free English could be mapped to specific keywords from a controlled vocabulary. To find these keywords, terms found in the request were expanded along narrower-than links in a semantic network constructed from a thesaurus of terms. The system obeyed a fundamental principle of bibliographic searching: that only specific applicable keywords from a controlled vocabulary should be used in a search. The system enabled users who were unskilled in bibliographic searching to conduct highly precise searches of bibliographically-indexed databases. Shoval's system applied this property in a small system using a limited thesaurus of business terms.

The LEXX expert system uses new coding, algorithms, and thesaurus construction techniques, and applies the property found by Shoval both to interpreting user requests and to indexing incoming medical information.

As a natural language interface, LEXX can help users translate an abstract notion of the information they would like to the specific keywords that will retrieve relevant data. Requests can be entered in free English, using relatively non-technical terms that are known to such users as medical students or medical librarians.

For example, the request list cognitive and sensory disorders finds five diseases related to both cognitive and sensory disorder, which are listed in the table below. Even when it is operated with a thesaurus that is only partially complete, LEXX can be used as an effective exploratory tool for developing searches for medical information.

Rank Ordered List of Search Terms

```
1.# = = = = = > #AUDITORY-IMPERCEPTION#3
2.# = = = = = > #DEVELOPMENTAL-RECEPTIVE-DYSPHASIA#3
3.# = = = = = > #CENTRAL DEAFNESS#3
4.# = = = = = > #CONGENITAL-WORD-DEAFNESS#3
5.# = = = = = > #CONGENITAL-WORD-BLINDNESS#3
```

The numbers at the end of the entries indicate that the terms are semantically "narrower-than" all of the key terms in the information request, and are appropriate search terms for disorders relating to both sensory and cognitive deficits. Additional search terms related to either cognitive disturbance or sensory disturbance were also found.

The request inflammatory diseases of the spine and peripheral nervous system results in the following useful search terms:

Rank Ordered List of Search Terms

```
1.# = = = = = > #ACUTE-ASCENDING-SPINAL-PARALYSIS#3
2.# = = = = = > #INFLAMMATORY-SPINE-DISEASE#3
3.# = = = = = > #SPINAL-ARACHNOIDITIS#3
4.# = = = = = > #SPONDYLITIS#3
5.# = = = = = > #ANKYLOSING-SPONDYLITIS#3
```

As an indexing system, LEXX processes medical texts and selects a set of terms that specifically indicate the topics of the text. These terms are then used as the indexing keywords associated with the text. The terms are drawn from one of a set of thesauri of medical terms.

The neuropathology report and table below show actual results of a test of LEXX automated indexing. LEXX processed the full text of the report and produced the terms shown in the table as the highest ranking index terms for the material in the report. The neuropathology report is from a patient with leukemia who died from an intracerebral hemorrhage secondary to a leukemia induced coagulation disorder.

Neuropathology Report

Microscopic examination of the cns sections reveals the following. The cerebral cortex and basal ganglia demonstrate recent subarachnoid hemorrhage and an extensive meningeal infiltration by leukemic cells. In addition cerebral edema and multiple extensive leukemic infiltrates of the white matter are noted. There is diffuse anoxic and ischemic changes noted. The leukemia cells disclose the same characteristics as in all systemic organs. These cells are immature myeloid. The spinal cord and cerebellum demonstrate minimal to modest subarachnoid hemorrhage associated with meningeal infiltration by similar blast cells. This infiltration is also seen between the folia. There is autolytic change noted in the cerebellum. Edema and mild ischemic changes of anterior born neurons is seen within the cord. Intracerebral hemorrhage multiple acute secondary to leukemia acute myelogenous. Minimal subarachnoid hemorrhage temporal lobes brainstem spinal cord. Cerebral edema brain weight 1,560 grams. The leukemic infiltrate is extensive and is that clinically seen in leukemia phases when the white count is greater than 300,000 thousand. This level of white count leads to disruption of the poorly supported cerebral vessels and subsequent subarachnoid hemorrhage even in the face of an adequate platelet count. No opportunistic infections were noted. Selected coronal sections of the cerebral hemispheres.

Rank Ordered List of Index Terms

1. #NERVOUS-SYSTEM#RANK = = >#44
2. #CENTRAL-NERVOUS-SYSTEM#RANK = = >#43
3. #CEREBELLUM#RANK = = >#7
4. #LEUKEMIA#RANK = = >#6
5. #INTRACEREBRAL-HEMORRHAGE#RANK = = >#6
6. #SPINAL-CORD#RANK = = >#6
7. #CEREBRAL-EDEMA#RANK = = >#6
8. #ISCHEMIA#RANK = = >#5
9. #TELENCEPHALON#RANK = = >#5
10. #BRAIN-STEM#RANK = = >#5
11. #CEREBRAL-HEMISPHERE#RANK = = >#5
12. #BASAL-GANGLIA#RANK = = >#5
13. #CEREBRAL-CORTEX#RANK = = >#5
14. #WHITE-MATTER#RANK = = >#5
15. #MENINGES#RANK = = >#5
16. #SECONDARY-HEMORRHAGE#RANK = = >#5

At this time, we are constructing four LEXX thesauri, averaging 6,000 terms and 30,000 semantic links. The three largest thesauri each approach 8,000 terms and 40,000 links. An NLM R01 grant to continue construction of the thesauri and further develop LEXX has been approved. One end product of the grant will be a merged thesaurus allowing indexing of any material pertaining to the clinical neurosciences. The ultimate goal, which we believe will be attainable through automated thesaurus construction, will be a thesaurus covering all of the medical sciences.

It appears to be feasible to automate much of the construction of the LEXX thesauri. Our psychiatry thesaurus derives its terms from the MeSH headings used to index the MEDLINE database. We will complete the thesaurus, so that it includes all 14,000 MeSH headings. We will then select the 20 to 50 journals that authoritatively define a particular medical specialty and process the last 10 years of each journal with LEXX and the MeSH thesaurus. The top 10,000 to 20,000 terms (by frequency of use) found in the journals will constitute a complete and current thesaurus of the terms used in that specialty. Broader-than and narrower-than semantic links will be found by looking up the terms in the MeSH hierarchy. Morphological variations will be found by looking up the terms in a dictionary. The result will be an entirely automated thesaurus containing keywords, variations, and narrower-than and broader-than semantic links. Further manual work will be required to add synonyms and the "associated-with" and "perspective" semantic links that we have included in our thesauri.

LEXX has recently been ported from our MicroVAX II and Sun development systems to a microcomputer. The microcomputer, an AT&T 6300+, successfully compiled the LEXX software and built the largest of our thesauri, the neuropathology thesaurus of 8,000 terms and 40,000 semantic links. Performance on the 6300+ proved to be entirely acceptable for interactive use, even on unconstrained searches such as "brain disease."

The BOOLE module is the collection of Boolean search utilities that are used for all information retrieval in MARS. AND, OR, and NOT searches are supported, as well as a relational query language. With the relational query language, any parenthetic search request using a valid combination of AND, OR, and NOT expressions can be executed. Docsets containing the results of previous searches can be incorporated in a query. Keywords suggested by LEXX can also be referenced by number in DBASE queries issued from within LEXX. For example, the expression "(au:einstein & (abs:relativity | abs:relativistic))" would, given a suitable database, yield bibliographic references that have "Einstein" in the author field and the words "relativity" or "relativistic" in the abstract. The query language will be modified to accept input directly from LEXX, and will be mated with the PALINURUS coaching system.

4.3.3.1. The PALINURUS Interface Assistant

The MARS system will be used by a wide variety of users, most of them with limited experience in using computers. It will not be easily possible to train all users, and the problem will be complicated by the high turnover in some categories of University Health Center employees. MARS hardcopy documentation will be designed for concision and ease of use. To prevent its loss, the documentation will be attached in some way to MARS workstations. However, even the best documentation in the world will not allow inexperienced users to learn how to use MARS as rapidly and easily as we require. In the PALINURUS module, we will use expert system technology to try to solve the problem of making a complex system easily available to end users.

Usually, programs in large-system environments have been adapted for use by novice computer users with a combination of two strategies. The first strategy is to provide a navigational system for users, often a panel-driven or graphic interface. Panel-driven interfaces do not usually require much computational power to run, but they don't discriminate between experienced and inexperienced users. All users must proceed through the panels of the interface. Both panel and graphic interfaces are poor vehicles for complex services, such as MARS cross-field Boolean searches. Frequently, only a subset of a program's capabilities can be made available through a panel or graphic interface; to use advanced functions, users must learn to use a second interface. The second strategy is to subset the function provided by a program. In this strategy, an attempt is made to restrict the user in some way to the relatively simple functions that may be needed by most users most of the time. Subsetting a program's capabilities makes the program easier to document and simplifies training, but again, users may have a difficult time learning to use advanced functions of a program. Neither of these strategies entirely responds to the needs of an entirely naive user who simply wants to get something done. These users, who are the users that MARS must serve, must make a detour—to a help system or documentation—before they can use a program to perform their task. Users are, however, goal-oriented; they are more likely to experiment and quit in frustration than to turn aside from their goal to consult documentation. Interfaces may give some useful feedback in the form of error messages. However, these are notoriously curt and obscure; usually, the user must turn to message documentation for help.

MARS will use a third strategy to make itself easily accessible to users. That is, the MARS system itself will coach users who are having difficulty with the system. An expert system, the PALINURUS module, will monitor user inputs. If an error occurs, the system will attempt to diagnose the error and will offer instructions and examples for correcting it. If a simple syntactical error has occurred, such as a missing parenthesis, the system will display the corrected command and ask if it should be executed. There are several advantages to this approach. Firstly, the system does not penalize experienced users to help novices; experienced users will not see the coaching system unless they make an error. Secondly, there is only one command language for all users. Novices will not have to learn a new grammar when they learn how to make more sophisticated requests for information. Most importantly, novices do not have to take any action—such as invoking a help system—to get assistance. The system responds constructively to any input, correct or incorrect, that is given to it. An expert system monitoring commands will use more computational power than a panel-driven interface. However, the incremental cost in power will not be large. When correct requests are entered, there will be no additional cost: the expert system will be invoked only if the request is not intelligible. The bulk of the expert system's processing will involve pattern matching, which can be performed very rapidly. We expect that the expert system will be able to run in MARS microcomputer work stations, so that no computational burden will fall on the local server or central data processing machines of the MARS network.

At first, the expert system will only discriminate among a few major types of incorrect input. Its assistance will be restricted to offering brief instructions and correct examples. We will elaborate the system through the protocol analyses that are planned for the MARS interface. As we learn more about the errors that users make, we will incorporate more sophisticated logic and more precise coaching into the system. The goal will be to produce a fully generalized input monitor that can be configured to assist users of any program.

4.3.4. Medical Expert Systems: QMR, EEG, DDD, RAD

QMR, EEG, DDD, and RAD are expert systems that are to be made available to clinicians through the MARS system. All four systems are being developed at the University of Pittsburgh.

QMR is a general-purpose internal medicine diagnostic system, operating with the one of the most comprehensive computerized internal medicine knowledge bases in existence. It is the most recent enhancement of the INTERNIST-1 program, and is being developed by Dr. Randolph

A. Miller and the Section for Medical Informatics of the School of Medicine. QMR retains the basic function of INTERNIST-1: evaluating a set of manifestations and patient demographics and producing a differential diagnosis. QMR adds the capacity to explore manifestations and differential diagnoses in interactive sessions. A user will be able to ask for information about a particular illness or manifestation, and can ask for the system's reasoning in including or excluding an illness from a differential diagnosis.

EEG provides interfaces to the EEGs used by the University of Pittsburgh Epilepsy Center, and will be used to digitize multiple channels of analog EEG data in real time for analysis and inclusion in patients' electronic medical records. Intelligent analysis capabilities will be added to this system as well.

The DDD, or Data-Driven Decision-making expert system will be an automated system for monitoring physiologic and laboratory data in real time. Its expert system will be able to give warnings when danger signs appear in physiologic or lab data. It will also analyze the indications and suggest underlying causes and ameliorative courses of action.

The RAD neuro-imaging expert system is a tool for neuroradiologists and neurosurgeons. RAD has direct interfaces to the GE CT and MRI scanners in use at the University Health Center. From CT or MRI scans, the system is capable of generating arbitrary two dimensional images. A lesion can be visualized, for example, in any projection that a user wishes to see. The system can also generate 3-dimensional views of brain structures from stacks of CT or MRI slices. Utilities have been provided for manipulating images: patient images can be merged with or compared to models from a stereotaxic atlas or the MARS archives using Boolean AND, OR, or NOT operations.

At its current stage of development, RAD is an image management system, allowing users to manipulate patient images, images from a computerized stereotaxic atlas, and images from the MARS archives. Pattern recognition-capabilities and a diagnostic expert system are to be added to the system so that it can aid in interpretation of CT and MRI scans.

4.4. Electronic Mail, Educational, and Support Services

In addition to producing an archival system for medical information, the Office of Biomedical Informatics has major responsibilities for preparing the University Health Center community for a transition to electronic management of medical information.

The Office is currently providing a rapidly expanding electronic mail service which has immediate productivity benefits and also provides an important vehicle for increasing computer literacy. Selective database services using MARS software are being started, and a variety of classes, manuals, and educational materials for electronic mail and the MARS software are being prepared.

There are currently 100 electronic mail users on the system, from diverse groups including the staffs of the Falk and WPIC Libraries, the Center for Medical Ethics, the Neuropathology Laboratory, the University of Pittsburgh Epilepsy Center, and the Section for Medical Informatics. The number of users will shortly be expanded to 250 users to include most members of the IAIMS planning Task Forces. Our goal is to provide electronic mail and database services to 1000 users, spread throughout the University Health Center, at the end of 18 months.

To educate the eventual prime users of the MARS system, plans are being laid to add the first year classes of the Medical School and the School of Nursing during 1988. Within three years, all students and staff in these schools will be served by the Biomedical Informatics systems.

The National Library of Medicine has recently approved an IAIMS grant request submitted by the Office of Biomedical Informatics for funding of an IAIMS educational program. The coordinator of the program will work with the Office of Biomedical Informatics to put in place a complete educational program for users of the MARS system.

4.5. Conversion from LISP to C

Originally, the MARS software was written largely in the LISP language. Most MARS software has now been converted to the C language. This conversion has resulted in much faster operation and has extended our ability to run on microcomputers.

Much of the improvement in performance stems from the opportunity that C provides to optimize system management functions. For example, we have been able to implement explicit paging schemes to reference the large databases that MARS programs use. These paging mechanisms are much less costly in terms of code size and speed than the fully generalized paging mechanisms provided in LISP environments. Additionally, garbage collection, a lengthy process in LISP environments, now requires only that pointers to free storage buffers be set back to zero. Perhaps most significantly, the C implementation dispenses with most of the alphanumeric string comparisons that had to be performed in the LISP versions of MARS software. By translating terms into 16 bit digits in a data dictionary, LEXX processing, for example, can be done as numeric comparisons. Since 16 bit manipulation is the native mode for many microcomputers, LEXX and the Boolean search utilities of the database management modules run on these systems with little unnecessary overhead. While we have not yet developed satisfactory benchmarks for comparing performance in LISP and C, we estimate that we have attained a 10-fold increase in execution speed.

As MARS development proceeds, we will implement a caching strategy and register variables to further increase the execution speed and compactness of the MARS code.

4.6. Implementation Schedule

4.6.1. Near-Term Plans—1988 to 1990

The developmental efforts for this two year period will be directed toward consolidation of the MARS software and toward preparation of the University Health Center population for the transition to computerized medical information management.

Software development will be completed and modules will be taken through several cycles of beta testing to improve interfaces and functionality. Modules will also be thoroughly documented. Thesauri will be extensively developed to provide full natural language interface and automated indexing capabilities. In selected areas, depending on resources, clinical services will be extended. A major effort will be directed toward integrating the operational MARS modules with the upgraded versions of the Presbyterian and Falk information systems.

The electronic mail system will extended to 1,000 users, the full complement that we expect to serve with the MARS system. In association with the IAIMS educational coordinator, computer literacy and MARS-specific training programs and documentation will be prepared.

4.6.2. Medium and Long-Term Plans—1990 to 1992

During the last two years of the MARS project, the full scale system will be implemented for text and data. Modules that incorporate images into the electronic medical record will be deployed. Medical diagnostic support modules such as QMR and RAD will be brought on line as part of the system. Prototype systems providing data driven decision making in the style of the HELP system (the DDD module) will be incorporated into the central processing units of the MARS system. A new five-year plan will be formulated to continue this work.

Glossary[1]

Access time: The total time required to find, retrieve, and display data after initiation of a retrieval command. Access time is usually measured at its worst, or the longest possible time it takes to get from one section of the medium (tape, disc, disk) to another. This is generally a matter of minutes on videotape, two or fewer seconds on videodisc or CD, and milliseconds or microseconds on a computer.

Analog: The representation of numerical values by physical variables such as voltage, current, etc. Information which steadily flows and changes. Continuously variable quantities whose values are analogous to the quantitative magnitude of the variables. Since the information carried is steadily flowing and continually changing, there is commonly some degradation in fidelity when broadcasting, recording, or subsequently rerecording an analog signal. This is caused in large part by the electrical circuits that it is sent through. Electrical "noise" weakens and distorts the signal. Analog devices are characterized by dials and sliding mechanisms.

Analog video: A video signal that represents an infinite number of smooth gradations between given video levels. By contrast, a digital video signal assigns a finite set of levels.

Authoring language: A specialized, high-level, plain-English computer language which permits non-programmers to perform the programming function of courseware development. The program logic and program content are combined. Generally provides fewer capabilities or options than an authoring system.

Authoring system: Specialized computer software which helps its users design interactive courseware in everyday language, without the painstaking detail of computer programming. In an authoring system, the instructional logic and instructional content are separate. Allows greater flexibility in courseware design than an authoring language.

Bandwidth: The range of signal frequencies that a piece of audio or video equipment can encode or decode; the difference between the limiting frequencies of a continuous frequency band. Video uses higher frequency than audio, thus requires a wider bandwidth.

CAV: Constant Angular Velocity. A mode of videodisc playback in which a disc rotates at a constant speed, regardless of the position of the reading head or stylus. Thus, each frame is separately addressable. In optical videodisc technology, each track contains two video fields that comprise one complete video frame. CAV discs revolve continuously at 1,800 rpm (NTSC) or 1,500 rpm (PAL), one revolution per frame. Program time is 30 minutes per side on a 12" disc, 14 minutes per side on an 8" disc. All VHD discs run in CAV, at 900 rpm (NTSC) and 750 rpm (PAL). Each track contains four fields (i.e., two frames). All transmissive optical videodiscs are also formatted for CAV play.

CD-ROM: See compact disc-read only memory.

CD-ROM drive or CD-ROM player: A device that retrieves data from a disc pressed in the CD-ROM format. Differs from a standard audio compact disc player by the incorporation of additional error correction circuitry. Often lacks the necessary D/A converter to play music from standard compact discs.

CED format: The CED (capacitance electronic disc) system has grooved media and uses a stylus in physical contact with the disc surface, reading capacitance signals embedded on the disc. Developed for the consumer marketplace by RCA under the trade name SelectaVision; abandoned by RCA in 1984.

Chapter: One independent, self-contained segment of a computer program or interactive video program.

Chapter search: A function of most videodisc players which allows specific chapters to be accessed by chapter number.

Clean room: An equipment room in a videodisc or compact disc pressing plant that is maintained virtually dust-free to reduce particle contamination of discs during the mastering and replication process.

CLV: Constant Linear Velocity, an alternative format for reflective optical videodiscs. CLV (or "extended-play") discs allow twice as much play time (up to one hour) per side, but many of the user-control capabilities of the CAV format are forfeited (e.g., no still-framing is possible). The CLV disc can be read in linear play only, but can provide chapter search capability.

With CLV videodiscs, the revolution speed varies with the location of the pickup to ensure a constant data rate. CLV optical videodiscs vary in speed from 1800 rpm at the inner track to 600 rpm at the outer edge. Program time is 60 minutes per side (12″ disc) or 20 minutes per side (8″ disc).

All compact discs are played in CLV mode.

Combi-player or combination player: A single player that can accommodate a variety of disc formats. Units currently available can play 8″ and 12″ videodiscs as well as 4.75″ compact discs and CD Videos.

Compact disc (CD) or compact audio disc: A 4.75″ (12 cm) optical disc that contains information (usually musical) encoded digitally in the CLV format. Popular format for high fidelity music, offering 90 dB signal/noise ratio, 74 minutes of digital sound, and no degradation of quality from playback.

The standards for this format (developed by NV Philips and Sony Corporation) are known as the Red Book. The official (and rarely-used) designation for the audio-only format is CD-DA (compact disc-digital audio). The simple audio format is also known as CD-A (compact disc-audio). A smaller (3″) version of the CD is known as CD-3.

Compact disc + graphics (CD+G): A CD format which includes extended graphics capabilities as written into the original CD-ROM specifications. Includes limited video graphics encoded into the CD subcode area. Developed and marketed by Warner New Media.

Compact disc-interactive (CD-I): Under development. A compact disc format (scheduled for release in 1989) which will provide audio, digital data, still graphics, and limited motion video.

The standards for this format (developed by NV Philips and Sony Corporation) are known as the Green Book.

Compact disc-read-only memory (CD-ROM): A 4.75″ laser-encoded optical memory storage medium with the same constant linear velocity (CLV) spiral format as compact audio discs and some videodiscs. CD-ROMs can hold up to 600 megabytes of data or the equivalent of 200,000 typed pages.

CD-ROMs require additional error-correction information than the standard prerecorded compact audio disc. The standards for this format (developed by NV Philips and Sony Corporation) are known as the Yellow Book.

Compact disc-video (CDV or CD Video): A CD format introduced in 1987 that combines 20 minutes of digital audio and six minutes of analog video on a standard 4.75″ compact disc. Since its introduction, many firms have renamed 8″ and 12″ videodiscs as CDV, capitalizing on the consumer popularity of the compact audio disc.

Compact videodisc (CVD): Under development. An analog/digital hybrid capable of delivering interactive mixed-media applications. Can deliver either 10 (CLV) or 20 (CAV) minutes of full motion video. Developed by SOCS Research, licensed by Mattel for toy and other applications. Originally known as interactive compact videodisc (ICVD).

Comprehension verification: An interactive technique in which the viewer's comprehension of what has been seen is tested before the viewer may proceed through the program. Absent a correct response, the viewer is either looped back through the same material or branched off to a different set of materials. If correct, the viewer may proceed through the program.

Compress: To reduce certain parameters of a signal while preserving the basic information content. Compressing usually reduces a parameter such as amplitude or duration of the signal to improve overall transmission efficiency and to reduce cost.

Compressed audio: A method of digitally encoding and decoding up to 40 seconds of voice-quality audio per individual disc frame, resulting in a potential for over 150 hours of audio per 12″ videodisc. By using a buffer to store the audio information, a limited amount of audio may be delivered to accompany a still-frame image. Also known as still-frame audio.

Compressed video: A video image or segment that has been digitally processed using a variety of computer algorithms and other techniques to reduce the amount of data required to accurately represent the content—and thus, the space required to store that content.

Courseware: Instructional software, including all discs, tapes, books, charts, and computer programs necessary to deliver a complete instructional module or course.

Delivery system: The set of video and computer equipment actually used to deliver the interactive video program. A delivery system may comprise as little as a videodisc player with on-board microprocessor, a monitor, and a keypad—or may extend to an external computer, two or more monitors, and a variety of peripherals.

Density: The closeness of space or data distribution on a storage medium, e.g., a magnetic drum, magnetic tape, optical disc, or CRT. The higher the density, the higher the resolution—or more compact the storage.

Diagnostic-prescriptive model: An interactive technique, using the results from an assessment of the students' knowledge, interests, and/or abilities to affect the instruction which follows. The process is cyclic; the student leaves the cycle when an assessment shows that all of the goals of the lesson have been met.

Dialog or dialogue: An exchange of information between human operator and the program/technology. The term is mostly used to infer a continuing interactive response between both operator and program/technology.

Digital: A method of signal representation by a set of discrete numerical values, as opposed to a continuously fluctuating current or voltage.

Digital audio: Audio tones represented by machine-readable binary numbers rather than analog recording techniques. Analog audio is converted to digital using sampling techniques, whereby a "snapshot" is taken of the audio signal, its amplitude is measured and described numerically, and the resulting number is stored. More frequent sampling results in a more accurate digital representation of the signal.

Digital Video Interactive (DVI): Under development. A technology that allows real-time compression and decompression of graphics and full-motion video for recording on CD-ROM, videodiscs, magnetic disks, or other digital storage media. Developed by RCA's David Sarnoff Research Center and scheduled for release in 1989.

Digitize: To register a visual image or real object in a format that can be processed by a computer; to convert analog data to digital data.

Disc: Flat, circular rotating medium that can store and replay various types of information, both analog and digital. "Disc" is often used in reference to optical storage media, while "disk" refers to magnetic storage media. Often used as short form for videodisc or compact audio disc (CD).

Disk: Alternative spelling for "disc." Generally refers to magnetic storage medium on which information can be accessed at random, or radially (as opposed to sequentially). Floppy disks are small, portable storage vehicles; hard disks can store much more data. (Optical discs typically contain up to 500 to 1,000 times the storage capacity of the same size magnetic medium.)

DRAW (direct read after write): Type of optical discs that can be locally recorded but not erased. Recorders use a high-power laser to burn pits into a heat-sensitive layer beneath the surface of a recordable disc. Information is then read by a lower-power laser.

Drive: That part of a computer-based system (such as a personal computer) into which floppy disks, tapes, CD-ROMs, or videodiscs, other optical or magnetic media are inserted when they are being used to input, process, or output information.

Dual-channel audio: The capability to reproduce two audio channels, playing them either simultaneously or independently. A characteristic of all optical videodisc systems.

EIDS: Electronic Information Delivery System. A combination microcomputer/videodisc-based audio-visual training system, contracted by the US Army in November 1986 as the Army-designated standard stand-alone computer-based instructional system.

EIDS refers both to the hardware configuration, provided by Matrox Electronics under the initial contract, and to the standard for courseware (i.e., EIDS-compatible).

Electronic publishing: The delivery of information via computer or other electronic medium; closely parallels the concept of traditional print publishing, except for medium of delivery. Content is held in a storage device for delivery on a computer screen, rather than printed on paper.

Encode: To convert information to machine or computer-readable format (frequently binary numbers) representing individual characters or groups of characters in a message. Encoding is one step in the process of converting an analog signal into a digital signal. The three steps are sampling, quantizing, and encoding.

Field: One-half of a complete television scanning cycle (1/60 of a second NTSC; 1/50 of a second PAL/SECAM). When interlaced, two fields combine to make one video frame.

Field dominance: In videodisc mastering, the order of the video fields established on the videotape during edits or transfers. A tape with field one dominance has a new picture beginning on field one; with field two dominance, the new picture begins on field two. The field dominance of the master tape determines on which field the videodisc frames will begin.

Flow chart: A diagram or map of interactive logic which represents the possible paths a viewer may take through a program and is comprised of standard symbols for program segments, decision points, clues, responses and logic flow.

Frame: A single, complete picture in a video or film recording. A video frame consists of two interlaced field of either 525 lines (NTSC) or 625 lines (PAL/SECAM), running at 30 frames per second (NTSC) or 25 fps (PAL/SECAM). Film runs at 24 fps.

Frame address: In videotape and optical videodiscs, each frame has an address or frame number. A frame address is put on each disc or tape frame in the form of a frame address code.

Freeze-frame: A single frame from a segment of motion video or film footage held motionless on the screen. Unlike a still frame, a freeze-frame is not a picture intended to appear motionless, but is one frame taken from a longer motion sequence.

Generic courseware: Educational courses that are not specific to one organization and thus appeal to a broader market; as opposed to custom courseware, which primarily meets the needs of one specific client or audience.

Generic software: Computer software that is not specific to one organization, and thus, appeals to a broader market.

Generic videodisc: Videodisc material that can be used with courseware developed by more than one organization; discs associated with the subject matter but not with a particular course.

Hertz (Hz): The standard unit of measuring frequency. One Hz is equal to one cycle (or vibration) per second. One kilohertz (KHz) equals 1,000 cycles per second, and one megahertz (MHz) equals 1,000,000 cycles per second. Named after German physicist Heinrich Hertz (1857–1894).

High Sierra format: A standard format for placing files and directories on CD-ROM discs proposed by an ad hoc committee of computer vendors, software developers, and CD-ROM system integrators. (Work on the format proposal began at the High Sierra Hotel at Lake Tahoe, Nevada.) A revised version of the format was adopted by the International Standards Organization as ISO 9660.

High-level language: A computer programming language designed to facilitate use of computers by people. One statement in a high-level language may be translated to many assembly language or machine code instructions. High-level languages are also designed to be machine independent, in contrast to assembly level language. Examples of high-level languages are BASIC, Pascal, FORTRAN, etc.

HyperCard: An Apple Macintosh-based software product developed by Apple Computer. Using the philosophy of hypertext, the program enables users to randomly organize information in a manner like that of his own thinking.

Hypermedia: An extension of hypertext that incorporates a variety of other media, in addition to simple text.

Hypertext: The concept of non-sequential thinking/working/creating that enables users to link information together through a variety of paths or connections. Hypertext empowers users to seek greater depths of information by moving between related documents along thematic lines or accessing definitions and bibliographic references without losing the context of the original inquiry.

The term was coined by Theodore Nelson in the early 1960s. Hypertext is the driving concept behind Apple's HyperCard software program.

Individualized instruction: Software that modifies its instructional method or content based on student feedback to optimize learning.

Instant jump: The feature of some videodisc players that allows branching at imperceptible speeds between frames within certain minimum distances, usually one to 200 frames away. The branch occurs during the vertical blanking interval between images.

Instructional designer: Overseer and developer of any educational program; frequently used with interactive video design and development and computer-assisted learning design and development.

Instructional design: The methodology and approach used to deliver information in a manner that achieves learning. Some interactive programming aspects include question strategy, level of interaction, reinforcement and branching complexity.

Intelligent videodisc player: A videodisc player with processing power and memory capability built into it.

Interactive: Involving the active participation of the user in directing the flow of the computer or video program; a system which exchanges information with the viewer, processing the viewer's input in order to generate the appropriate response within the context of the program; as opposed to linear.

Interactive media: Media which involves the viewer as a source of input to determine the content and duration of a message, which permits individualized program material.

Interactive still video: A technology that captures images on a reusable two inch (2″) floppy diskette that can then be combined with graphic overlays, menus, branching, authoring and other interactive elements, to permit the easy in-house production of effective, inexpensive and immediately available interactive programs based on examples taken from the learner's own environment.

Interactive video: The fusion of video and computer technology. A video program and a computer program running in tandem under the control of the user. In interactive video, the user's actions, choices, and decisions genuinely affect the way in which the program unfolds.

Interactivity: A reciprocal dialog between the user and the system.

Interface: The component that links two or more pieces of equipment and enables them to communicate, or process and manipulate information. An interface is needed between a computer and a videodisc player.

Kilobyte (K or KB): A term indicating 1,024 bytes of data storage capacity. A typical personal computer might have 128K of memory.

Language: A medium of communication between computer and programmer. Some computer languages include BASIC, COBOL, Pascal, FORTRAN, and C.

Laser: 1. Light Amplification by Stimulation of Emission of Radiation. An amplifier and generator of coherent energy in the optical, or light, region of the spectrum. In the laser videodisc system, a laser is used to read the micropits on the videodisc which contain the picture and sound information.

2. Generic name for reflective optical videodisc format promoted by NV Philips, Pioneer Video, Hitachi, Sony, and others. See optical videodisc, reflective optical videodisc; also videodisc formats.

Laser disc (LD): Common name for reflective optical videodisc. LaserDisc is a trademark of Pioneer Electronics USA for its reflective optical videodisc products.

LaserFilm: A videodisc made of photographic film that uses solid state laser technology for recording and playback. Developed by McDonnell Douglas.

LaserVision (LV): Trade name for reflective optical videodisc format promoted by NV Philips, Sony, Pioneer, Hitachi, and others.

Levels of Interactive Systems: Three degrees of videodisc system interactivity proposed by the Nebraska Videodisc Design/Production Group in 1980.

• Level One system: Usually a consumer-model videodisc player with still/freeze frame, picture stop, chapter stop, frame address, and dual-channel audio, but with limited memory and limited processing power.

• **Level Two system:** An industrial-model videodisc player with the capabilities of Level One, plus on-board programmable memory and improved access time.

• **Level Three system:** Level One or Two players interfaced to an external computer and/or other peripheral processing devices.

• *NOTE:* Some commentators have advocated additional levels (Four, Five, and up), suggesting that the addition of digital audio, touch screens, etc. creates new levels of interactivity. However, the industry has not settled on any single standard for these higher levels, and any innovation mentioned with such "higher levels" all fall categorically into Level Three.

Levels of Interactivity: Derived from levels of interactive systems. Levels One, Two, and Three refer to the interactive design features available with each respective hardware configuration. Does not relate to the quality, relative value, or degree of sophistication.

Magneto-optics: An information storage medium that is magnetically sensitive only at high temperatures, while stable at normal temperatures. A laser is used to heat a small spot on the medium, allowing a normal magnet to change its polarity. The ability to tightly focus the laser greatly increases the data density over standard magnetic media.

Master: 1. An original audio tape, videotape or film. Used for broadcast or to make copies.

2. The process of producing master, mother, and stamper video discs, which are used for replicating videodiscs.

Master videodisc: First stage disc in videodisc manufacture. On the master disc, conductivity to receive the converted video signal is produced by evaporation or plating. The disc is then nickel-plated.

Medium: In computing, a substance or object on which information is stored. Its plural is media.

Memory: The location in which computer-based equipment stores recorded information, either permanently or temporarily. Usually measured in kilobytes or megabytes.

Menu: A table of contents or index listing major modules of information available on a videodisc or other computer program.

MOR: Magneto-optic recording combines magnetic and optical technologies.

Mother disc: Second stage disc in videodisc manufacture. From the nickel-plated master, a mother disc is formed and coated with remover. The mother disc is then nickel-plated. From the mother, several daughters are made and used in pressing.

Motivational device: A design element which arouses and sustains interest or regulates activity for the purpose of causing the student to perform in a desired way.

Mouse: A hand-held, rolling remote control device for a computer which guides the cursor on the computer screen.

NAPLPS: North American Presentation Level Protocol Standard (pronounced "nap-lips"). Visual computer standard for graphic communication protocol that provides a method for creating pictures and compressing them into relatively short blocks of digital data for storage and transmission over low-bandwidth channels. NAPLPS is one standard protocol for videotex.

NTSC: National Television Systems Committee of the Electronics Industries Association (EIA) that prepared the standard specifications approved by the Federal Communications Commission, in December 1953, for commercial color broadcasting.

NTSC format: A color television format having 525 scan lines; a field frequency of 60 Hz.; a broadcast bandwidth of 4 MHz.; line frequency of 15.75 KHz.; frame frequency of 1/30 of a second; and a color subcarrier frequency of 3.58 MHz. See also PAL, SECAM.

OMDR: Acronym for the Matsushita/Panasonic line of Optical Memory Disc Recorders. An 8″ or 12″ write-once videodisc which is not compatible with laser videodisc players from Hitachi, Philips, Pioneer, and Sony.

Optical digital data disc: A catch-all phrase for any optical disc used to store digital information.

Optical disc player: The playback device for an optical videodisc.

Optical memory: A generic term for technology that deals with information storage devices that use light (usually laser-based) to record, read, or decode data.

Optical videodisc: A videodisc that uses a laser light beam to read information from the surface of the disc. The information in optical videodiscs is encoded in the form of microscopic pits pressed into the disc surface. The pits or holes modulate the laser in a manner that can be decoded by the videodisc player. Information stored in these pits is "read" by a laser beam and transmitted to a decoder in the player. See reflective optical videodisc, transmissive optical videodisc.

OROM or optical read-only memory: A 5.25″ laser-encoded optical memory storage medium, which features a concentric circular format and constant angular velocity (CAV). OROMs have faster access time than CD-ROM discs, but less storage space (250 megabytes as opposed to 500).

Overlay: The facility to superimpose computer-generated text and/or graphics onto motion or still video.

PAL format: Phase Alternation Line; the European standard color system, except for France. See also NTSC, SECAM.

Pit: The microscopic physical indentation or hole found in the information layer of a videodisc. Pits on reflective optical discs modulate the reflected beam. Pits in transmissive discs block the beam or allow it to pass through the disc. Pits on VHD discs cause a detectable change in electrical capacitance. In all cases, variations in the pits carry the information.

PMMA: Polymethyl methacrylate. A rigid, transparent acrylic plastic used to manufacture many laser videodiscs.

Pre-mastering: The stage in the production of a videodisc when the master tape (generally 1″ Type C NTSC master helical videotape) is checked and prepared for final transfer onto the master disc, from which all subsequent discs will be pressed.

Pre-production: All design tasks (flow-charting, story-boarding, script-writing, software design, etc.) that lead up to the actual shooting of material on video or film.

Program: 1. To plan a computation or process for computer operations, including coding, numerical analysis, specification of printing formats, etc.

2. A set of instructions or steps that tells the computer exactly how to handle a complete problem.

3. Material on a tape or disc viewed by an audience.

Programmer: One who prepares or writes programs for a computer.

PROM: Programmable Read-Only Memory. A type of nonvolatile, semiconductor read-only memory component that can be programmed by the user once, and thereafter only read.

Random access: The ability to reach any piece of data on a storage medium in a very short time.

Read-only memory (ROM): 1. A computer storage medium which allows the user to recall and use information (read) but not record or amend it (write).

2. The smaller part of a computer's memory, in which essential operating information is recorded in a form which can be recalled and used (read) but not amended or recorded (written).

Receiver: An electronic device (such as a television or radio) capable of receiving and displaying a broadcast signal.

Reflective optical videodisc format: Reflective laser videodiscs contain their information imbedded as pits or holes in reflective surfaces sandwiched between layers of polymethyl methacrylate (PMMA). The shiny surface reflects the laser light into a mirror, which in turn reflects it to a decoder. The clear PMMA protects the information from dirt and superficial scratches. Reflective discs must be turned over to read information on both sides.

Because this format uses a laser instead of a stylus to retrieve information, there is no physical contact between the reading mechanism and the disc itself, hence no wear or degradation during playback. Promoted by NV Philips, Sony, Pioneer, Hitachi, and others. See also Laser, LaserVision, optical videodisc, videodisc formats.

Remote control: Command of a computer or interactive videodisc program through an electronic device independent of the computer or disc player (i.e., keypad, touch screen, joy stick, mouse).

Replicates: Videodisc copies pressed from the stamper disc.

Replication: The mass reproduction of prerecorded videodiscs or compact discs.

Repurposing: The process of modifying the content of an existing program to accomplish a task other than the one for which it was originally designed. Often, Level One consumer videodiscs are repurposed for Level Three use.

Retrofitted Videodiscs: A method of using existing broadcast quality video, film and/or videodisc segments to create a new videodisc. The intent is to minimize production costs and development time.

RGB (Red-Green-Blue): A type of computer color display output signal comprised of separately controllable red, green, and blue signals; as opposed to composite video, in which signals are combined prior to output. RGB monitors typically offer higher resolution than composite.

RS-232C: A standard serial interface between a computer and its peripherals. Various peripherals (including some videodisc players) equipped with an RS-232C computer port can be plugged directly into a compatible computer. The RS-232C is increasingly becoming a standard feature of computers and their peripherals.

Sampling: The process of taking measurable slices of an analog signal at periodic intervals. Obtaining the values of a usually analog function by making automatic measurements of the function at periodic intervals. A step in the process of converting an analog signal into a digital signal.

Sampling rate: 1. Rate at which slices are taken from analog signals when converting to digital.

2. Frequency at which points are recorded in digitizing an image. Sampling errors can cause aliasing effects.

Search: In interactive video systems, to request a specific frame, identified by its unique sequential reference number, and then to instruct the player to move directly to that frame (forwards or backwards) from any other point on the same side of the disc or tape.

Search time: The amount of time required by a computer or disc player to locate specific data in the storage medium.

SECAM format: "Sequential couleur a memoire" (sequential color with memory), the French color TV system also adopted in Russia. The basis of operation is the sequential recording of primary colors in alternate lines. See also NTSC, PAL.

Segment: Any material with a start and stop frame; a motion sequence as well as a series of still frames meant to be accessed together.

SelectaVision: Trade name for RCA's defunct CED videodisc format.

Shared disc or sharedisc: Videodisc which is produced jointly by several parties, each receiving a portion of the disc space for its own purpose. Often produced to bring down production costs.

Simulation: Representation of a system, sub-system, situation or device, with a degree of realism. The simulation mode enables users to learn the operation of equipment without damaging it or harming themselves or others. Extremely useful in training applications which involve potentially dangerous activities.

Software: The programs, routines, subroutines, languages, procedures, videodiscs, charts, workbooks—in fact, everything that isn't hardware used in a computer or videodisc system.

Step frame or step: 1. A function of optical videodisc players which permits the user to move either forward or reverse from one frame to the next.

Still frame: 1. A single film or video frame (1/24 or 1/30 of a second, respectively) presented as a single, static image.

2. Refers to information recorded on a frame or track of a videodisc that is intended to be retrieved and displayed as a single, motionless image. Playback is achieved by repeating the play of the same track, rather than going on to the next; as opposed to a freeze-frame, which stops the action within a motion sequence.

Surrogate travel: One application of interactive videodisc in which physical travel is precisely simulated using disc and computer, allowing the user to control the path taken through the environment. Vicarious travel disc systems have been used for tours of nuclear power plants and for high-level security systems. Also known as "vicarious travel."

TED or TelDec format: An early videodisc system developed jointly by Germany's Telefunken and Britain's Decca. It employed a flexible plastic foil disc read by a prow-shaped stylus. However, the first discs were only ten minutes long, and picture quality was poor. The system appeared only briefly on the European market in 1975.

Test: Any strategy by which a response to the video courseware is elicited, and which results in the measurement of understanding by program logic.

Touch screen: A video and/or computer display which acts as a control or input device under the physical finger touch of the user. Basic functions are executed by touching or stroking certain parts of the screen, and specific responses made by touching appropriate words, messages, or pictures as they appear.

Different touch-screen technologies use infrared grids, small wires separated by air spaces, changes in electronic capacitance, acceleration detection, plastic membranes, or other methods.

Transmissive optical videodisc format: Transparent videodisc which allows the laser beam to pass through the disc to the detector. Originally developed by Thomson/CSF (France), which introduced a player that could read both sides of a disc by changing the laser's focal point.

The only transmissive system currently on the market is the McDonnell Douglas Electronics Company (MDEC) LaserFilm system, which uses one-sided discs.

VHD format: Video High Density. A grooveless capacitance videodisc system which uses a broad stylus to pick up information. VHD discs rotate at a constant 900 rpm, contain four video fields per revolution, and can accommodate one hour of material per side without loss of special features. The discs are housed in a jacket which is inserted into the player and then removed, leaving the disc.

The format, developed and marketed by Matsushita/JVC, is now available only in the Japanese market. The same player can handle both NTSC and PAL format discs.

145

Video: A system of recording and transmitting information which is primarily visual, by translating moving or still images into electrical signals. These signals can be broadcast (live or pre-recorded) using high-frequency carrier waves, or sent through cable on a closed circuit.

The term video properly refers only to the picture—but as a generic term, usually embraces audio and other signals which are part of a complete program. Video now includes not only broadcast television, but many non-broadcast applications—such as corporate communications, marketing, home entertainment, games, teletext, security, and even the visual display units of computer-based technology.

Videodisc: A generic term describing a medium of information storage which uses thin circular plates of varying formats, upon which video, audio, and data signals may be encoded (usually along a spiral track) for playback on a video monitor. For purposes of this book, the term videodisc will refer to the reflective optical or laser videodisc format unless otherwise noted.

Videodisc formats: reflective optical videodisc or laser; transmissive optical videodisc; CED or capacitance electronic disc; VHD or Video High Density (see separate entries under each).

Videotex: A collective name for systems which use the domestic TV receiver to display data from a central computer transmitted to the set, either via coaxial cable or telephone link.

WORM (write-once/read-many) memory: A type of permanent optical storage that allows the user to record original information on a blank disc, but does not allow erasure or change of that information once it is recorded.

Write: To transcribe recorded data from one place to another, or from one medium to another. Information from the computer is written to a disk, rather than on a disk.

Endnotes

1. Rockley L. Miller, Vicki L. Reeve-Dusenberry, John H. Sayers, eds., Videodisc and Related Technologies: A Glossary of Terms. First Printing, February 1986 Revised, July 1988; Future Systems Inc. aka The Videodisc Monitor. Selected terms used with permission.

Bibliography

Books

Adler, Mortimer J. *The Paideia Program: An Educational Syllabus*. New York: Macmillan Publishing Company, 1984.

Agee, Warren K.; Ault, Phillip H.; and Emery, Edwin. *Introduction to Mass Communications, Sixth Edition*. New York: Harper & Row, 1979.

Bertolotti, M. *Masers and Lasers: An Historical Approach*. Bristol, England: Adam Hilger Ltd., 1983.

Binder, Roberta H., *Videodiscs in Museums: A Project and Resource Directory* (Falls Church, VA: Future Systems, Inc., 1988).

Borg, Walter R., and Gall, Meredith D. *Educational Research: An Introduction, Fourth Edition*. New York: Longman, Inc., 1983.

Brand, Steward. *The Media Lab: Inventing the Future at MIT*. New York: Viking Penguin, Inc. 1987.

Carpenter, Edmund, and Heyman, Ken. *They Became What They Beheld*. New York: Ballantine Books, Inc., 1970.

Daynes, Rod, and Butler, Beverly, eds. *The Videodisc Book: A Guide and Directory*. New York: John Wiley and Sons, Inc., 1984.

DeBloois, Michael; Maki, Karen Clauson; and Hall, Arno Ferrin. *Effectiveness of Interactive Videodisc Training: A Comprehensive Review*. Falls Church, Va.: Future Systems Incorporated, 1984.

Gayeski, Diane M., and Williams, David V. "Interactive Video in Higher Education." In *Video in Higher Education*, p. 67. Edited by Ortrun Zuber-Skerritt. New York: Nichols Publishing Company, 1984.

Gayeski, Diane M., and Williams, David V. *Interactive Media*. New Jersey: Prentice-Hall, Inc., 1985.

Goslin, David A., ed. *Handbook of Socialization Theory and Research*. New York: Rand McNally & Company, 1969.

Greeno, J. G., and Simon, H. A. "Problem Solving and Reasoning." Included in *Stevens' Handbook of Experimental Psychology, Revised Edition*. Eds. R. C. Atkins, R. Herrnstein, G. Lindzey, and R. D. Luce (New York: Wiley, 1987).

Gross, Lynne Schafer. *The New Television Technologies*. Dubuque, Iowa: Wm. C. Brown Company, Publishers, 1983.

Heinich, Robert; Molenda, Michael; and Russell, James D. *Instructional Media and the New Technologies of Instruction*. New York: John Wiley and Sons, 1985.

Holzner, Burkart, and Nehnevajsa, Jiri, eds. *Organizing for Social Research*. Cambridge: Schenkman Publishing Company, 1982.

Iuppa, Nicholas V. *A Practical Guide to Interactive Video Design*. White Plains, N.Y.: Knowledge Industry Publications, Inc., 1984.

Iuppa, Nicholas V., and Anderson, Karl, *Advanced Interactive Video Design: New Techniques and Applications* (White Plains, NY: Knowledge Industry Publications, Inc., 1988).

Lambert, Steve, and Ropiequet, Suzanne, eds. *CD ROM: The New Papyrus*. Redmond, Wash.: Microsoft Press, 1986.

Miller, Rockley L., et al. *Videodisc and Related Technologies: A Glossary of Terms*. Falls Church, Virginia: Future Systems, Incorporated, 1986.

Moehlman, Arthur H., et al. *A Guide to Computer-Assisted Historical Research*. Austin, Texas: University of Texas Press, 1969.

Parsloe, Eric, ed. *Interactive Video*. United Kingdom: Sigma Technical Press, 1983.

Reigeluth, Charles M., ed. *Instructional-Design Theories and Models: An Overview of Their Current Status*. New Jersey: Lawrence Erlbaum Associates, 1983.

Rilke, Rainer Maria. *Letters to a Young Poet*. New York: W. W. Norton & Company, Inc., 1954.

Rogers, Everett M. *Diffusion of Innovations, Third Edition*. New York: The Free Press, 1983.

Runes, Dagobert D., ed. *The Diary and Sundry Observations of Thomas Alva Edison*. New York: Philosophical Library, Inc., 1948.

Saettler, Paul. *A History of Instructional Technology*. New York: McGraw-Hill, 1968.

Schneider, Edward W., and Bennion, Junius L. *Videodiscs*. Englewood Cliffs, New Jersey: Educational Technology Publications, 1981.

Schwartz, Ed. *The Educators' Handbook to Interactive Videodisc.* Washington, D.C.: Association for Educational Communications and Technology, 1985.

Sigel, Efrem, et al. *Video Discs: The Technology, the Applications and the Future.* New York: Van Nostrand Reinhold Company, 1980.

Souter, Gerald A., *The DISConnection: How to Interface Computers and Video* (White Plains, NY: Knowledge Industry Publications, Inc., 1988).

Toynbee, Arnold J. *A Study of History. Vol. 3: The Growths of Civilizations, 8th ed.* London: Oxford University Press, 1963.

van Someren, Alex. *Interactive Video Systems.* London: Century Communications, 1985.

Wurtzel, Alan. *Television Production, Second Edition.* New York: McGraw-Hill Book Company, 1983.

Interviews

Elmquist, Thomas L. 3M Company, St. Paul, Minnesota. Interview, 12 June 1986.

Ferralli, Anthony and Kathryn. At Residence, Erie, Pennsylvania. Interview, 29 April 1986.

Fiedler, James N., and Jones, George. DiscoVision Associates, Costa Mesa, California. Interview, 13 June 1986.

Kerfeld, Donald J. 3M Company, Vadnais Heights, Minnesota. Interview, 12 June 1986.

Messerschmitt, John C. Philips Subsystems and Peripherals Inc., New York, New York. Interview, 11 June 1986.

Petruso, Sam P. Millcreek Education Center, Erie, Pennsylvania. Interview, 29 April 1986.

Price, Frank M., and Prudhon, Lou L. 3M Company, St. Paul, Minnesota. Interview, 12 June 1986.

Salmon, Verel R. Millcreek Education Center, Erie, Pennsylvania. Interview, 29 April 1986.

Troeltzsch, Lloyd A. 3M Company, St. Paul, Minnesota. Interview, 12 June 1986.

Yeazel, Lynn A. Airporter Inn, Costa Mesa, California. Interview, 13 June 1986.

Lecture

Gant, Rus. "Interactive Videodisc: Current Developments and Future Trends." Classroom lecture presented at the University of Pittsburgh, Pittsburgh, Pennsylvania, 19 June 1986.

Periodicals

Abramsom, Albert. "Letters." *Television: Journal of the Royal Television Society* 21,2 (March/April 1984): 87–88.

Baird, M. H. I. "Letters." *Television: Journal of the Royal Television Society* 21,3 (May/June 1984): 131–132.

Bairstow, Jeffrey. "CD-ROM: Mass Storage for the Mass Market." *High Technology* 6,10 (October 1986): 44–51.

"Balfour Rolls Out ByVideo Kiosks for Colleges." *The Videodisc Monitor* 4,10 (October 1986): 3.

Balson, Paul M.; Ebner, Donald G.; Mahoney, James V.; Lippert, Henry T.; and Manning, Diane T. "Videodisc Instructional Strategies: Simple May Be Superior to Complex." *Journal of Educational Technology Systems* 14,4 (1985–86): 273–281.

Balson, Paul M.; Manning, D. Thompson; Ebner, Donald G.; and Brooks, R. Franklin. "Instructor-Controlled Versus Student- Controlled Training in a Videodisc-Based Paramedical Program." *Journal of Educational Technology Systems* 13,2 (1984–85): 123- 130.

Bear, George G. "Microcomputers and School Effectiveness." *Educational Technology* 24 (January 1984): 1–15.

Beck, Melinda et al. "A Nation Still at Risk," *Newsweek* May 2, 1988. pp. 54–55.

Bejar, Isaac I. "Videodiscs in Education: Integrating the Computer and Communication Technologies." *BYTE* 7,6 (June 1982): 78–104.

Bennion, Junius L., and Schneider, Edward W. "Interactive Videodisc Systems for Education." *Journal of the SMPTE* 84,12 (December 1975): 949–953.

Blackman, James A.; Albanese, Mark A.; Huntley, Jean Sustik; and Lough, Loretta K. "Use of Computer-Videodisc System to Train Medical Students in Developmental Disabilities." *Medical Teacher* 7,1 (November 1, 1985): 89–97.

Bloom, Benjamin S. quoted in Robert J. Trotter, "The Mystery of Mastery." *Psychology Today* 20,7 (July 1986): 32–38.

Bolt, Richard A. "Conversing With Computers." *Technology Review,* February/March 1985, pp. 35–43.

Boraiko, Allen A. "LASERS: A Splendid Light." *National Geographic* 165,3 (March 1984): 335–363.

Bork, Alfred. "Education and Computers: The Situation Today and Some Possible Futures." *T.H.E. Journal* 12,3 (October 1984): 92- 97.

Bosco, James. "An Analysis of Evaluations of Interactive Video." *Educational Technology,* May 1986, pp. 7–17.

Bosco, James J. "Interactive Video: Educational Tool or Toy?" *Educational Technology,* April 1984, pp. 13–19.

Bowen, William. "The Puny Payoff From Office Computers." *Fortune,* May 26, 1986, pp. 20–24.

Boyer, Peter. "Public TV: That Delicate Balance." *New York Times,* October 25, 1987, sect. 2, p. 1, 40.

Broadbent, Kent D. "A Review of the MCA Disco-Vision System." *Journal of the SMPTE* 83,7 (July 1974), 554–559.

Brody, Herb, "Picking Up the Pieces of RCA," *High Technology Business* (May 1988): 41–44.

Brody, Herb, "Rising Stars in Consumer Electronics," *High Technology* 6, 12 (December 1986): 28.

Buckeley, William M., "Computers Failing As Teaching Aids," *The Wall Street Journal* 6 June 1988, sec. 2, p. 17.

Buckley, Jerry. "A Blueprint for Better Schools," *U.S. News and World Report.* January 18, 1988. pp. 60–65.

Cambre, Marjorie A. "Interactive Video." *Instructional Innovator* 29,6 (September/October 1984): 24–25.

Carter, Alex, and Wedman, John. "A Survey of Classroom Media Use." *Instructional Innovator* 29,6 (September/October 1984): 36- 37, 41.

Cash, Joan "Picture Power: Optical Discs and Video Computing Come of Age," *Museum News* 66, 6 (July/August 1988) 58–60.

Cash, Joan. "Spinning Toward the Future: The Museum on Laser Videodisc." *Museum News,* August 1985, pp. 19–31.

"CD Spotlight." *The Videodisc Monitor* 4,10 (October 1986): 10.

Christie, Ken. "One Year in the Life." *The Videodisc Monitor* 2,1 (January 1984): 12–14.

Cohen, Peter A.; Ebeling, Barbara J.; and Kulik, James A. "A Meta-Analysis of Outcome Studies of Visual-Based Instruction." *Educational Communication and Technology Journal* 29,1 (Spring 1981): 26–36.

Cohen, Vicki Blum. "Interactive Features in the Design of Videodisc Materials." *Educational Technology,* January 1984, pp. 16–20.

"Conversations with John Messerschmitt." *Videography* 9,1 (January 1984): 52–58.

Cook, Peter R. "Electronic Encyclopedias." *BYTE* 9,7 (July 1984): 151–70.

"Developing Technology: Major Industry Milestones." *Broadcast Engineering* 21,5 (May 1979): 60–61.

ETC Targets 3,3 (Educational Technology Center, Cambridge, MA, Fall 1986).

Ebner, Donald G.; Manning, Diane T.; Brooks, Franklin R.; Mahoney, James V.; Lippert, Henry T.; and Balson, Paul M. "Videodiscs Can Improve Instructional Efficiency." *Instructional Innovator* 29,6 (September/October 1984): 26–28.

Farr, Kenneth E. "Phonovid—A System for Recording Television Pictures on Phonograph Records." *Journal of the Audio Engineering Society* 16,2 (April 1968): 163–167.

"Federal Judge Orders U.S. to Issue Patent to Man who Invented Laser." *Video Computing,* January/February 1986, p. 18.

Ferralli, Anthony, and Ferralli, Kathryn. "Interactive Video in Education: A New Approach." *The Videodisc Monitor* 3,6 (June 1985): 14–15.

Ferralli, Anthony, and Ferralli, Kathryn. "Videotex Takes Interactive Video Across Any Distance." *E-ITV* 18,1 (January 1986): 16–19.

Freiberger, Paul. "The Videodisc Connection." *Popular Computing* 3,11 (September 1984): 67–69.

Friedman, Susan G., and Hofmeister, Alan M. "Matching Technology to Content and Learners: A Case Study." *Exceptional Children* 51,2 (October 1984): 130–134.

"GE/RCA Puts Full Motion Video on CD." *The Videodisc Monitor* 5,4 (April 1987): 1.

Gannon, Joyce. "Apple Founder Considering City Site," Pittsburgh Press May 24, 1988, pp. 21–22.

Gale, Larrie E., and Brown, Bruce L. "A Theory of Learning and Skill-Acquisition Applied to Interactive Video: Activities at the David O. MacKay Institute, Brigham Young University." *Studies in Language Learning* 5,1 (Spring 1985): 105–114.

Gardner, R. N.; Rinehart, T. A.; Johnson, L. H.; Freese, R. P.; and Lund, R. A. "Characteristics of a New High C/N Magneto- Optic Media." *Proceedings of SPIE—The International Society for Optical Engineering* 420 (Arlington, Virginia: June 1983), pp. 242–247.

Gayeski, Diane M. "Interactive Video: Integrating Design 'Levels' and Hardware 'Levels'." *Journal of Educational Technology Systems* 13,3 (1984–85): 145–151.

Getter, Ric. "Army to Purchase 400,000 Discs by 1990." *Video Manager,* March 1986, pp. 1, 12.

Ginsberg, Charles P. "The Birth of the VTR." *Video Pro* 5,2 (March 1986): 22–26.

Grabinger, R. Scott. "An Evaluation of Three Authoring-Language Software Packages." *Tech Trends* 30,4 (May/June 1985): 20–23.

"Grapevine." The Videodisc Monitor 4,9 (September 1986): 6. Halloway, R. E. "The Videodisc in Education: A Case for Gradualism." *Videodisc/Videotex* 11 (Spring 1982): 2.

Hafner, Katherine M., and Brandt, Richard, "Steve Jobs: Can He Do It Again?" *Business Week,* October 24, 1988, pp. 74–80.

Hann, Becky. "IBM: Its Own Best Customer." *The Videodisc Monitor* 4,9 (September 1986): 18–19.

Hannafin, Michael J. "Empirical Issues in the Study of Computer-Assisted Interactive Video." *Educational Communication and Technology Journal* 33,4 (Winter 1985): 235–247.

Hannafin, Michael J. "Options for Authoring Instructional Interactive Video." *Journal of Computer-Based Instruction* 11,3 (Summer 1984): 98–100.

Hawker, Pat. "Letters." *Television: Journal of the Royal Television Society* 23,3 (June 1986): 165–166.

Hawker, Pat. "The Pioneers of Television." *Television: Journal of the Royal Television Society* 20,6 (November/December 1983): 273- 279.

Hawker, Pat. "Television's Spring Review of Books (The Secret Life of John Logie Baird by Tom McArthur and Peter Waddell)." *Television: Journal of the Royal Television Society* 23,2 (April 1986): 104–5.

Haynes, George R. "Actively Interactive in Pittsburgh." *Video Computing,* September-October 1986, pp. 8, 12.

Helgerson, Linda. "Videodisc for the Storage of Maps." *International Television* 3,4 (April 1985): 38–44.

Hittinger, W. C., and Sonnenfeldt, R. W. "Foreword." *RCA Review* 39,1 (March 1978): 3–5.

Hoban, Phoebe. "Artificial Intelligence." *Omni* 8,11 (August 1986): 24, 111.

Holmgren, J. E.; Dyer, F. N.; Hilligoss, R. E.; and Heller, F. H. "The Effectiveness of Army Training Extension Course Lessons on Videodisc." *Journal of Educational Technology Systems* 8,3 (1979- 80): 263–274.

Hon, David. "Interactive Training in Cardiopulmonary Resuscitation." *BYTE* 7,6 (June 1982): 108–120, 130–138.

Hrbek, George W. "An Experimental Optical Videodisc Playback System." *Journal of the SMPTE* 83,7 (July 1974): 580–582.

Hutchinson, Joseph C. "The Language Laboratory—How Effective Is It?" *School Life* 46,4 (January/February 1964): 14–17, 39–41.

Ingersoll, Bob. "Plastic Platters Vie for Role in Home TV Playback Battle." *Product Engineering,* August 17, 1970, pp. 49- 50.

"Integrated CD-ROM, Videodisc System." *The Videodisc Monitor* 4,8 (August 1986): 3.

"Interactive Video on a Shoestring." *Instructional Innovator* 29,6 (September/October 1984): 29, 40.

Ivey, Henry F. "Optics at Westinghouse," *Applied Optics* 11,5 (May 1972): 985–992.

Jarvis, C. Stan, "1988: The 30th Anniversary of the Videodisc," *The Videodisc Monitor* 6, 5 (May 1988): 15.

Jarvis, Stan. "Videodiscs and Computers." *BYTE* 9,7 (July 1984).

Jarvis, Stan and Booth, Steve, "A Century of Optical Disc Development," *Videodisc News* (July–August 1982): 22.

Jerome, Jonathan A., and Kaczorowki, Edward M. "Film-Based Videodisc System." *Journal of the SMPTE* 83,7 (July 1974): 560- 563.

Kirchner, Glenn; Martyn, Don; and Johnson, Chris. "Simon Fraser University Videodisc Project: Part Two: Field Testing an Experimental Videodisc with Elementary School Children." *Videodisc/Videotex* 3,1 (Winter 1983): 45–58.

Kulik, J. R.; Bangert, R. L.; and Williams, G. W. "Effects of Computer-Based Teaching on Secondary School Students." *Journal of Educational Psychology* 75 (1983): 19–26.

Laub, Leonard. "The Evolution of Mass Storage." *BYTE* 11,5 (May 1986): 161–172.

Laurillard, Diana M. "Interactive Video and the Control of Learning." *Educational Technology,* June 1984, pp. 7–15.

"LDCA Optimistic on Consumer Market," *The Videodisc Monitor* 6, 8/9 (August/September 1988): 11.

Levenson, Phyllis M.; Morrow, James R.; and Signer, Barbara. "A Comparison of Noninteractive and Interactive Video Instruction About Smokeless Tobacco." *Journal of Educational Technology Systems* 14,3 (1985–86): 193–202.

Manning, D. Thompson; Ebner, Donald G.; Brooks, Franklin R.; and Balson, Paul. "Interactive Videodiscs: A Review of the Field." *Viewpoints in Teaching and Learning* 59,2 (Spring 1983): 28–40.

Manning, D. Thompson; Balson, Paul; Ebner, Donald G.; and Brooks, Franklin R. "Student Acceptance of Videodisk-Based Programs for Paramedical Training." *T.H.E. Journal* 11,3 (November 1983): 105-108.

"Matrox Wins EIDS Contract." *The Videodisc Monitor* 4,11 November 1986): Special Bulletin.

"Matrox Wins EIDS: Sony Protests." *The Videodisc Monitor* 4,12 (December 1986): 1.

McClain, Larry. "A Friendly Introduction to Videodiscs." *Popular Computing,* April 1983, p. 79–80.

"MDEC in First Major Application." *The Videodisc Monitor* 3,5 (May 1985): 1.

Melmed, Arthur S. "The Technology of American Education: Problem and Opportunity. *T.H.E. Journal* 14,2 (September 1986): 77–81.

Merrill, M. David. "Peter Dean Lecture: Where is the Authoring in Authoring Systems?" *Journal of Computer-Based Instruction* 12,4 (Autumn 1985): 90–96.

Miller, Rockley L., and Sayers, John H. "EIDS Watch." *The Videodisc Monitor* 4,8 (August 1986): 3.

Miller, Rockley L., and Sayers, John H. "Integrating Laserdisc Technology in Industry and Education." *The Videodisc Monitor* 4,8 (August 1986): 18.

Morris, Jon D. "The Florida Study: Improvement in Student Achievement and Attitudes Through Variations in Instructional Television Production Values." *Journal of Educational Technology Systems* 12,4 (1983–84): 357–368.

Morris, Jon D. "The Florida Study: Improving Achievement Through the Use of More Dynamics in TV Production." *T.H.E. Journal* 12,3 (October 1984): 104–107.

Mullin, John. "Discovering Magnetic Tape." *Broadcast Engineering* 21,5 (May 1979): 80–82.

"N. A. Philips Scales Down U.S. Videodisc Efforts." *The Videodisc Monitor* 4,8 (August 1986): 5.

The National Task Force on Educational Technology. "Transforming American Education: Reducing the Risk to the Nation." *T.H.E. Journal* 14,1 (August 1986): 58–67.

Nugent, Gwen C. "Pictures, Audio, and Print: Symbolic Representation and Effect on Learning." *Educational Communication and Technology Journal* 30,3 (Fall 1982): 163–174.

Nugent, Gwen C.; Tipton, Thomas J.; and Brooks, David W. "Task, Learner, and Presentation Interactions in Television Production." *Educational Communication and Technology Journal* 28,1 (Spring 1980): 30–38.

Ohles, John F. "The Microcomputer: Don't Love It To Death." *T.H.E. Journal* 13,1 (August 1985): 49–53.

Onosko, Timothy. "Let There be Light." *Creative Computing* 11,9 (September 1985): 43–49.

Oravecz, John D. "CMU, NeXT, See Union of Computer, Education" Pittsburgh Press, February 24, 1987. sect. C, pp. 9, 12.

Ottenberg, Jill. "Discs Get Heavy Play in the Arcade." *Videography* 9,1 (January 1984): 22–28.

"Panosonic Introduces 12" Optical Memory Disc Recorder," *The Videodisc Monitor* 6, 6 (June 1988): 6.

Pea, R. D. "Beyond Amplification: Using the Computer to Reorganize Mental Functioning." *Educational Psychologist* 20,4 (1985): 167–182.

"Philips Shows CD-Video, Revives Laservision." *Television Digest with Consumer Electronics* 26,47 (24 November 1986): 10–11.

"Pioneer, LDCA Announce 'Compact Laserdisc' Format." *The Videodisc Monitor* 4,9 (September 1986): 5.

"Pioneer Offers New Player, Initiatives," *The Videodisc Monitor* 6, 5 (May 1988): 1.

"Pioneer Releases 'Special Interests', "*The Videodisc Monitor* 6, 6 (June 1988): 6.

"Pioneer Shows New Line." *The Videodisc Monitor* 4,10 (October, 1986): 1.

Pogue, Richard E. "Authoring Systems: The Key to Lesson Development." *Journal of Educational Technology Systems* 13,2 (1984–1985): 75–81.

"Practical Advice from a Videodisc Designer: An Interview with Ken Christie." *Museum News,* August 1985, p. 31–34.

Price, Frank. "Video: Disc Dynamics." *Audio-Visual Communications* 20,2 (February 1986): 40–43.

Reigeluth, Charles M.; Bunderson, C. Victor; and Merrill, M. David. "What Is the Design Science of Instruction?" *Journal of Instructional Development* 1,2 (Spring 1978): 11–16.

Reigeluth, Charles M., and Garfield, Joanne M. "Using Videodiscs in Instruction: Realizing Their Potential Through Instructional Design." *Videodisc and Optical Disk* 4,3 (May/June 1984): 206- 215.

Reilly, Claire. "Two-Way Computer Tutors." *Audio-Visual Communications* 19,1 (January 1985): 30–34, 92–93.

Rice, Philip, and Dubbe, Richard F. "Development of the First Optical Videodisc." *Journal of the SMPTE* 91,3 (March 1982): 277- 284.

Rodesch, Dale F. "Interleaving Multiple Channels on Videodisc for Rapid Interactivity." *The Videodisc Monitor* 4,3 (March 1986): IA-ID.

Rogers, Michael, "Here Comes Hypermedia," *Newsweek,* October 3, 1988, pp 44–45.

Rogers, Michael and Sandza, Richard, "Computers of the '90's: A Brave New World," *Newsweek,* October 24, 1988, pp. 52–57.

Roth, Judith Paris. "The Coming of the Interactive Compact Disc." *High Technology* 6,10 (October 1986): 46.

Schwartz, John, *et al,* "Steve Jobs Comes Back", *Newsweek,* October 24, 1988, pp. 46–51.

Shanker, Albert, "Impatience Short-Circuits Reform: Tough Problems Need Time and Effort," Where We Stand Column, *The New York Times,* 13 March 1988, sec. 4, p. 9.

Shanker, Albert, "An Open Letter to Education Secretary Bennett," Where We Stand Column, *The New York Times,* 1 May 1988, sec. 4.

Shanker, Albert. "Our Profession, Our Schools: The Case for Fundamental Reform." American Educator 10,3 (Fall 1986): 10–17, 44–45.

Shanker, Albert. "Impatience Short-Circuits Reform: Tough Problems Need Time and Effort," Where We Stand Column, *The New York Times,* 13 March 1988. sect. 4, p. 9.

Shao, Maria, *et al,* "A Campus Groan: I've Got the Computer, So Where's the Software?" *Business Week* October 24, 1988, p. 82.

Sieger, Joshua. "Television's Spring Review of Books (The Secret Life of John Logie Baird by Tom McArthur and Peter Waddell)." *Television: Journal of the Royal Television Society* 23,2 (April 1986): 103–104.

Sinnett, Dennis, and Edwards, Sheila. "Authoring Systems: The Key to Widespread Use of Interactive Videodisc Technology." *Library Hi Tech* 2,4 (Issue 8, 1984): 39–46.

"Smithsonian and IVC Establish National Demonstration Laboratory." *The Videodisc Monitor* 4,8 (August 1986): 1.

"Special Report: The Year in Review." *The Videodisc Monitor* 4,1 (January 1986): I-D.

"Teachers Still Not Full-Fledged Professionals, Study Says," Pittsburgh Press. April 12, 1988. p. A-6.

"Television Pioneering." *Broadcast Engineering* 21,5 (May 1979).

Thorkildsen, Ron, and Friedman, Susan. "Videodiscs in the Classroom." *T.H.E. Journal* 11 (April 1984): 90–95.

Thorne, K. G. "The Teldec Video Disc." *Television: Journal of the Royal Television Society* (November/December 1972): 133–138.

Turner, Judith Axler. "For Apple Computers Founder, Time for a New Vision." *Chronicle of Higher Education.* June 10, 1987. p. 19.

"Videodisc Sails the World." *The Videodisc Monitor* 4,9 (September 1986): 1, 3.

Waddell, Peter. "Letters." *Television: Journal of the Royal Television Society* 21,3 (May/June 1984): 132–133.

Waddell, Peter. "Letters." *Television: Journal of the Royal Television Society* 23,3 (June 1986): 164–165.

Ward, Bernie. "Centers of Imagination." *Sky,* September 1985, pp. 72–78.

Waters, Harry F., et al. "The Age of Video." *Newsweek,* December 30, 1985, pp. 44–53.

Waters, Harry F., "The Future of Television," *Newsweek* (October 17, 1988): 85.

Wiegand, Ingrid. "Interactive Here and Now: Keeping it Rolling on Tape." *Video Manager,* March 1986, p. 10.

Wilson, Roger. "VHD—The United Kingdom Market Story." *Videodisc and Optical Disk* 5,2 (March/April 1985): 148–155.

Winslow, Ken. "Here Come the Home Video Discs." *Popular Electronics* 8,5 (November 1975): 38–44.

Wolf, Emil. "Einstein's Researches on the Nature of Light." *Optic News,* Winter 1979, pp. 24–39.

Zakariya, Sally Banks. "Here's Why Most Schools Don't Use Videodiscs - Yet." *The American School Board Journal,* June 1984, p. 26.

Ziaukas, Tim. "200 Years and Counting." *Pittsburgh Magazine,* October 1986, pp. 43–48.

Ziff, Richard. "Magnetic Tape's Impact on Broadcasting." *Broadcast Engineering* 21,5 (May 1979): 78–80.

Press

Crutchfield, Will. "Next Home Stereo Advance: Digital Tape Cassettes in 1987." *The New York Times,* 24 October 1986, pp. 1, 50.

"Firm Pushes High-Tech Training Video." *The Pittsburgh Press,* 11 August 1986, pp. B4, B6.

Freedman, Alix M., and Hudson, Richard L. "DuPont and Philips Plan Joint Venture to Make, Market Laser-Disk Products." *The Wall Street Journal,* 30 October 1985, p. 4.

Hotz, Lee. "The Laser: CMU, Westinghouse Experts Beam as New Technology Spreads to All Fields." *The Pittsburgh Press,* 28 August 1983, p. E1.

Modoono, Bill. "NFL Unveils a Replay Official to End the Arguments Over Calls." *The Pittsburgh Press,* 7 September 1986, p. D8.

Perlez. "Improvement in Teachers is Viewed as Threatened." *The New York Times,* 6 July 1986, p. Y14.

"RCA Offering Product Refunds." *The Pittsburgh Press,* 26 November 1984, p. B6.

Thornton, Matthew. "Convocation: Pitt's Bicentennial Celebration Kicks Off." *The Pitt News,* 22 October 1986, p. 1.

Promotional Releases

"ARDEV Interactive Photographic Film Videodisc System" (Promotional release from ARDEV Company, Inc.).

Schiering, Rolf W. "The TeD Videodisk System" (a TeD press information release. The unspecified date appears to be late 1975).

Reports

Published

Becker, Henry Jay. Instructional Uses of School Computers: Reports from the 1985 National Survey (The Johns Hopkins University: Center for Social Organization of Schools, June 1986), pp. 1–10.

Moore, Omar Khayyam. "From Tools to Interactional Machines," in New Approaches to Individualizing Instruction, report of a conference to mark the dedication of Ben D. Wood Hall, Educational Testing Service, Princeton, N.J., 11 May 1965.

Ragosta, M.; Holland, P. W.; and Jamison, D. J. Computer- Assisted Instruction and Compensatory Education: The ETS/LAUSD Study. Project Report Number 20 (Princeton, N.J.: Educational Testing Service, June 1982).

Reid, J. C., and MacLennon, D. W. Research in Instructional Television and Film. (Washington, D.C.: U.S. Government Printing Office, 1967).

Unpublished

Balkovich, Edward E., et al. "Project Athena: An Introduction" (Project Athena prospectus, Massachusetts Institute of Technology, 1983), pp. 1–40.

"Educational Technology Center, Second Year Report" (Harvard Graduate School of Education, November 1985).

Eggert, John. "Lessons Learned in the Development and Implementation of Computer-Based/Interactive-Video Instruction" (Center for Instruction Development and Evaluation, University of Maryland, no date given), pp. 5–7.

Gale, Larrie E., and Barksdale, Karl. "The Development and Formative Evaluation of 'Interactive Digame' Courseware: A Cooperative Project of Brigham Young University and the Provo City School District." Report prepared at Brigham Young University, Provo, Utah, 13 June 1986, pp. 1–12.

Gant, Rus. "Introducing Interactive Video Information Systems into the Educational Environment" (Transcription of presentation at the Seminar on Interactive Video and Laser Disc Technology, University of Pittsburgh, 31 May 1985), pp. 1–31.

Kryder, Mark H. "The Magnetics Technology Center: Description and Proposal" (Received from Mark H. Kryder, 25 September 1986), pp. 1–20.

May, Leslie Steven. "Corporate Experience in Evaluating Interactive Video Information System Courses" (Bedford, Mass.: Digital Equipment Corporation, Educational Services, August 1984), pp. 1–9.

Moes, Robert J. "The CD ROM/CD-I Puzzle: Where Do the Pieces Fit?" paper presented at the National Online Meeting, New York City, N.Y., 6–8 May 1986, pp. 1–11.

"Philips in the Age of Optical Disc Media" (A report received from John Messerschmitt on 11 June 1986), pp. 1–12.

Index